THIS BOOK IS FROM THE LIBRARY OF

NAME : ....

ADDRESS : ....

....

....

THE FIRST WORLD WAR

WRITTEN BY ALEXANDRA CHURCHILL

ILLUSTRATED BY STEPHEN SMITH

UNIFORM

For Charlie, the biggest kid I know. AC
A huge thanks must go to Alex for all her enthusiasm, hard work, expertise, knowledge & vision that made this project a reality. SS

Published in 2021 by
Uniform, an imprint of Unicorn Publishing Group
5 Newburgh Street
London
W1F 7RG
www.unicornpublishing.org

ISBN 978-1-914414-20-6

Designed by Alexandra Churchill & Stephen Smith
Printed in Turkey by FineTone Ltd.

WHAT'S INSIDE?

What was the First World War?

The First World War was fought between 1914 and 1918. Officially, it began on 28th July 1914 and finally ended after more than four years on 11th November 1918...

...In that time more than thirty countries declared war on each other. Most of these fought on the side of the Allies. Russia, France, Belgium and Great Britain were joined by the likes of Serbia, Italy, Romania, Japan, Montenegro, Portugal, the Hejaz, Greece, Siam (Thailand), China, Brazil and the USA. Lots of countries fought as part of the British Empire; including India, Canada, Newfoundland, which was separate at the time, the West Indies, Australia, New Zealand and South Africa.

The opposing side was known as The Central Powers. Germany was joined by Austria-Hungary, which was one country at the time, Turkey (The Ottoman Empire) and Bulgaria.

It wasn't the first war in the world, but it was the first time that so many countries, on so many continents, had been involved in one conflict.

What's in a name?

There are different names for the First World War. Sometimes it is called World War One, but you will often hear it called The Great War. This isn't because people thought it was brilliant. This name was used a lot before the Second World War happened, and it just meant big.

Why Did Europe Go To War?

EUROPE

NORWAY
FINLAND
SWEDEN
ESTONIA
DENMARK
LATVIA
LITHUANIA
E. PRUSSIA
RUSSIAN EMPIRE
GREAT BRITAIN
HOLLAND
GERMAN EMPIRE
POLAND
BELGIUM
BOHEMIA
GALICIA
FRANCE
SWITZERLAND
AUSTRIA-HUNGARY
CROATIA
ROMANIA
ITALY
BOSNIA
MONTENEGRO
SERBIA
BULGARIA
SPAIN
ALBANIA
GREECE
OTTOMAN EMPIRE

Think of all the great powers as a person...

Germany was like a teenager, excited and wanting to make its mark. It had only been a country since 1871, and was still working out where it fit in on the world stage. Germany had big ideas for the future, and this made other nations nervous.

Britain and France were like grown adults, with an established place, big empires and a way of behaving that they had learned over many years. They liked the way things were and did not want anyone to challenge them, but naturally, countries like Germany wanted to catch them up.

The Austro-Hungarian Empire and Russia were like very old men. They had been very powerful, but by 1914 the way they did things was out of date and tired. It couldn't go on and one thing was certain: When these old orders collapsed, it would create a big mess, because countries would want to take up the power the old leaders had lost and they would not all agree on how to divide it up.

3

A Game of Thrones

Europe before the First World War was full of Kings and Queens, or what we call monarchies. Some had been around for centuries. How many names and countries do you recognise from 1914?

Kaiser Wilhelm II
Germany

King George V
Britain

Tsar Nicholas II
Russia

King Albert I
Belgium

Emperor Franz Josef I
Austria-Hungary

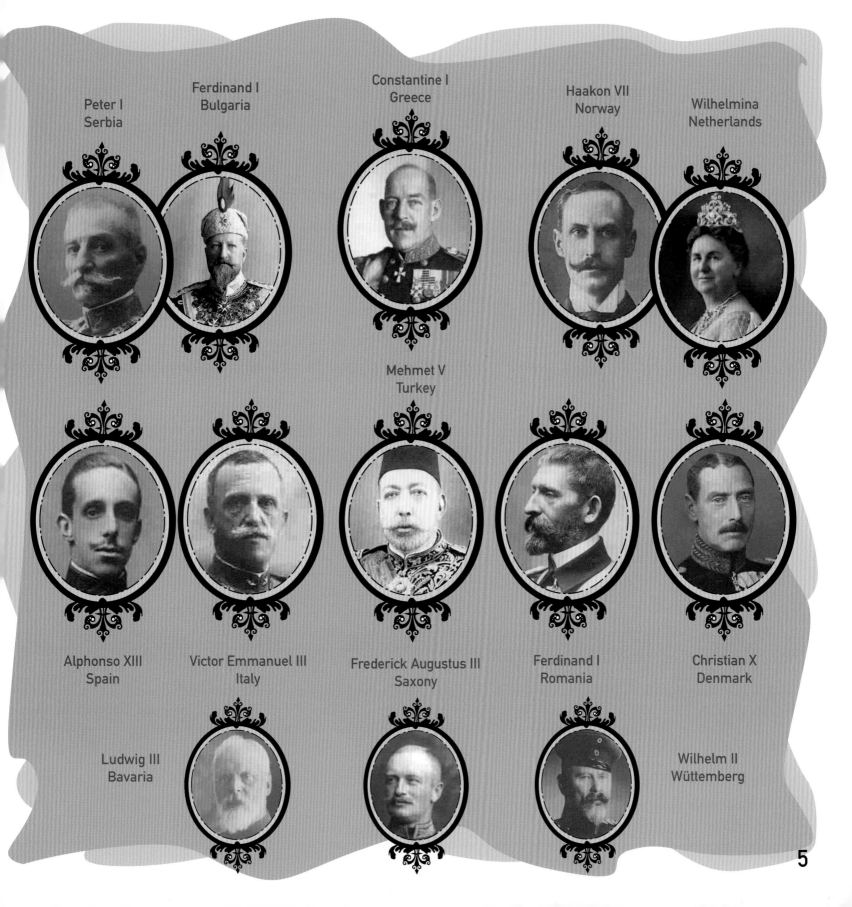

Peter I
Serbia

Ferdinand I
Bulgaria

Constantine I
Greece

Haakon VII
Norway

Wilhelmina
Netherlands

Mehmet V
Turkey

Alphonso XIII
Spain

Victor Emmanuel III
Italy

Frederick Augustus III
Saxony

Ferdinand I
Romania

Christian X
Denmark

Ludwig III
Bavaria

Wilhelm II
Wüttemberg

5

Alliances and Treaties

There are lots of long term causes of the First World War. These happened in the years building up to 1914. **Foreign Policies** are the choices that countries make about how to connect with the world around them. These choices affected how nations got along. These policies contributed to the war in 1914.

Alliances and Treaties are official agreements or friendships between two countries.

Germany was close to its neighbour, Austria-Hungary, and also had a treaty with Italy, but in the years just before the war, neither country was taking this important document very seriously.

France and Russia had signed an alliance together. Later, Britain joined them. This made Germany feel left out. Russia also looked upon Serbia like a little brother or sister, and Britain had a treaty with Belgium, so there were lots of links that meant that other countries would want to stick up for each other if their friends were in a fight!

Militarism

All of the tension that existed between the powers led to what we call **militarism**. This means that they were all very interested in making sure that they were stronger than other nations. Before the war, making sure that you had the biggest army was important to countries like Russia and Germany.

By 1914, Germany could put together an army of nearly four million men. Austria-Hungary had what we call a strength of three million.

France could also find four million men. But don't forget, Russia was friends with France, and was so huge, that it could find nearly six million!

Britain could not match these numbers because it was traditional that nobody in the country would ever be forced to serve in the army. In 1914, Britain could put together 975,000 men. And then there were much smaller countries. The strength of the Belgian Army in 1914 was less than 150,000, and in Serbia it was 200,000. You can see, when you add up the Allied numbers, why Germans felt like other countries were ganging up on them.

The Naval Arms Race

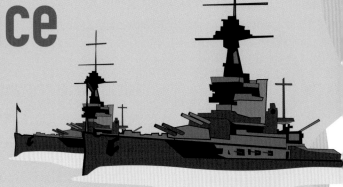

It was not only armies that made countries nervous. Before 1914, Britain and Germany were locked in a race to have the biggest and best navy in the world.

Britain had decided they would always make sure that the Royal Navy was much bigger than anyone else's fleets. But in the years before the war, Germany worked very hard to make their navy something really special too. Each time one country spent money on ships, the other would spend more. We call this the naval arms race. Britain won, but it made the two countries trust each other less.

DREADNOUGHTS

This was just the name of a ship. It meant feareless: dread-nought means dread (or fear) nothing. It was a traditional name from the time of Elizabeth I. But when it was used to name an amazing new type of ship in 1906, and the powers started to build more and more of them, it became a nickname for all of them.

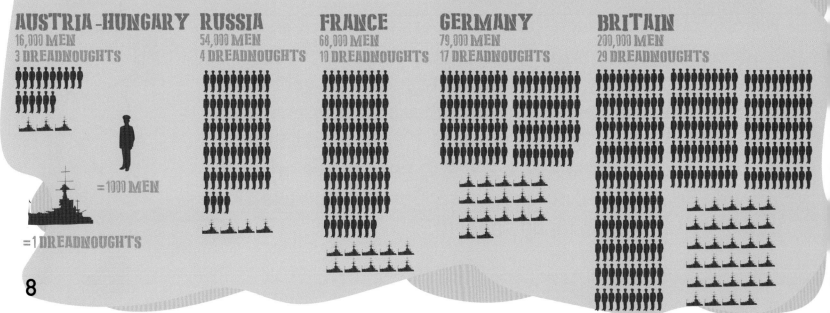

AUSTRIA-HUNGARY
16,000 MEN
3 DREADNOUGHTS

RUSSIA
54,000 MEN
4 DREADNOUGHTS

FRANCE
68,000 MEN
10 DREADNOUGHTS

GERMANY
79,000 MEN
17 DREADNOUGHTS

BRITAIN
200,000 MEN
29 DREADNOUGHTS

=1000 MEN

=1 DREADNOUGHTS

The Last Straw

Lots of little events had almost made Europe go to war in the years before 1914. But we call one the catalyst for the beginning of the war. This means it was one last thing that tipped everyone over the edge and made them fight each other.

It happened in the Balkans, where many people were angry about being part of the Austro-Hungarian Empire and wanted to leave. On 28th June 1914, the heir to the throne, a man named Archduke Franz Ferdinand, and his wife were shot and killed by a Serbian terrorist.

Austria was afraid of Serbia trying to ruin her empire, and the country used the killing as an excuse to declare war. Then things got out of hand. Russia sided with Serbia, then Germany sided with Austria. Then Germany declared war on France, because they were friends with Russia, and decided that to beat them, they would need to march through Belgium. When their troops entered Belgium, who didn't want to be involved, Belgium asked for help and then Britain declared war on Germany. The First World War had begun.

Gavrilo Princip was the man who fired the gun that killed the Archduke and his wife. He was born in Obljaj, in Bosnia into a Serbian family. He was only 19 when he shot the duke. He wanted Slavs to be freed from Austro-Hungarian rule.

Why Did This Become a World War?

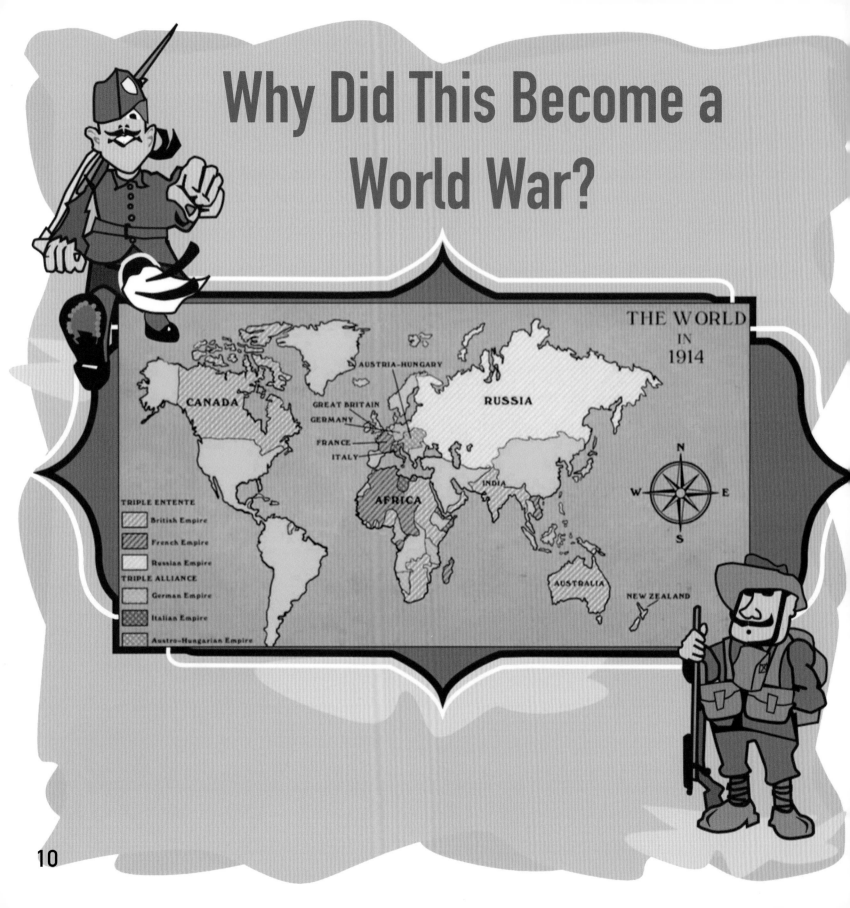

THE WORLD IN 1914

CANADA

AUSTRIA-HUNGARY
GREAT BRITAIN
GERMANY
FRANCE
ITALY
RUSSIA
INDIA
AFRICA

TRIPLE ENTENTE
British Empire
French Empire
Russian Empire

TRIPLE ALLIANCE
German Empire
Italian Empire
Austro-Hungarian Empire

AUSTRALIA
NEW ZEALAND

The world in 1914 looked very different to what you see today. A lot of it was divided into Empires. Britain, France, Austria-Hungary and Russia still had big Empires. Italy, Belgium, Japan, Portgual and Germany all had smaller ones. The rules vary, but if a country was part of someone else's empire, it could be called a colony.

The way that colonies were divided up between the Great Powers was another cause of the war, because everyone always wanted their Empire to be the biggest and the best. On the map, you can see which countries belonged to which power in 1914.

In most cases, if a power joined the war, their colonies automatically did too. This meant that men and women from all over the world would fight. For example, France's colonies included countries we now know as Morocco, Algeria and Vietnam.

There were also countries like Canada, New Zealand, South Africa and Australia, who had been colonies but were now self-governing. They made their own decisions and were called dominions. They still felt very close to Britain. When the war started, they wanted to help Britain win, and so they chose to go to war too.

1914

Men and women rushed to be involved with the war. Lots of people expected it to be over very quickly and didn't want to miss out!

Mobilisation

These Russian soldiers are part of the cavalry, which meant that they fought on horseback. In this photo they are getting ready to leave for war in 1914.

Once a country had declared war, it needed to mobilise its army. Organising food, travel, weapons, horses and equipment for thousands of men and then taking it all to another country was a hard job.

For years before 1914, Britain, France, Germany, Russia and Austro-Hungary had all been working on very complicated plans for how to do this. This meant that they could mobilise very quickly. All around the world, men were getting on boats and trains to go to war.

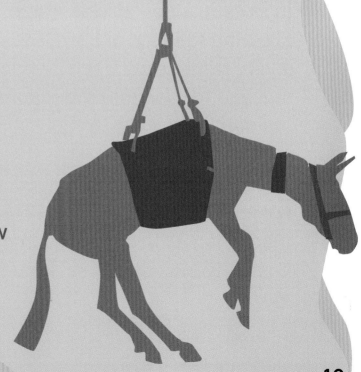

Recruitment

While armies were moving in the first weeks of the war, thousands more men were desperate to enlist.

Some of them wanted to serve their country. They joined the army because they were patriotic. For some, war was an adventure and a chance see the world. For others, it was simply a better paid job than the one they had at home.

In Britain, a poster was made showing the face of Lord Kitchener, a very famous soldier. The posters told young men that their country needed them to go to war.

Thousands of men answered, and on one day in September 1914 more than 33,000 men volunteered! It usually took a year to recruit that many.

These men are all waiting to join the army in Britain. In August and September 1914 there were queues like this all over Europe.

Even before the First World War, British soldiers were called 'Tommies'. This comes from a longer nickname: 'Thomas Atkins'. Nobody is exactly sure why this was chosen as a name to reflect all soldiers. One idea is that it was chosen by the famous Duke of Wellington, who remembered a particularly brave man by that name who had died under his command at the Battle of Boxtel in 1794.

The French Army had a nickname too. The soldiers were called 'Poilus', which means hairy! At the time, most of the men came from the countryside, and the name stuck on account of their big beards and bushy moustaches!

Austria-Hungary

Belgium

Serbia

Germany was incredibly proud of its army in 1914. It was the best in Europe. Other soldiers nicknamed German soldiers 'Fritz' or another name which was less friendly: 'Huns'. They were especially known for their spiky picklehaube helmets. Soldiers from other countries liked to collect them as souvenirs.

Russia

What did Soldiers Look Like?

Weapons

At the beginning of the war, the French soldier was armed with the Lebel Model 1886. When introduced, this was the first military firearm in history to use smokeless powder ammunition. However, by 1914 the Lebel was old and a bit out of date.

The main rifle of the Austro-Hungarian soldier was the Steyr-Mannlicher M.1895,

The most common rifle used by soldiers of the British Empire was the famous Short Magazine Lee-Enfield Mk. III, introduced in 1907. The Lee-Enfield was shorter than most rifles and was known for being accurate and fast shooting.

German soldiers usually carried the Mauser Gewehr 98. Mauser rifles were known for being accurate and strong weapons. They were sent to many other countries before the war, including Belgium and Serbia.

The Russian army's rifle was the 7.62mm Mosin-Nagant M.1891.The Mosin-Nagant was a reliable and rugged rifle and one of the most produced firearms of all time. During the First World War many were given to Russia's allies or captured by the Central Powers and reissued.

The Western Front

Germany needed to pass through both Belgium and Luxembourg so that they could then turn south and try to invade France. Luxembourg had a tiny army and let them pass straight away. Belgium, however, refused to let them in and so Germany declared war and marched across the border on 4th August 1914. The Germans sent nearly two million men. The little Belgian Army would never be able to beat them, but they would do a very good job of annoying the Germans and holding them up.

The Belgians had tried to protect themselves, in case they were ever attacked, by building massive forts. In some places the walls were six metres thick and made of concrete! But they got a nasty surprise at towns like Liège and Namur when the German invaders brought up what we call super heavy artillery. Artillery gets more 'heavy' the bigger the guns are and the bigger the shells are that they fire. To destroy Belgium's forts, the Germans used massive shells nearly half a metre wide. They made a horrific noise when they were fired, and when they landed the explosion was so big they shook the ground all around and destroyed everything nearby. Even the German soldiers were surprised at what these shells could do.

This photo shows the damage to one fort at the town of Namur in Belgium, caused by the German guns.

BRUSSELS

GERMANY

NAMUR

FRANCE

SIEGE OF NAMUR

LUX

19

When the forts had fallen, King Albert and the Belgian Government knew that they could not hold on to the capital, Brussels. They packed up all the important papers, and the country's gold, and left for the next biggest city, Antwerp, before the Germans arrived. They were going to try to run the country from there.

These are Belgian refugees. Thousands of people ran away from their homes because they were scared when armies began fighting in their towns and villages. A name for people who see a war, but not in uniform is **civilians**.

Antwerp was protected by forts, too. It had two rings of them around it, for extra protection. But once again the German guns destroyed them. By now help had begun to arrive to assist the very tired Belgian Army. Britain sent some cavalry, some soldiers and a special unit called the Royal Naval Division.

At the beginning of the war, Britain had more sailors and volunteers to serve in the navy than they knew what to do with, so they formed the naval division to serve on land as soldiers. The man who decided to send them to Belgium in 1914 was Winston Churchill, a name you might be familiar with! However, all of the help arrived too late and the Belgians were forced to give up Antwerp too. Once again they left before the German soldiers arrived, and carried on marching west.

These Belgian soldiers have stopped to rest in Brussels. There were not enough of them to defend the city, so they were forced to leave it to the German armies so that they could choose to fight another day.

Meanwhile, whilst the Germans were invading Belgium, the French armies were carrying out their own plan. This was called Plan 17. At the beginning of the war they were very keen on the spirit of the offensive. This seems silly now, but their plan was to attack everything, all the time, because your enemy couldn't beat you if you were always going forward! It was brave, but unfortunately, it meant that they were not very well prepared at all when things started to go wrong. They had no practice going backwards!

The French were still very angry about the result of a war with Germany in 1870. Germany had humiliated France and taken control of the lands along the border between the two countries. France wanted them back. The main French attack took place near Strasbourg, in September. It went well at first, but then the German armies fought back and the French had to retreat. A similiar thing happened to the French attacks in the Ardennes.

By now, the British Expeditionary Force, or BEF had arrived and moved into Belgium to help. British soldiers fought their first battle of the First World War. The Battle of Mons took place on Sunday, 23rd August 1914. Mons was a terrible place to try and fight a battle, because of all the mining work that happened nearby, and compared to the kind of battles that were to come, it was tiny. 1,600 British soldiers were killed, wounded or taken prisoner. The result of the day was a draw, with the British leaving the town in order to regroup.

This picture shows British soldiers unloading horses from their ship upon arriving in France at the beginning of the war.

Before August had passed, 75,000 French soldiers had died. 27,000 were killed on 22nd August 1914 alone. Compare that to the first day of the Battle of the Somme, which is the worst day in the history of the British Army. On that day, 19,000 men died. The French Army suffered very badly at the very beginning of the war.

23

What Happened Next?

BRITAIN   HOLLAND
BELGIUM
R. Seine   GERMANY
R. Marne
Paris
SWITZERLAND
FRANCE

Schlieffen Plan

The Germans were aiming for Paris, to try and make France surrender and leave the war. Then the Germans would be able to move all of their soldiers to the east to try and beat Russia. This was called the Schlieffen Plan, and it was named after the man who designed it.

So far the British, French and Belgian armies had failed to stop the German plan, and now they began a two week withdrawal we call the Great Retreat. The German armies continued to chase the British and French armies south towards Paris, and it looked as though the war might be over very quickly. The troops were all mixed up, filthy and hungry. Some men marched more than 100 miles. A lot of them were reservists, which meant they were only part-time soldiers, and they weren't very fit. Lots of them collapsed and could not walk any further. It looked like Germany might win the war and Europe held its breath.

With things looking very bad for the Allies, General Joffre, in command of the French armies, had a brilliant idea. He pulled men from anywhere he could and made them into a new army. He then threw them forward to attack through a gap that began to appear between the two advancing German forces. This battle is called the First Battle of the Marne. Sometimes in France it is called the 'miracle' on the River Marne, because it looked like all was lost, then suddenly the French troops, with the help of the British, managed to stop the Germans from reaching Paris.

Allied forces
German forces

In this photo, French soldiers take a break at the Marne, which is a river to the northeast of Paris. This is as close as the German armies got to taking the French capital in 1914.

The cavalry tried to play a traditional part in the opening weeks of war, when armies were on the move. Many units on different sides still wore their colourful, old-fashioned uniforms. The German cavalry in Belgium lost lots of men and horses trying to charge the Belgian Army.

This photo shows some Belgian cavalry riding off into action.

At Néry on 1st September, British cavalry were getting ready to move south again when they were suprised by Germans. Both sides got down from their horses to fight, and a battery (a small group) of Horse Artillery with their horse-drawn guns, spent two and a half hours fighting a big group of German field guns. The German cavalry began to run out of ammunition and more British arrived and ran them off. They were forced to leave most of their guns behind.

One of the last cavalry charges in history, when all of the horses ran at the enemy, happened on the night of 9th September when the French cavalry charged a German airfield at Soissons.

Once the Western Front was dug, the war became very still, with no open spaces, and barbed wire everywhere, the cavalry on all sides were unable to charge the enemy anymore. At first they waited to the rear, in case a collapse occurred in the enemy line and they could rush up, but until the end of the war there was no point. Neither could they carry out their normal jobs, like going out to see what the enemy was up to. You'd find it very hard to ride a horse across No Man's Land without being spotted!

For most of the war the cavalry went into battle without their horses. A similar pattern occurred on the Eastern Front, though it took longer. After hundreds of years of being very special in armies, during the First World War cavalrymen saw most of their work made impossible or t aken over by new inventions, like aeroplanes.

This photo shows German Uhlans. They were a very famous type of cavalry.

You can see from this photo, that the first trenches on the Western Front were very different to the complicated networks with lots of defences that were dug later on.

Now it was the turn of the German armies to retreat, as they were pushed north again. They finally managed to dig in along the banks of the River Aisne in the middle of September, The First Battle of the Aisne was a draw, The British and French armies tried to push the Germans further back, but they refused to move. The first trench systems were dug and the Western Front as we know it was born.

So how did the Western Front come to stretch from the North Sea to Switzerland?

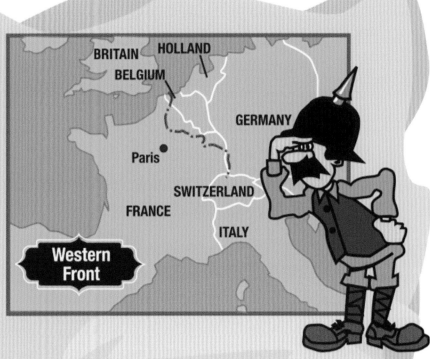

This photo shows soldiers from the German invasion force arriving in Brussels.

We call the ends of a line made by an army the flanks. One of the easiest ways to beat another army is to get behind it, and this means getting around the flanks. For the rest of 1914, armies raced to do this, moving further and further north until they reached the sea. By the time they were done, they had created a front that was more than 400 miles long! We call this The Race to the Sea.

The German Armies had one more chance to win the war in 1914. By October, the BEF had left the River Aisne and swapped with some French troops to be closer to the English Channel. This made more sense as it was easier to send them supplies from home. They had also met up with a second British group that had landed to try and help defend Belgium, but had been forced back as German soldiers captured most of the country.

It was here that the first fighting took place near the famous town of Ypres (Eep, or Ee-per. British soldiers called it Wipers!) The First Battle of Ypres lasted for nearly a month, with the worst of the German attack landing on British and French soldiers again and again. On 31st October, the German Army broke the British line, and they could have pushed through and perhaps won the war. The day was saved by men of the Worcestershire Regiment, who came and filled the gap.

In this photo you can see how much damage was done to the town square in Ypres by shells during the war.

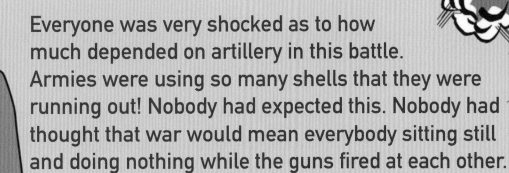

Everyone was very shocked as to how much depended on artillery in this battle. Armies were using so many shells that they were running out! Nobody had expected this. Nobody had thought that war would mean everybody sitting still and doing nothing while the guns fired at each other.

By the end of the battle in November, many thousands of soldiers had been killed on all sides, and the Ypres Salient had been created, A salient just means a bulge, as you can see from the map. It's a bad thing to try and defend one in a war, because your enemy can shoot at you from three different directions at once! The 'dreaded' salient was a dangerous place to be and before the war was over it would claim many lives.

When this battle was over, everyone began digging trenches here, too. Just like on the Aisne, for the next three years, the armies facing each other would hardly move at all!

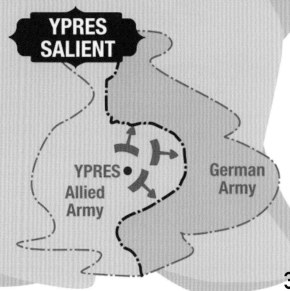

YPRES SALIENT

YPRES
Allied
Army

German
Army

Whilst the British and some French troops were fighting at Ypres, the Belgian Army was further north. They fought the Germans at the same time in the Battle of the Yser river. (EE-ser)

Like during the fighting at Ypres, the Germans looked very strong. In the end, the Belgian Army took the decision to flood some of the land to hold back the enemy. They opened gates at Nieuport to let the water past, and it created a water-logged area a mile wide that the Germans could not cross. This meant that one tiny corner of Belgium remained in Belgian hands during the whole of the First World War.

In this photo, Belgian soldiers are looking at some of the flooded land at a place called Ramscapelle.

The Christmas Truce that you will hear about most was something very odd that happened on the Western Front in 1914. It was not planned, but on Christmas Day, in some parts of the line men from both sides of the trenches climbed out into No Man's Land and began to fraternise with each other. This means socialising and being friendly with someone who is supposed to be your enemy,

One officer of the Royal Welsh Fusiliers walked along the lines and was amazed to see British soldiers scampering about wearing German field hats. One man even emerged from the enemy trenches carrying the gift of a heater. The officer shared a cigarette, talked about football and swapped details with a German officer before they decided that it was probably better if the men were not getting a good look at each others' defensive positions.

After 1914, this sort of fraternisation was frowned upon on the Western Front by the British Army. In fact, any officers who let truces take place at Christmas faced serious punishment. On the Eastern Front, however, much bigger truces continued throughout the war, including one that involved hundreds of regiments at Easter 1917.

The Eastern Front

Russia had arranged 'Plan 19' before the war, and on 17th August their armies invaded Eastern Prussia. This was terrible for Germany, because this area was so close to their capital, Berlin. The opposing armies met each other at the Battle of Tannenberg at the end of the month. The Germans used railways very well to move their troops about, and the Russian forces were so badly beaten that their commanding officer committed suicide. A whole Russian army was destroyed, and thirteen generals captured! However, as bad as this was, the Russians were not forced out of East Prussia.

But while the Russians were being beaten in East Prussia, they were also fighting Austro-Hungarian forces in Galicia. Here things went better for them. They forced their enemy out of Galicia completely and captured the city of Lemberg. Nearly half a million Austro-Hungarian soldiers were killed, wounded or captured, which was more than 30% of the men they could put together. The Russians also advanced 100 miles!

DID YOU KNOW?

The Eastern Front was much, much bigger than the one in France and Belgium. It was nearly 1,000 miles long!

EASTERN
FRONT

NORWAY

SWEDEN

RUSSIA
EMPIRE

DENMARK

BRITAIN

HOLLAND

BERLIN

WARSAW
LODZ

EAST PRUSSIA

POLAND

BELGIUM

TANNENBERG

KOW
PRZEMYSL

FRANCE

GERMAN
EMPIRE

LAPANOW LIMANOWA

GALICIA

SILESIA

SWITZERLAND

AUSTRO-
HUNGARIAN
EMPIRE

ITALY

ROMANIA

SPAIN

SERBIA

BULGARIA

ALBANIA

OTTOMAN
EMPIRE

FRENCH
ALGERIA

FRENCH
TUNISIA

GREECE

When this happened, the Russians also surrounded an important fortress at Przemyśl (you pronounce this 'Zye-mis'). As well as its forts, the town was surrounded by 30 miles of trenches and 650 miles of barbed wire! The Russian troops began a siege, and it was the longest one in the whole war. Life under siege is always difficult, especially for civilians. At Przemyśl food began to run out and people began to fight amongst themselves. There was a lot of anti-semitic feeling against people living in the town.

Anti-Semitism has been a problem all over the world for hundreds of years. It is a special term used when someone discrimates against people because they are Jewish. The worst example is the Holocaust during the Second World War, though not all of the victims were Jewish.

This photo shows the town of Przemśl a bit later in the war. You can see that, like Ypres in Belgium, it has been badly damaged.

There was also fighting in Poland on the Eastern Front in 1914. At the time, bits of Poland were part of Germany, Austria and the Russian Empire. By October lots of Russian troops were arriving there. Thousands of men from Siberia came together around Warsaw, and the Germans advanced, so that they faced each other across the Vistula River. After heavy fighting, both the Germans and the Austro-Hungarians were forced to retreat, and when winter weather stopped the fighting, they found themselves in a good positon to continue advancing on Silesia in Germany.

In November, although winter had already arrived, three Russian armies prepared to try and invade Silesia. The Germans were heavily outnumbered, but decided to attack first and take the initiative. Again they rushed troops to battle on trains, and managed to force the Russians to retreat back towards Warsaw, giving up the important city of Łodz.

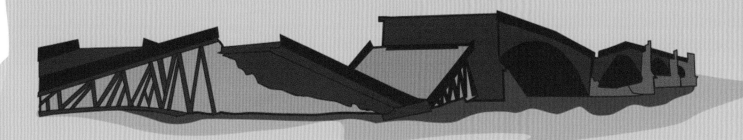

In this photo you can see some of the thousands of men from Siberia ready to fight as part of the Russian Army in Poland in 1914.

The Russian Army in the First World War included soldiers from countries we know today such as Finland, Ukraine, Belarus, Latvia, Uzbekistan and Georgia. There were also lots of different ethnic groups, like Cossacks and Tartars.

The Austro-Hungarians were hoping that all of this later fighting for Russia against Germany meant that their front would be quiet for winter, but they would be disappointed. At the beginning of December, with the Russians eager to reach Krakow, lots of fighting took place around the towns of Limanowa and Łapanów. The Russian forces had to retreat, ruining their chances of reaching Hungary and forcing them back across the Carpathian mountains.

These soldiers from Austria are getting ready to go on patrol. The weather on the Eastern Front in the winter of 1914 was very cold. Lots of men died as a result of exposure, as well as in battle.

Asia and the Pacific

GERMAN SAMOA

At the beginning of the war Japan joined the side of the Allies against Germany and the Central Powers. Germany had a small colony at Tsingtao (now Qingdao, China) The Japanese decided to attack it, and sent ships from the Imperial Navy at the end of August. The Royal Navy sent ships to support the siege, and Japanese soldiers were sent ashore. They were joined eventually by both Indian and British troops. Kaiser Wilhelm was very angry at the thought of losing Tsingtao, and said: 'It would shame me more to surrender Tsingtao to the Japanese than Berlin to the Russians.' The German garrison held out for two months but was defeated in November. The Allies took control of the port and the surviving German troops were taken prisoner. This left the German East Asia Squadron without a port, which meant that the Kaiser's ships had to go on something of a suicide run across the Pacific. Admiral Von Spee said, 'I am quite homeless. I cannot reach Germany... I must plough the seas of the world doing as much mischief as I can, until my ammunition is exhausted, or a foe far superior in power succeeds in catching me.'

In this photo, Japanese sailors are on their way to land at Tsingtao.

TSINGTAO

JAPAN

CHINA

TSINGTAO

Just as Japan had attacked Tsingtao, other Allied nations moved against German colonies in the Pacific.

At the end of August, troops from New Zealand arrived in German Samoa, in the Pacific. The landings were not opposed by anyone on the islands and they were occupied by the New Zealand Government on behalf of King George V.

A similar thing happened in German New Guinea. Australian troops occupied Kaiser-Wilhelmsland and the surrounding islands. Only one battle took place, on 11th September 1914, when the power station at Bita Paka was attacked. Six soldiers were killed and four wounded. These were the first Australian casualties of the First World War.

This photo shows soldiers from New Zealand. After landing in Samoa, they pulled this German Imperial flag down from a Government building.

The War At Sea

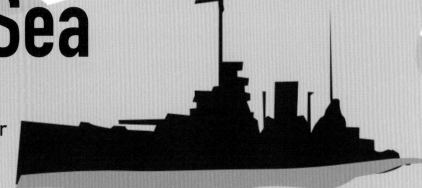

The war at sea began very quickly and the work of the Royal Navy involved lots of different things. First of all, it was their job to get the army onto the European mainland safely, transporting men and protecting troop ships. In the opening weeks of the war, Royal Navy men were also sent to support war on the Western Front. A huge piece of work that also started straight away was the blockade of the Central Powers. Royal Navy ships would stop merchant ships as they passed through the northern passages from the Atlantic into the North Sea, board them, send them to a British port to assess their cargo and either keep them, or send them on their way.

The Royal Navy also disrupted lots of Germany's global communications. They cut the main telegraph cables in the English Channel on 5th August, but also destroyed German wireless stations at Dar-es-Salaam, the Palau Islands and atTanga. This would be like turning off the internet today! Early fighting at sea was carrried out by smaller ships. Two famous cruisers belonging to Germany were *Goeben* and *Breslau*. At the start of the war, their job was to try and stop France from bringing their colonial soldiers to Europe from North Africa. The Allied navies hunted all over the Mediterranean for them. The cruisers managed to reach Constantinople (now Istanbul) and were given to the Ottoman Navy. This was important because the Ottoman Empire was not yet part of the war and it began a chain of events that led Turkey to join the Central Powers in November 1914.

VENICE KOSOVO
BLACK SEA
ROME ISTANBUL
ALGIERS
MEDITERRANEAN SEA GREECE
BASRA
TRIPOLI
ALEXANDRIA JERUSALEM
SUEZ
CAIRO
OTTOMAN
EMPIRE
RED SEA
MECCA

Lots of work was going on underwater too. All navies laid mines to destroy each others' ships. They would lay, or drop, tens of thosaunds all over the world before the war was over.

Submarine warfare was very new in the First World War. Underwater craft had been around for a number of years, but this was the first conflict in which they played a proper part in naval warfare. In German they were called Unterseeboots, and this was shortened to U-Boats.

Both Britain and Germany initially used submarines mainly to try to pick off ships and damage each others' fleets. Both used them against civilian shipping too. Eventually though, Germany would have a very different philosophy. Because they had lost the naval arms race, and their fleet was weaker, they tried to use their U-Boats to make up for Britain's advantage. This made the rest of the world very angry.

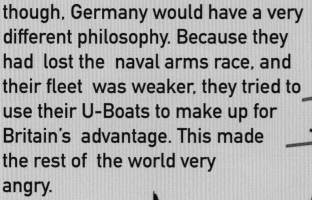

On 22nd September 1914, a German submarine scored a huge victory over the Royal Navy. Early in the morning the U-9 attacked a group of British ships. Three armoured cruisers were sunk. Aboukir was destroyed first, then Hogue was hit by two torpedoes. Finally, the Cressy was hit and turned upside down before she too sank. Losing three ships before breakfast in one day was humiliating for the Royal Navy, and more than 1,400 sailors were lost in the disaster.

Before it happened, one naval officer had nicknamed the ships 'the Live Bait Squadron' because owing to the age of the crews and their lack of experience, they were considered to be at risk. *Hogue*, *Aboukir* and *Cressy* were all due to be replaced as soon as new ships were finished.

The crew of the submarine were treated as heroes in Germany. Postcards like this one were made to celebrate their victory.

The Kapitänleutnant of U-9 was Otto Weddigen. He was killed in March 1915. After firing a torpedo at HMS *Neptune*, his submarine was chased by HMS *Dreadnought*. The British ship rammed the U-boat and cut it in two. There were no survivors.

Admiral von Spee commanded the German East Asia squadron, made up mainly of cruisers. On 1st November 1914, he ran across a British squadron off the coast of Chile. Von Spee's ships outnumbered the Royal Navy, and it was an easy victory for the Imperial German Navy at the Battle of Coronel. Two British ships were sunk and 1,660 men lost.

The Royal Navy did not have to wait long for revenge. Alarmed at what had happened, the British Government sent two modern battle-cruisers towards South America. The Battle of the Falkland Islands took place on 8th December 1914. Von Spee attempted to raid the British base at Stanley. Unfortunately for him, it was a clear day, and his ships were spotted quickly. They were chased and all but two were sunk by British ships, including the two newly arrived battlecruisers. Six German ships were lost and more than 2000 sailors lost or taken prisoner.

SOUTH AMERICA

CORONEL

SOUTH ATLANTIC

FALKLAND ISLANDS

STANLEY

On 16th December 1914, German ships attacked the British coastal towns of Scarborough, Hartlepool, West Hartlepool and Whitby. The raid occurred early in the morning, with lots of people on their way to work or to school. The German ships fired more than 1,000 shells into Hartlepool alone, hitting the steelworks, gasworks, seven churches and 300 houses. Nearly 100 civilians were killed, including children, and nearly 500 more were injured. People in Britain were outraged, not only with the German Navy, who they called 'baby killers', but with the Royal Navy, for failing to stop the attacks. 'Remember Scarborough' became a propaganda slogan for recruitment.

REMEMBER SCARBOROUGH!

ENLIST NOW

In this photo, children are looking at shell fragments displayed in a shop window in Hartlepool after the German naval raid.

One more important event happened for the Royal Navy in 1914. Back then, there was no Royal Air Force. The Army had the Royal Flying Corps (RFC) and the Navy had the Royal Navy Air Service. (RNAS).

On Christmas Day the RNAS carried out a raid near Cuxhaven using very early aircraft. Seven aeroplanes carrying bombs set out to cause damage to huge sheds that housed German airships.

The raid on Cuxhaven went forward in bad weather, and it was not very successful, but it is important because it was the first time that the Royal Navy carried out an attack using a combined force of ships and aeroplanes. Ships called Seaplane Carriers took the seaplanes close to Germany, and from there, they took off for the coast.

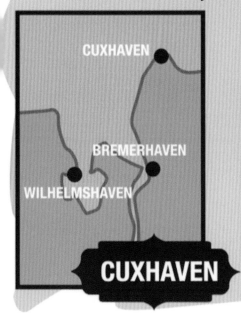

CUXHAVEN
BREMERHAVEN
WILHELMSHAVEN

CUXHAVEN

Taking photos in the middle of an air raid in 1914 was impossible, but artists had a lot of fun imagining what it might have looked like!

47

The Balkans

At the very beginning of the war, Austro-Hungarian troops tried to invade Serbia. They began shelling the capital, Belgrade, as early as 29th July 1914. These were the first shots of the First World War.

The Austro-Hungarians crossed the Drina River into Serbia on 12th August. But the Austro-Hungarians made some terrible mistakes, and at the Battle of Cer in August they were forced to retreat.

In September, Serbia was pressured by her allies to launch an offensive against Austria-Hungary in what became known as the Battle of the Drina. This did not go well. The Austro-Hungarians managed to stop the Serbian offensive, then push them back, but they couldn't get any further. The small Serbian army was now exhausted and running out of equipment and shells, and when the Austro-Hungarians launched a third invasion in November, the Serbians lost control of their capital, Belgrade.

This photograph shows Serbian soldiers relaxing in a trench.

But by December the Allies had sent them what they needed, and the Serbians attacked again at the Battle of Kolubara. They managed to take back Belgrade. However, Serbia was too small to replace all of the men who had been lost, and would need lots of help from Allied troops if she hoped to beat the Austro-Hungarian forces.

To make things worse, Serbia also suffered from a huge outbreak of Typhus beginning at the end of 1914. It is possible that this epidemic killed more than 150,000 Serbs. Lots of doctors and nurses volunteered to go to Serbia to help. Margaret Neill Fraser was a famous lady golfer as well as a nurse, Louisa Jordan was a nurse from Glasgow and Elizabeth Ross was a doctor. She had also worked as a surgeon on ships and treating the sick in what is now Iran before the war. All three became victims of typhus themselves whilst helping the sick and died in Serbia.

What is Typhus?

Typhus is an infectious disease that thrives in dirty conditions. In the First World War it was carried by lice and was a problem particularly on the Eastern Front. It causes high temperatures, fever and a rash.

1915

A year of trial and error, all nations would struggle to understand this new, industrial warfare and how they might win the war.

The Western Front

One of the first things we think about when someone mentions the First World War is trenches. We've already seen that the first ones were just ditches in the ground, but very quickly, all the nations involved in the war worked hard to make trenches easier to defend and more comfortable to live in.

Different countries had different ways of doing things, but the picture on the next page gives you a general idea of what a British trench looked like on the Western Front.

Trench conditions could be terrible. After all, you were living in the ground. In bad weather it was impossible to stay dry, or clean. Men had to live in them for days on end, surrounded by rats and vermin and with the enemy ready to shoot at them the second they showed too much of themselves above the parapet. Sometimes the enemy's trenches were only a few metres away and they could hear each other. Sometimes men would even talk to each other across No Man's Land!

This photo shows a trench in France at the beginning of 1915, and just how wet they could get!

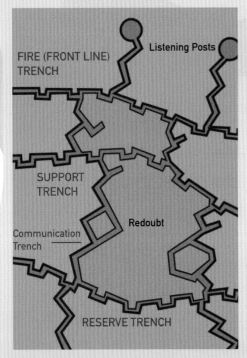

FIRE (FRONT LINE) TRENCH

Listening Posts

SUPPORT TRENCH

Communication Trench

Redoubt

RESERVE TRENCH

This system has three lines of trenches, and all of them would be full of men, in case the enemy decided to attack. They were connected by communication trenches so that men could move about without showing their heads above ground. You can see that they have also dug a little further into No Man's Land, so that men could edge closer to the enemy and see if they could hear what they were up to at listening posts. There is also a redoubt. This is a stronghold full of machine guns and more men. If the trenches are attacked, the enemy might get inside the system, but it will be very difficult for them to get past the redoubt too.

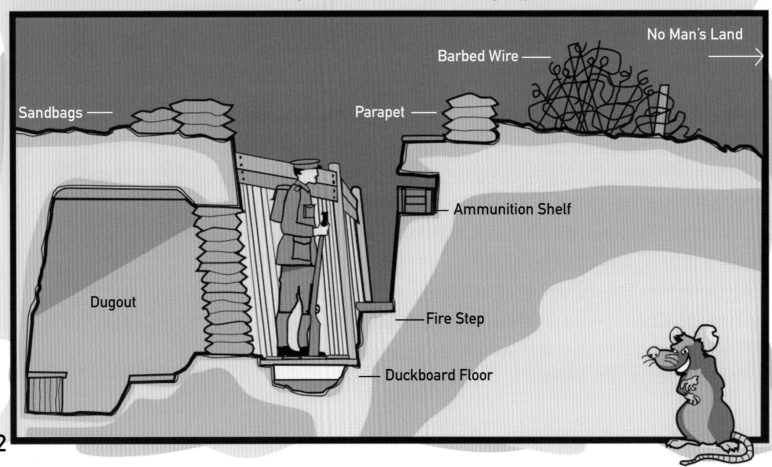

No Man's Land

Barbed Wire

Sandbags

Parapet

Ammunition Shelf

Dugout

Fire Step

Duckboard Floor

1915 was a new year and the Allies had thought hard about what to do. After the First Battle of Ypres, the plan for the Allies on the Western Front was always to wait for better weather and then to attack the Germans, trying to push them out of France and Belgium.

If you're the German Army, you're not in a hurry. Of course, if you can conquer the whole of France and Belgium you can win the war, but let's not forget: you have already managed to get into those countries. If you just stay put, you are still not losing, so you have more time to think about what to do.

This was a new type of warfare for everyone. All of these trenches had been dug and nobody quite knew how to approach the idea of attacking them. The general plan used a lot at the beginning of the war was this:

The Allies would attack, try to punch a hole in the German line of trenches, and then throw lots of men forward. These men would rush through the gap where the Germans had been beaten, and get behind their line. This would cause the German network to collapse, because there would be so much confusion.

Let's not forget the artillery. In the First World War, artillery became the king of the battlefield. Suddenly it looked very important. You have all of these big guns, and all of these trenches. It's dangerous to send men into them, but what if you use the guns to smash the enemy trenches to bits and THEN send your men forward? They're going to stand a much better chance. Even on days when you are not attacking the enemy in a battle, you can cause damage to his network of trenches with your guns, without putting soldiers at risk.

You don't have to just attack the enemy's trenches. Big guns, heavy guns like the one in the drawing could fire an exploding shell for miles. This means that you can attack your enemy's infrastructure. This is a word used to describe everything that helps your enemy function. So, train stations, where his troops might arrive; or headquarters, where his generals might be planning a battle. Or even church towers. These were very useful for men to climb up in and get a good view of the surrounding countryside. You don't want your enemy to do this. Within a few months of war, there was hardly a church tower left standing on the battlefield in Flanders.

We'll see a bit later on, too, that armies even found a way to use artillery shells to protect their men when they went into battle.

This photo shows a more typical British gun. It's called a field gun. This would have been used for things like smashing barbed wire before attacks

The French were determined to try and push the Germans out of their country. General Joffre thought that if they cut the enemy's access to the rail lines, they could destroy the Germans' method of getting supplies to their soldiers. This meant capturing towns and cities under enemy control, like Lens, Lille and Douai. There was an attack in late December called the First Battle of Artois, where the French wanted to take back high ground on the ridge called the Notre Dame de Lorette. It did not come to much. The enemy's trench lines were just too good, and nobody had any experience of how to attack them. The world was discovering a new industrial type of warfare, and it seemed at this point to the French that whatever they did, it was not going to be possible to make the German Army leave quickly.

General Joffre was in command of all of the French forces. His nickname was 'Papa Joffre' and he was a national hero.

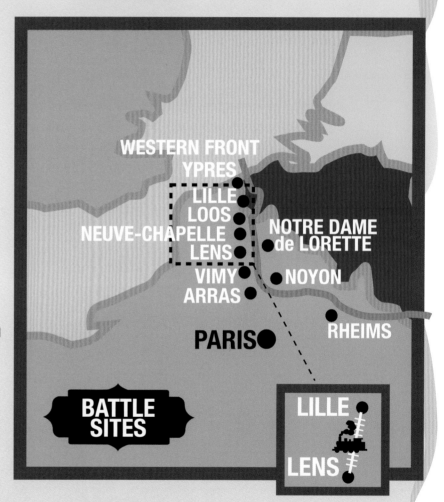

WESTERN FRONT
YPRES
LILLE
LOOS
NEUVE-CHAPELLE
LENS
NOTRE DAME de LORETTE
VIMY
ARRAS
NOYON
RHEIMS
PARIS

BATTLE SITES

LILLE
LENS

This photo shows a machine gun. You can see the soldier's gas mask is ready to use on his hat.

Below, you can see French soldiers preparing a meal.

In this photo soldiers are wearing early types of gas mask.

In the photo underneath you can see an example of a French fire trench.

This photo shows German troops on board a train at the front.

Above you can see a photo of German prisoners. They don't look sorry that their war is over!

The work of building and repairing trenches was never finished. In this photo you can see that the German Army have even brought an elephant to war to do some heavy lifting!

The photo below shows some troops from Bavaria in a trench.

For the British Expeditionary Force, the first effort of moving the German soldiers in front of them came at Neuve Chapelle in France. A combination of British and Indian soldiers. They made a good start, but were unable to break the German lines like they wanted to. It turned out that it was easy to get inside the enemy network of trenches, but by the time the German Army rushed men to that spot to help defend it, it was very hard to get out the other side and cause the collapse that was needed.

In this photo Indian soldiers are lining up to have minor wounds treated at a dressing station.

This photo shows the town of Neuve Chapelle. You can see that a lot of it has been destroyed. Right at the front you can also see graves where soldiers have buried men who have been killed.

Very early in the war, all sides were learning how difficult it was to keep communications with soldiers after the attack had begun because there were no radios or mobile phones. Armies were using more soldiers in battle than before, and again, they had no experience of how to do it. All telephone calls had to be made using land lines that they quickly laid down, but as soon as the shells started flying they smashed them to pieces.

This meant that the generals could not issue the right orders, because as soon as their men left their sight, they might have no idea what they were doing! During the First World War, armies would try literally anything they could think of while they tried to work out a way around this problem, including using pigeons and even dogs to carry messages!

59

In this photo French soldiers have a message dog with them. A note would be tied to the animal's collar and they would be sent off to deliver it.

In this photo soldiers are using a lamp to send messages a long way by flashing light.

In this photo a soldier from the artillery is using a telephone to exchange information. This was one of the ways they would try to ensure that shells were landing in the right place. By talking like this they could make alterations.

In this photo men from the Royal Engineers are trying to put up telephone wires in a dangerous spot!

Meanwhile, the German commanders had decided to carry out their own attack. They chose to have another go at breaking the Allied lines around the Ypres Salient. The battle began at the end of April, when the German Army used poison gas for the first time on the Western Front. The first victims of this hideous new type of weapon were French colonial troops from Algeria and Morocco. The poor men were terrified. One officer who watched them said that they ran 'like madmen… shouting for water, spitting blood, some even rolling on the ground making desperate efforts to breathe'.

This photo shows French colonial troops. It was men from Morocco/Algeria who were the first victims of gas on the Western Front. Below is a photo of them going into action

The battle continued for nearly a month, with more gas attacks. It was significant because it was the first battle to include soldiers from Canada. At the outbreak of war, thousands of men had volunteered to go to Europe and fight with Britain. They began arriving at the end of 1914 and it was here that they fought for the first time.

Canadians were badly affected by gas during the Second Battle of Ypres. They were also not ready to fight this new type of war. However, twice during the Second Battle of Ypres they got one over on the German Army. This was the first time in history that colonial soldiers had defeated a European power in Europe.

The battle forced the Allies back, but the Germans did not take Ypres. It is very difficult to count how many soldiers became casualties. Casualties are all of the men who were killed, died because of gas poisoning, were wounded or taken prisoner.

This photo shows a Canadian recruitment poster.

In this photo Canadian volunteers are saying goodbye to their loved ones in Toronto.

One of the things that happens in a war, is that technology advances quickly. Fighting throws up lots of problems and they have to be solved very quickly to get an advantage on the battlefield. Like gas. Immediately someone needed to reply by making a brilliant gas mask. Here are some important inventions from 1915:

The artillery used Field Guns to shoot at trenches, but look how they fire. They have to shoot from a long way away, and the men in the trenches have to get other people to do this for them.

What soldiers needed was a big weapon that could fire from one trench to another, right in front of them, like this. Trench Mortars came in different sizes, but were used throughout the war. Their shells were big round bombs called 'toffee apples'!

Hand grenades, or hand-held bombs, had been around for hundreds of years, but they were not very good. In fact, the British Army thought they had no future, until during a war between Russia and Japan in 1905, they turned out to be useful when troops were dug in trenches. In 1915, British soldiers were given Mills Bombs for the first time. Once a man pulled the pin out, he had about seven seconds until the little bomb exploded in which to throw it. Bombs came in all shapes and sizes. The German Stielhandgranate was also introduced in 1915, and had a stick on it to help soldiers throw it further. Every country used hand-held bombs, and it is estimated that 75 million were produced in the First World War!

In this photo a Canadian soldier shows off his different bombs.

63

In this photo French troops are using a flame thrower. This is something else that arrived on the Western Front in 1915.

This photo shows some French soldiers with a bomb for attacking trenches. There were many, many different kinds in the First World War.

This photo shows a French soldier demonstrating how to throw one type of hand-held bomb.

In this photo soldiers are using a trench periscope to see over the top and into no mans land. These were a very useful invention because you didn't have to put your head up!

The German chemist Fritz Haber was the man who suggested using chlorine gas as a weapon. Chlorine was let out of cylinders, like when you fill a helium balloon, and then you would wait for the wind to carry the deadly green/yellow cloud towards the enemy.

It was a horrible invention. The gas would ruin a man's lungs if it was breathed in, they would feel like they needed a drink badly, or feel very sick. Their lungs would fill up with fluid, as if they were drowning. It was a very frightening, very painful thing to experience. When it first appeared on the battlefield in 1915, the world was shocked.

This photo shows a British soldier wearing a very early type of gas mask.

The Allies immediately needed to find a way to protect soldiers from gas. The first masks were just pads, like cotton wool. It sounds disgusting, but one of the early orders men were given was to wet them or even wet their handkerchiefs by soaking them with pee. There were buckets of it all around just in case! It was a very basic way to try and limit what the gas did to them.

The French Army was still very keen to push the Germans out of their country. General Joffre had not given up on his idea of taking back the railway lines and so he decided to try attacking again in Artois. The important place the French needed to take from the German Army was Vimy Ridge. This was a brilliant piece of high ground. Whoever had it could see exactly what their enemy was up to. The French Army started really well, and took the ridge, but then the Germans fought back and forced them off again. We call this a counter-attack. They were going to become a common problem in the war. It was not impossible to get INTO the enemy's trenches, but HOLDING them when they counter-attacked was very hard. You always need reserves in a battle. As men are killed, you put the reserves into the fight. In this case, the French reserves were not moved fast enough to be ready for when the Germans fought back. The Second Battle of Artois did force the Germans to stop their attack at Ypres, but 1915 was proving a horrible year for France. This battle alone used up more than two million shells, and more than 100,000 casualties. The German Army lost nearly that many men too.

This French soldier has been photographed looking at the ruined town of Arras.

These Moroccan soldiers have been photographed at Notre Dame de Lorette.

British and Indian troops were also part of the attacks in Artois. They first took part in the Battle of Aubers Ridge on 9th May. They were trying to punch two holes in the German line but failed to do this. They tried twice more, but still could not get past the German machine guns. The attack had been a complete failure, but the French wanted the British to try again. The Battle of Festubert began nearby on 15th May. The British Army did push the Germans back nearly two miles, but with the failure of the main French plan to capture Vimy Ridge, the Allies finally gave up attacking on 25th June. The British, Indian and Canadian forces suffered nearly 30,000 casualties.

This photo shows a very spacious British position on the Western Front.

67

Remember we talked about the artillery? And how nobody expected it to be the most important part of a big war? By early 1915, it had caused a big problem. Armies just did not expect to be firing so many shells, and they were not ready to make enough of them in their factories at home to keep the guns firing. It started to affect how battles were being fought, and not in a good way.

Another big problem was the type of shell they were used to making. Armies were used to using shrapnel shells. These explode a few feet from the ground, and spray little metal balls over a wide area. This is all very well and good when everybody was above ground.

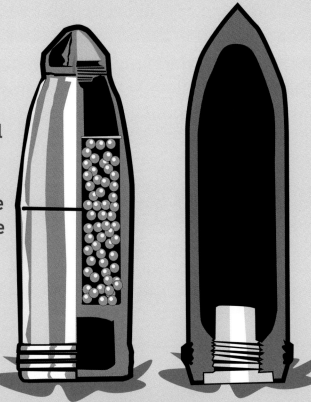

But these are not nearly so useful when everyone is hiding in trenches and dugouts. Armies needed more high-explosive shells instead. These are bombs that go bang on a specific target. But making them was different to making shrapnel shells. Lots of factories would need to change their way of doing things before they could make them in large numbers.

This photograph shows a munitions worker in France finishing off shell cases.

Herbert Asquith The British Prime Minister

In Spring 1915 there was a crisis in Britain about the shell shortage on the Western Front. Officers went to the press to tell the public that the guns were silent for a want of shells, and that Britain might lose the war because they could not keep up with the enemy in producing ammunition.

David Lloyd George The new Minister of Munitions

This led to a change of government. In times of crisis in the past, what has happened in Britain is that the major political parties have agreed to form a coalition government. This means men from different parties all agree to work together for the good of the country. In 1915, Asquith remained Prime Minister, but had to dismiss his own people and replace them with his political opponents to keep the country happy.

The most important change for the war effort was the creation of a new ministry, the Ministry of Munitions, which was to be led by David Lloyd George. This was going to be a whole government office responsible for producing all of the shells etc. that Britain needed to win the war.

The French were not done fighting in 1915. They really, really wanted the German Army to leave. They planned to attack again all along the Western Front. General Joffre was not only trying to attack German-held railways in Artois, 1915 was also spent attacking the enemy closer to Reims, in the area known as Champagne. (Yes, it's where the drink comes from!) The First Battle of Champagne finally ended in the middle of March, without success, but just like in Artois, the French Army was going to try again.

The Second Battle of Champagne is called Herbstschlacht, or Autumn Battle in German. This began on 25th September 1915, the same day as Loos and the fighting in Artois. France's Centre Army Group went forwards in the rain and managed to break the German line in four places. But they had pulled their artillery back to safety, and their reserves were ready to come up to plug the gaps in their line. The French tried hard to go forward again, but they started to run out of shells and on 3rd October General Joffre gave up on the idea of breaking the German line. The fighting eventually stopped on 6th November. The French had suffered 145,000 more casualties and Germany at least 72,500.

This photo shows hundreds of German soldiers captured in the Champagne

In this picture you can see an early cemetery made by German soldiers in the Champagne

The attacks on 25th September also included a Third Battle of Artois. The French were more concerned with the bigger fight going on in Champagne, and so they were trying to be careful about how many men and shells they used. They made some progress, but the attacks ended up yet another expensive failure with another 48,000 French casualties.

On the same day, the British Army would also be attacking at Loos. This was a horrible place to try and fight a battle, as it was built up and an area where a lot of mining took place. This means lots of uneven ground and lots of equipment etc. in the way. The leading British generals on the Western Front did not want to fight here, but the government ordered them to go ahead as the French had asked.

This photo shows the mining town of Loos. The big structure in the middle was a winding gear at a pit head. British soldiers nicknamed it Tower Bridge. Can you think why?

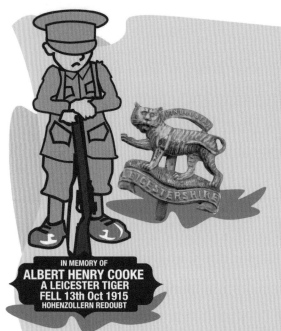

IN MEMORY OF
ALBERT HENRY COOKE
A LEICESTER TIGER
FELL 13th Oct 1915
HOHENZOLLERN REDOUBT

There were not enough shells to try and flatten the German lines to make it easier for the men attacking. Instead they were relying on using gas for the first time. Some of the gas did reach the Germans, but in other places it blew back on British soldiers. The General in charge of the battle, Sir John French, decided to watch the battle from a place that did not have a telephone, so he could not speak to his men in front.

Much like in French battles, the British soldiers did get into the German line, but were pushed out again.

In this photo you can see a German gun on display in London that was captured at Loos. Lots of people came to look at displays like this.

Fighting was fierce, especially at a German strongpoint called the Hohenzollern Redoubt; named after the Kaiser. There was a huge, very public argument after the battle about how slow reserves were to arrive and whose fault it was. When they did get to the battle they were exhausted and some of them were sent towards barbed wire where they would almost certainly be killed. Like all of the other attacks by the allies this year, it was eventually abandoned. In all, the fighting at the end of 1915 cost the British Army nearly 60,000 casualties.

Gallipoli

People disagreed about how to win the war. With things on the Western Front going nowhere at the end of 1914, politicians and generals began to take sides.

First of all there were the Westerners. These men believed that the Western Front was the most important and that this was the only place that the war would be won or lost. They thought that all of the Allied efforts should be put into the Western Front.

David Lloyd George

Winston Churchill

Then there were the Easterners. This group included politicians like David Lloyd George and Winston Churchill. They believed that the Western Front was going nowhere, and that the Allies should try something else at the same time. They came up with some pretty mad ideas for all over Europe, and one of these was to attack the Dardanelles.

The Dardanelles is a strip of water about 60 miles long that goes from the Aegean Sea to the Sea of Mamara. You can see from the map, that these straits connect Europe to Asia. Importantly, it's also a route through to Turkey and the capital of the Ottoman Empire. Today the city is called Istanbul, but during the First World War its name was Constantinople. One of the Easterners' plans was to conquer the Dardanelles, sail men into the Sea of Mamara and threaten Constantinople. If the city fell, then Turkey should be out of the war and Germany and the other Central Powers would suffer. But the Allies didn't have enough shells and enough men for the fronts they were already fighting on, so there were lots of arguments about whether to go ahead and try this.

Constantinople

GALLIPOLI

One of the biggest early supporters of the idea was Winston Churchill. From his job in charge of the Royal Navy, he said he thought that the Dardanelles could be forced using only ships. This is far less work than sending an army to attack across land, and so the government thought, why not? A force of British, French and even a Russian ship tried this in February 1915, but failed. The Turks had forts built all along the coast of a bit of Turkey near a town called Gallipoli, next to the straits, to protect them from invasion, and the Allied ships still couldn't get through.

On 18th March, 18 Allied battleships tried one last time to get up the straits, past Gallipoli and through the Sea of Mamara towards Constantinople. It was a terrible day for the Allies, and a huge victory for Turkey and the Ottoman Empire. Lots of ships were damaged and sunk. Even worse, the French ship *Bouvet* struck a mine and sank in just two minutes. She had a crew of more than 700 men, and only 75 survived.

This photo shows a view of Gallipoli from a battleship nearby

The Allied Governments decided now that they would send a small army to Gallipoli and approach Constantinople that way, over land. In Turkey they call Gallipoli 'Çanakkale' instead (Chan-ack-a-ley). It really wasn't a good plan and the Allies did not pay proper attention to how determined the Turkish soldiers might be to stop their country being invaded. Some of the men attacking Gallipoli were going to be British. They would be accompanied by a battalion from Newfoundland too, which was not yet part of Canada. The Royal Naval Division would be back in action, and there would be French soldiers. Almost straight away, Indian soldiers were sent to Gallipoli too.

OUTDATED VIEWS

Some of the Allies showed a lack of respect to the Turkish soldiers because at the time, many people believed that white men would always be better soldiers than men whose skin was a different colour. There were lots of attitudes to race during the First World War that make us feel uncomfortable now. How does that idea make you feel?

CAIRO
LUXOR
SUEZ CANAL
COLOMBO
COCOS ISLAND
AUSTRALIA
NEW ZEALAND
ANZACS

The Government also decided to use the volunteers from Australia and New Zealand. Thousands of young men had already been sent all the way to Egypt, and were busy training. They put them all together and made the Australia and New Zealand Corps. This was shortened to ANZAC, which has become a very famous word.

76

The Gallipoli landings began early on 25th April. British, French and Newfoundland men would all be arriving at the southern part of Gallipoli, called Cape Helles. Almost all of them would arrive in little boats, jump into the water and then run onto different beaches to claim them. This is called an amphibious landing (am-phib-ee-ous), like amphibians (say, a frog) they were going from water to land!

SUVIA BAY

FISHERMANS HUT   HILL 971

ANZAC

MAL TEPE

AEGEAN SEA

KILID BAHR PLATEAU

CHANAK

29 DIV BRITISH

KIRITHIA

Y

X

DARDANELLES

LANDINGS

W   V

S

KUM KALE

W Beach is often called Lancashire Landing, because the soldiers who were sent to take it first were men of the Lancashire Fusiliers. Not many Turkish soldiers defended the beach, but they had machine guns and they had put barbed wire and mines along the beach. It was a long, hard day of fighting, but things were worse at V Beach. Most of the attackers landed with the River Clyde. The beach was defended by a fort and by machine guns, and lots of men were killed. X, Y and S beaches were small, and they were hardly guarded by any Turkish soldiers at all.

The River Clyde was an old ship that was used to get men ashore. Soldiers were crammed inside, and then she was run up to the beach so that they could stay protected inside as long as possible, then spring out onto the beach. After the landings they used her to keep supplies in.

Z beach, which was further north, is only ever called 'Anzac', because it is where the men from Australia and New Zealand landed and it came to mean so much to those countries. At Anzac, the land leading away from the beaches is very steep and very diffcult to get across, without being shot at by the enemy!

They did manage to climb, but the Turkish carried out a counter-attack. Things got so bad at Anzac, that the generals in charge of the Australians and New Zealanders suggested that they all get back on their boats. But the general in charge of the whole Gallipoli campaign, Sir Ian Hamilton, ordered them to stay. They managed to stop the Turks, but did not manage to take the high ground above the beaches. You always want the high ground, because you don't want your enemy looking down on everything you are doing!

This photo shows soldiers at Anzac Cove.

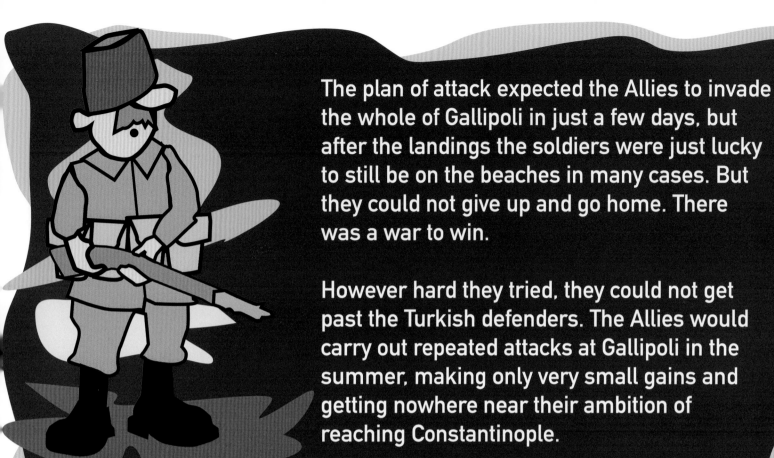

The plan of attack expected the Allies to invade the whole of Gallipoli in just a few days, but after the landings the soldiers were just lucky to still be on the beaches in many cases. But they could not give up and go home. There was a war to win.

However hard they tried, they could not get past the Turkish defenders. The Allies would carry out repeated attacks at Gallipoli in the summer, making only very small gains and getting nowhere near their ambition of reaching Constantinople.

In this picture you can see Indian artillerymen working at Gallipoli

79

This soldier is trying to smoke a cigarette at Gallipoli without being attacked by flies!

These men are cleaning uniforms. They are are trying to fumigate them and get rid of all of the lice and insects which can cause disease.

Conditions were different to those on the Western Front, but they were no nicer, even if it was sunny a lot of the time. Flies were everywhere. One soldier had a jar of jam sent to him by his family. He said that when he took the lid off, in the time it took him to pick up a spoon, the whole jar would be full of flies!

Disease was also a huge problem at Gallipoli, and again it was because of the dirty conditions. One of the worst was a horrible illness called dysentery (Dis-en-terry). This was caused by flies transferring germs, and gives you a very upset stomach, belly cramps, high fever and makes you vomit.

The Allies decided to try something very different to try to finish their invasion of Gallipoli. In August 1915, they decided to carry out landings at a new spot further north, called Suvla Bay. There were not many Turkish soldiers waiting for them, but yet again the Allies' attacks failed because they did not take the high ground. Lots more men were killed, and still the campaign had got nowhere. One New Zealand battalion that tried lost 711 of their 760 men.

There were no shops on Gallipoli for the Allies! Everything had to be brought by boat. Here men are sorting cans of safe drinking water for soldiers.

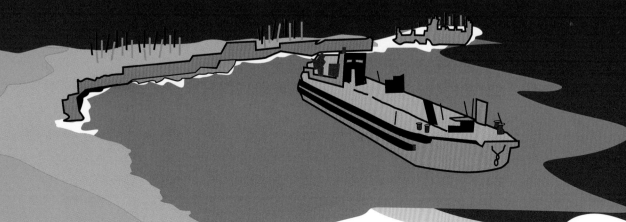

Soldiers will always try and make themselves comfortable. In this photo you can see that they have managed to take a gramophone into the trenches to listen to music!

In this photo some soldiers are sleeping, but another is playing a game with the enemy, by waving a helmet and pretending that a soldier is showing his head. We wonder if they shot at it!

It was clear that the invasion of Gallipoli would never be a success. In some places, the two sides did not even shoot at each other from their trenches anymore, and some men exchanged presents with each other by throwing them backwards and forwards. There was even a truce where everyone agreed not to fight for a while, so that they could all spend some time burying some of the many bodies lying about.

Then the weather started to get cold. The Allied soldiers only had summer clothes, and many got sick. Some of them even froze to death. The weather at Gallipoli can be frightening. Blizzards and flash floods also killed many soldiers on both sides.

At the end of the year, it was finally decided that the Allies would leave and give up trying to get to Constantinople this way. To take everyone off of Gallipoli safely would be a huge job. The sad thing is, this was the only really successful part of the whole Allied invasion of Gallipoli. The Allies broke what they couldn't take away, set fire to supplies they didn't want the Turks to have, and took away all they could carry in the middle of the night. It only took a few days in the end, but not one man was killed in the evacuation of Gallipoli and the operation was completed in January 1916.

The Gallipoli, or 'Çanakkale Savasi' campaign was a very expensive failure for the Allies. Nearly 60,000 Allied soldiers died and in the end they had to run away. Winston Churchill lost his job at the head of the Royal Navy, and the general who led the campaign, Sir Ian Hamilton, saw his career ruined.

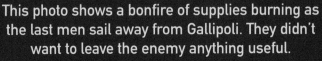
This photo shows a bonfire of supplies burning as the last men sail away from Gallipoli. They didn't want to leave the enemy anything useful.

For Turkey, Çanakkale Savasi is remembered as a heroic defence of their homeland against invaders. Nearly a quarter of a million men from the Ottoman Empire were killed, wounded, got sick or taken prisoner, or died of disease.

One man who helped the Ottoman Empire to victory was Mustafa Kemal. When the Empire collapsed, he later became Atatürk, the founding father of the Republic of Turkey. He is a national hero.

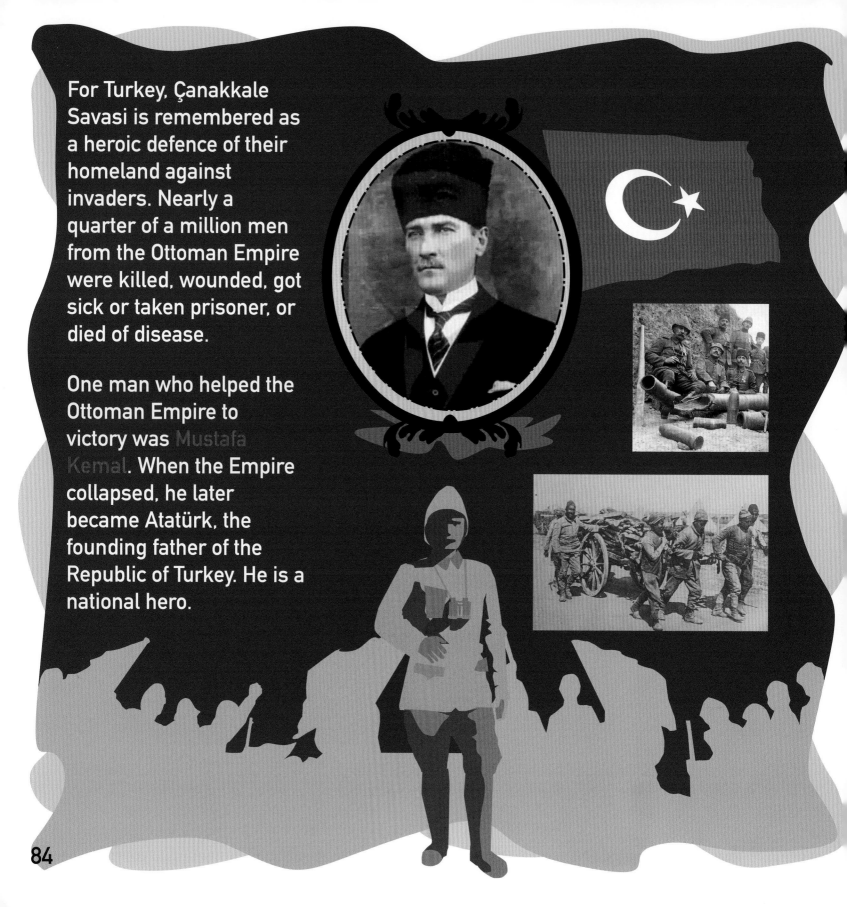

The Eastern Front

1915 was a year of mixed fortunes. In January the German and Russian armies fought the Battle of Bolimów. We already know how important railways are in war, and this village lay along the line between Łodz and Warsaw. Here the Germans used their poison gas for the very first time, but the wind blew it back towards them, instead of at the Russians, and then the cold weather froze it, so it was a failure.

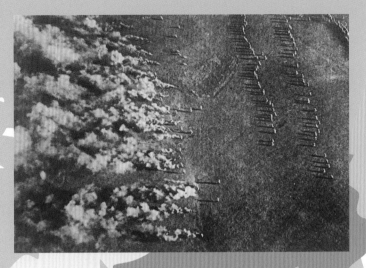

This photo shows a gas attack on the Eastern Front. Can you see the clouds?

Because of this, the Germans decided not to carry out their offensive after all, but the Russians did go forward. The Germans used their artillery to break up the attack and 40,000 Russians were killed, wounded or taken prisoner.

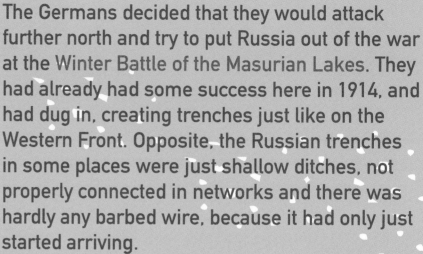

The Germans decided that they would attack further north and try to put Russia out of the war at the Winter Battle of the Masurian Lakes. They had already had some success here in 1914, and had dug in, creating trenches just like on the Western Front. Opposite, the Russian trenches in some places were just shallow ditches, not properly connected in networks and there was hardly any barbed wire, because it had only just started arriving.

The snow drifts were as tall as the men in some places, but the German troops advanced up to 75 miles in a week and the Russians ran away. They left their food behind, so the Germans did not go hungry. On 18th February, the Russian 20th Army Corps made a heroic last stand in Augustów Forest, but three days later they were forced to surrender. They did, however, give the main Russian force time to make a new defensive line by holding up the Germans. This battle was important, because it led to the Russian Army being forced from German soil and Germany got their foot through the door and into Russia.

But whilst Germany was doing well, Austria-Hungary would be trying to cross the Carpathian Mountains into Galicia in the direction of Przemyśl and Lemberg to attack more Russian armies. This was a very bad idea in the middle of winter. There were hardly any roads to supply the attack, and soldiers were more likely to die from the cold than they were at the hands of the enemy.

Nevertheless, General Conrad von Hötzendorf, in command of the Austro-Hungarians, sent his men in to attack here three times anyway.

Each time, it got worse, and in the end his forces fell back. If you add up all of the men on both sides who were killed, died because of the conditions, were wounded or taken prisoner, there are two million of them. That is more than the number of people that live in Vienna, the capital of Austria, today!

You can see in this photo just how much snow there was in the mountains. These are Austrian soldiers trying to have a look about.

Although we talk about Austria-Hungary and the armies that fought for its Hapsburg Empire, there were troops from many other places fighting under their flag. These included Bosnian muslims. Polish soldiers could have found themselves fighting other Poles in the Russian Army. And there were also men who might have identified, as Slavs, more with Russia, than they did with the country they were fighting for. Sometimes, without real justification, these men were blamed when things went wrong. This was definitely true of Czech soldiers after the Winter War in the Carpathians. They were blamed for the failure of the Austro-Hungarian attacks because of their ethnicity.

In this photo you can see Bosnian soldiers.

This photo shows a group of Czech soldiers later in the war.

Conditions on the Eastern Front were very different to the Western Front. During the first years of the war, the front moved a lot more than in the west, which meant that trenches were often less permanent, and so less 'nice' to live in for the soldiers.

The front was also enormous and the ground, or terrain, varied greatly from vast open plains to snow-covered mountains and from swamps and marshes to thick forests. In the summer, the soldiers suffered under sweltering heat, but during winter, the temperature could drop below -20 degrees causing frostbite and sometimes even death from exposure. Thousands of soldiers would freeze to death because they were not given proper winter clothing. In fact, often the weather claimed more lives than the actual fighting.

In this photo you see can some Russian soldiers having a snowball fight. But living outside in snow like this was not fun.

You can see from this photo how much damage was done to Przemyśl during the war.

Remember that in 1914 the Russians had begun a siege at the important fortress of Przemyśl (Zye-mis) on the River San? Austro-Hungarian troops inside managed to hold out for 133 days, before they finally surrendered in March 1915 and let the Russians in. This was embarassing for Austria-Hungary, especially as more than 100,000 soldiers surrendered to the enemy. When you think about how many men also died attacking the Carpathians because of the awful conditions, it really was a complete disaster for Austria-Hungary.

EAST PRUSSIA

WARSAW   POLAND

VISTULA   KRAKOW

PRZEMYSL

LODZ   LIMANOWA

LAPANOW   GALICIA

SILESIA

SANS

In this photo you can see Austro-Hungarian prisoners at Przemyśl.

The Gorlice-Tarnów Offensive was the Central Powers' biggest attacking effort of 1915. After the disaster in the Carpathian mountains, General Conrad threatened to have Austria-Hungary quit the war and leave Germany to fight Russia alone if they did not help him.

Eventually, the two countries agreed to work closer together this time, and it took 500 trains to bring all of the German soldiers into the right areas. They also brought together the big guns that had destroyed fortresses in Belgium in 1914.

WHAT DOES IT MEAN?

An offensive is just another name for a very big attack, that is going to last for a while,

In this photo, civilians are watching German and Austro-Hungarian soldiers moving backwards and forwards during the Gorlice-Tarnow Offensive.

The offensive began at the beginning of May and straight away the soldiers from the Central Powers began to destroy the Russian Army in front of them. On 3rd June, they took back Przemyśl, then they took vital oil fields, which they needed for the war effort, and carried on going towards Lemberg.

This time is known as the Great Retreat of 1915. In August, Warsaw fell to the Germans and by the end of the month the whole of Poland was in the hands of the Central Powers. The Germans tried to get Russia to make peace, but the Tsar said no. He had promised Britain and France that he would not do this without them. For Russia, the Gorlice-Tarnow offensive was completely humiliating. It's very hard to figure out how many men died, but nearly half a million Russian soldiers could have been killed, wounded or taken prisoner.

In this photo you can see an Austro-Hungarian soldier looking after a lot of Russian prisoners!

While the Gorlice-Tarnów offensive had been a great success, The man in charge of the Austro-Hungarian armies, Conrad von Hötzendorf, was unhappy that Germany got most of the glory for the victory. He still wanted to prove that his soldiers could fight too and win a victory of his own. He started putting a new army together, made up of mostly new troops with no experience.

In late August he launched the Black and Yellow Offensive (named after the Habsburg Dynasty's royal colours) in Volhynia, in what is today western Ukraine and Belarus. He wanted to capture the cities of Lutsk and Rovno, and while he did have some initial success, the Russians counter-attacked and the offensive got bogged down. Many of Conrad's inexperienced soldiers began to surrender in large numbers. It was a terrible failure, and the Austro-Hungarians lost more than 230,000 men as a result. As a joke, the offensive was quickly named 'Conrad's Autumn Swinery'.

The War at Sea

Dogger Bank is an area of the North Sea, about sixty miles away from the east coast of England. In the last Ice Age, it was actually part of a bridge of land linking Britain to Europe! For hundreds of years it has been used for fishing.

On 24th January 1915, Royal Navy ships located and attacked a German raiding squadron at Dogger Bank. The German ships fled, and the British chased them until they got close enough to start firing their guns. The *Blücher* was sunk, and some of her crew died, but whilst the Royal Navy ships were busy with her, the other German ships got away.

In this photo you can see the German ship *Blücher* sinking, and her crew climbing to safety.

TOP SECRET

The Royal Navy knew that the Germans would be at Dogger Bank because of intelligence.

Intelligence is hugely important in war. It means gathering knowledge about everyone else. You can do it openly, but it's where spies come in too!

The Royal Navy's intellgence included Room 40. It was a room on the first floor of the Admiralty building near 10 Downing Street. We think that the men working here intercepted, or heard, 15,000 German messages that came through telegraphs and wireless communications. They were codebreakers too. Their work was hugely important, especially, as we will see later on, when it came to the United States joining the war.

It was not only men who took part in secret work in the First World War. In this photo you can see both men and women at work in Room 40.

The Merchant Navy is what we call all British ships sailing for business purposes, but they got this name officially in 1928 because of their contribution to the First World War. Before then, we normally called it the Mercantile Marine.

It was impossible for merchant ships and crews not to become involved in the war. For a start, U-Boats would try to sink them because they carried important things like food. If you add up the weight of all the merchant ships that sank because of German submarines, they would weigh eight MILLION tons. That's more than the Great Pyramid at Giza! Nearly 15,000 merchant mariners from British ships alone were killed in the First World War.

But you must remember that many of the crew who died were not British. You could be from any country and sign on to a British ship as crew.

Merchant ships did not just carry on doing their normal work in wartime though; which was carrying goods and people backwards and forwards across oceans. In a lot of cases, governments had helped pay to build them. This meant that they could ask to use the ships during the First World War.

In this picture you can see *Lusitania*'s sister ship, *Mauretania*, painted in dazzle colours. She worked as a troop transport in the First World War.

Many ships, and with them their crews of men, women and even young boys, entered war service. They acted as troop transports. Furniture was ripped out and soldiers crammed in to sail them all over the world. They also acted as hospital ships. They would have big crosses painted on them to tell U-Boats that they were full of wounded men, hoping that they would leave them alone, but sadly this did not always work. More than 20 hospital ships were sunk in the First World War and we see a lot of women being killed, because they were working on board as nurses. One thing used to confuse U-Boats were dazzle paint schemes. This meant painting a ship in mad colours and patterns all over. It confuses your perception of a ship!

We have already looked at why the German Navy might try and use U-boats to make up for losing the naval arms race. If they couldn't meet the Royal Navy face to face and hope to win, they would have to try and find a different way. The British had set up a blockade, using their ships to stop ships with supplies getting to Germany, and so on 18th Feburary 1915, Germany publicly declared the waters surrounding Britain a war zone. They put warnings in newspapers and issued maps, and said that any boat flying an allied flag in these waters could be attacked and sunk by their U-boats.

They were not talking about military ships, but any ship. This meant that they were threatening to sink unarmed vessels carrying passengers. Ships could not just stop using these waters, so they developed ways to evade U-boats. They used dark paint so that they would be harder to see, they sailed in zag-zag courses so they would be harder to shoot at with torpedoes, and some of them even used the wrong flags so that they looked like they were from neutral countries.

A neutral country is one that doesn't want to get involved in a war. In the First World War; Spain, Switzerland, Denmark, Norway and Sweden are all examples of countries that never declared war.

WHO WAS LUSY?

Lusitania was one of the most famous ships in the world. She belonged to a company that still sails big cruise ships today, called Cunard. She was almost as big as *Titanic*, and faster. In fact, she was one of the fastest liners in the world. She was also luxurious. Even if you travelled in third class you would have been impressed! She was about eight years old when the war started, and had been nicknamed 'Lusy'. She worked on the North Atlantic, the most important route in the world. At the time there were no big aeroplanes, so boat was the only way to get to America. It took about five days to get from Southampton, England to New York, and was the most impressive way to travel. A trip on Lusy would be something you would brag to all your friends about!

The Government didn't ask to use Lusy, because she used too much coal, and so she stayed with Cunard, carrying passengers and mail. The *Lusitania* sailed from New York at lunchtime on 1st May 1915. She was just passing southern Ireland nearly a week later on her way to England when she was spotted by U-20. A torpedo was fired, and it hit the side of the ship. The ship was doomed. She sank in just eighteen minutes. She had enough lifeboats for everyone on board, but there was no time to get them away. Some turned over, some crashed into each other. The ship, was still moving and so dragged them along. Of the 48 boats, only six were launched successfully.

Captain Turner of the *Lusitania*

Walter Schwieger, commander of U-20

Lusy was 787 feet long. That's as long as 21 London buses parked end to end in a line!

A German medal celebrating the sinking of the *Lusitania*

The ship turned over on her side. Lots of boats left for the site immediately to try and help, but the water was so cold that many people did not survive long enough for them to arrive. Almost 1,200 people died, including nearly 100 children. It happened on 7th May 1915. It was a disaster nearly on the same scale as the sinking of RMS *Titanic* in 1912.

The world was outraged at what had happened to the ship, but in Germany people celebrated. A medal was even made for people to keep as a souvenir of the sinking.

Nearly 800 survivors were first taken to Ireland, where many of them needed to be treated in hospital.

This photo shows a victim of the *Lusitania* arriving home in America to be buried. The men dealing with the coffin have taken their hats off as a mark of respect.

At the beginning of 1915, the United States was the most important of all the neutral countries. Both the Allies and the Central Powers would have loved to have America on their side, but much more important was making sure that she did not side with your enemy. America was a rich country, and could have a big effect on the war. When Lusy was sunk, 128 Americans were killed and this was big news. Surely now Americans would be so angry that they would want to enter the war against Germany? But it did not happen. After a lot of publicity, it turned out that Americans would still rather stay neutral. Not everybody hated Germany. There were millions of people living in America whose heritage was German, and millions of people with Irish heritage too, who did not want to side with Britain. Lots of Americans just wanted to stay at peace, and Germany promised soon afterwards not to do anything like this again.

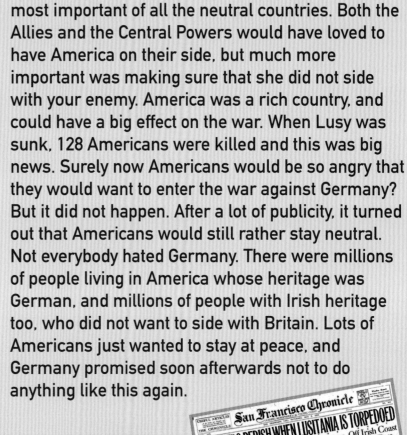

The Balkans

Bulgaria declared war on Serbia on 14th October 1915 and joined the Central Powers. Until then they had stayed out of the conflict. They had only just fought a war in 1912-13 and were not ready for another. The decision about which side to join was based on who would guarantee the best prizes at the end. Bulgaria was only a small country compared to some of the other powers, but it was going to have a big effect on the war.

Serbia was rightly terrified at the thought of Bulgaria becoming their enemy. They lined up half of their entire army along the border between the two countries, but to survive being invaded, they were going to need a lot of help from the Allies. But the Allies already had too much too do on the Western Front, Gallipoli, and everywhere else. They would have liked Greece to join the war and help instead.

This photo shows Bulgarian soldiers leaving for war.

In October 1915, Austria-Hungary, Germany and Bulgaria all invaded Serbia at different points. The Bulgarian Army took the towns of Niš and Pirot. It was all too much for the small Serbian army, still badly suffering after the typhus outbreak and the fighting of 1914. The country was quickly overrun with enemy troops and Serbian soldiers fell back toward Kosovo. Bulgaria decided to chase them as hard as they could.

This postcard celebrates the invasion of Serbia by the Central Powers

In these photos you can see some Bulgarians about to have their dinner!

Vladimir Putnik was in command of the Serbian Army. He was 70 in the First World War, and had fought in every Serbian war since 1876.

Just like in Belgium, lots of refugees left their homes to get away from the war

Now Serbia needed to save its army from complete destruction. Serbian soldiers and civilians began a long, terrible retreat through the mountains, in the middle of winter, towards Albania. As far as the army was concerned, about 150,000 men made it there, but they had lost everything and were taken away to the island of Corfu, where Serbia would have to begin building an army all over again.

The Great Retreat happened in horrible conditions.

In this photo you can see some Serbian women helping to carry wounded soldiers.

The Allies did finally arrive in the Balkans. French troops trying to help the Serbian Army fought the Battle of Krivolak against the Bulgarians in November. They did not defeat them, but they did distract them and give the Serbian soldiers time to get away. British troops had arrived to help too. They were attacked by Bulgarians in December, at the Battle of Kosturino, and forced to retreat. The Allies decided to go back to the city we now call Thessaloniki. The front that was formed for the rest of the war, we call the Macedonian Front, or, normally, just Salonika.

This photograph shows some of the supplies and equipment that the Allies took with them to Salonika

In this photo you can see British soldiers relaxing in a trench on the Salonika front.

It was not a big victory for the Central Powers, and the war had yet another static front, but they could now use the railway that ran between Berlin and Constantinople without the Allies getting in the way.

The force sent to Salonika was truly international. In the first picture, you can see French soldiers watering their horses.

In the photo below, you can see Indian troops moving supplies.

MACEDONIA • KRIVOLAK

KOSTURINO •

GERMANY
AUSTRIA-
HUNGARY
ITALY

The Italian Front

Before the First World War, Italy was part of the **Triple Alliance**. This meant that on paper she was friends with Germany and Austria-Hungary. But the bit of paper was quite old by this point, and the governments involved had not been looking after the agreement.

At first Italy stayed out of the war, but then the government began to realise that if they made an agreement with the right side, the country might gain more land and other benefits if they turned out to be on the winning side. They began to talk to both the Central Powers and the Allies to see who would give them the best deal. It turned out to be the Allies, and on 3rd May 1915, Italy officially 'revoked', or took back, their membership in the Triple Alliance. On 23rd, Italy declared war on Austria-Hungary and joined the Allies.

Lots of Italians were confused about why they should join a war. Lots of them didn't even really think of themselves as Italian, because it had only been one big country for 45 years!

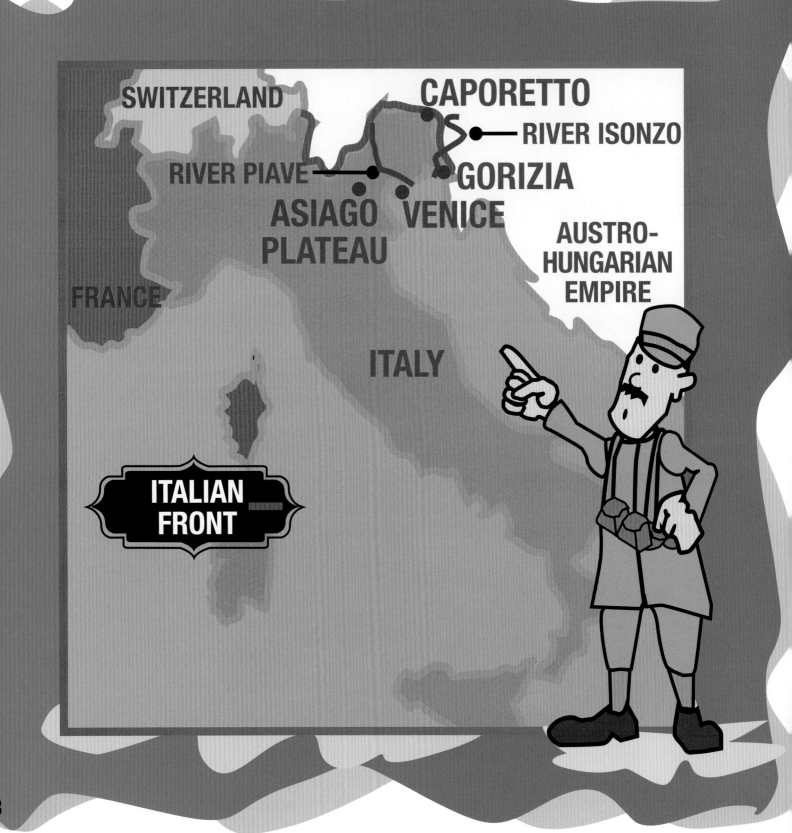

SWITZERLAND

CAPORETTO

RIVER ISONZO

RIVER PIAVE

GORIZIA

ASIAGO PLATEAU

VENICE

AUSTRO-HUNGARIAN EMPIRE

FRANCE

ITALY

ITALIAN FRONT

The Italian front was very unique in the First World War. It was about 400 miles long, like the Western Front, but stretched through very high mountains in the Alps, all the way down to the Adriatic Sea. It was a completely different kind of war, as you can see from the pictures, to the one being fought in France and Belgium. When Italian and Austro-Hungarian soldiers had to dig trenches, it was not in mud, it was in solid rock and even through glaciers! As you can see from the pictures, even moving equipment about could be almost impossible! Conditions could be very dangerous. In one month in 1916, 10,000 men were killed by avalanches!

In these pictures you can see how difficult life could be on the Italian Front. In the first photo, Austro-Hungarian troops are climbing a mountain wall for an attack. You can also see that sometimes it was easier to get about on skis! And in the bottom picture you can see how both sides approached the idea of getting a gun up the side of a mountain!

Often is was very hard to even climb up to the front!

This is what a the front looked like on top of a mountain!

Sometimes it was easier to send men to the bottom of the mountain in a lift like this, especially if they were wounded.

In this photo you can see men in Milan making animal skins into warm clothing for Italian soldiers.

General Luigi Cadorna was in charge of the Italian armies in 1915. He was 64 years old when Italy joined the war and close to retirement . He was very keen on attacking warfare, very strict, and not easy to get along with. The First World War would cause a lot of damage to his reputation.

The man in charge of the Italian soldiers, General Cadorna, liked attacking right from the front and very bravely, but this kind of fighting means that many, many soldiers are lost. His plan at the beginning of Italy's war was to attack on the River Isonzo. From here, Italy's armies would get into what is now Slovenia, take Ljubljana and then be on their way to the Austro-Hungarian capital, Vienna.

ITALIAN FRONT

RIVER IZONZO

ITALY

VENICE

ISONZO

The Italians would end up fighting many, many battles to get across the River Isonzo. The first started on 23rd June 1915. The Italians had double the amount of men as the Austro-Hungarians, and they started well, but the enemy had the high ground and had blocked the way up very well.

The Austro-Hungarians managed to fight back the Italians. Just like on the Western Front, the attack fizzled out and troops began digging trenches. In the end, the Italians had not taken very much ground at all, and by 7th July the battle was over.

In this photo, you can see Italian troops on the Isonzo front.

Cadorna wanted to try again almost straight away, this time using heavier artillery. He used almost the same plan. It was simple and very tough. Use lots of big shells and then throw his men at the Austro-Hungarian barbed wire and defences. Then they would take the enemy trenches. This was an even stranger plan when you consider that his armies lacked rifles, shells and even wire-cutters to try and get through the enemy defences.

The Second Battle of Isonzo started on 18th July. Men fought each other close together using the bayonets on the end of their rifles, swords, knives and everything else they could get their hands on. This terrifying fighting did not end until both sides started to run out of ammunition at the beginning of August. Italy had lost 43,000 men and Austria-Hungary had lost 48,000.

This photo shows General Cadorna inspecting Italian troops at the time of the Second Battle of the Isonzo.

2

ISONZO

3. ISONZO

Morale is a feeling. It's what we use to describe how large groups of people are feeling during the war. When a big battle is won, morale is high. In this case, morale among Italian soldiers was very low.

Remember that the Austro-Hungarian Army was made up of men from lots of different places? These men are from Bosnia.

General Cadorna then let his armies recover from the fighting of the summer before he tried once again. In this time, he had gathered together a lot more artillery. The Third Battle of the Isonzo started on 18th October and once again casualties were very high on both sides. The Italians fought hard but the Austro-Hungarians pushed them back again.

Italian soldiers were not impressed with Cadorna's methods, and some of them ran away! He was starting to pay attention to the difficult mountains he was fighting in, and how he spread his troops out, but morale was low.

But despite his latest failure, less than a week after the third battle, Cadorna sent his men into the **Fourth Battle of the Isonzo** on 10th November. Most of the fighting was aimed at trying to take Gorizia. Yet again, casualties were very high. At Mount Sei Busi alone, the Italians tried five times to take the mountain and failed. Eventually, the snow arrived, supplies dried up and both sides gave up.

In these first four battles, Italy had about 60,000 men killed. The type of attacks that Cadorna liked were very costly, and they had not brought him victory. The Austro-Hungarians had lost so many men that they asked Germany for help. At this time, Italy and Germany had not yet declared war on each other.

4

ISONZO

Zeppelins

A Zeppelin was what we call a rigid airship. This means it was not just a big balloon, but that it also had a strong frame. They were named after the man who developed them. In the end, the name was used for rigid airships generally, and not just the ones he designed. Underneath the balloon was a big compartment. They were used to carry passengers before the war, but the German forces loved them too! They used them for gathering intelligence on all different fronts, but more importantly they used them as aerial bombers.

Zeppelins bombed Paris, but the city got very good at defending itself. Aeroplanes patrolled the skies waiting to attack them if they showed up. The Zeppelins also had to fly over forts protecting the city. About 25 people were killed in Paris by airship bombs. There were plans to bomb St. Petersburg (which was renamed Petrograd to sound more Russian). This never went ahead, but Naples in Italy was bombed during the war too.

IT IS FAR BETTER
TO FACE THE BULLETS
THAN TO BE KILLED
AT HOME BY A BOMB

JOIN THE ARMY AT ONCE
& HELP TO STOP AN AIR RAID

GOD SAVE THE KING

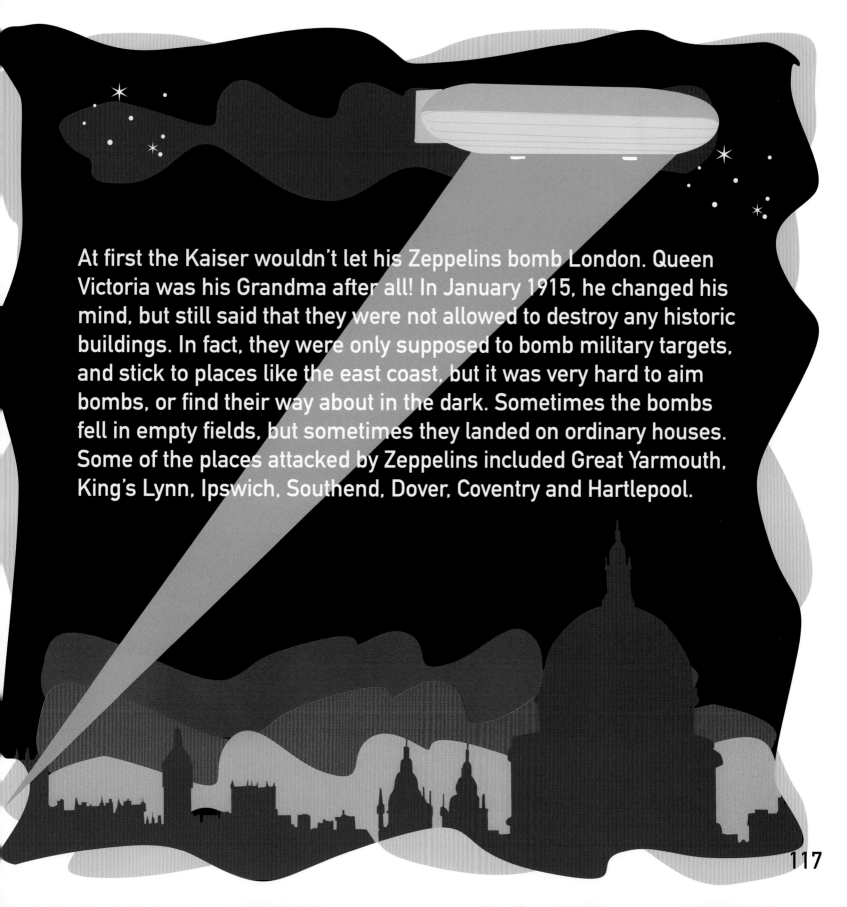

At first the Kaiser wouldn't let his Zeppelins bomb London. Queen Victoria was his Grandma after all! In January 1915, he changed his mind, but still said that they were not allowed to destroy any historic buildings. In fact, they were only supposed to bomb military targets, and stick to places like the east coast, but it was very hard to aim bombs, or find their way about in the dark. Sometimes the bombs fell in empty fields, but sometimes they landed on ordinary houses. Some of the places attacked by Zeppelins included Great Yarmouth, King's Lynn, Ipswich, Southend, Dover, Coventry and Hartlepool.

Zeppelins were very bad for morale. Men, women and children could just be asleep in their houses and a bomb could fall on them. In the First World War, in Britain alone, more than 500 people died in Zeppelin bombings. This had never happened in history before, and was a terrifying thought. People called the airships 'Baby-Killers'.

Of course this meant that everyone wanted to shoot them down. The most famous time this happened was on 2nd September 1916. In the biggest Zeppelin raid so far, Sixteen German airships set out for London. One of the airships was the new SL-11. It dropped a few bombs on Hertfordshire and then made its way to London. Flying a slow aeroplane, a pilot called Lieutenant William Leefe Robinson caught up with it and began shooting. The airship caught fire and crashed to the ground near the village of Cuffley in Hertfordshire.

In these photos you can see how much work needed to be done after the airship was shot down over Cuffley. It made quite a mess!

Lots of people in London watched the airship crash. Many artists tried to recreate what they saw and people bought postcards like this one to remember the famous event.

1916

Finally, the thousands of recruits from 1914 and 1915 were ready to fight, and nations had managed to properly equip them. Lots had been learned, but would it be enough to secure victory?

Allied Planning

The Allies knew exactly what they wanted to do on the Western Front in 1916. They wanted a big offensive on the Somme,

Why another big offensive now? - The Allies still needed to push the Germans back into their own country. They felt ready now. Remember all of those men that rushed to volunteer in 1914? They would be ready to fight in large numbers by the summer of 1916. Also, remember the shell shortage? All of the work to make enough ammunition for this huge new war had been paying off. There were lots of munitions available in 1916, so things looked good for the Allies.

What is the Somme? - The Somme is an area of Northern France, based around a river of the same name. Before 1916, although there were trenches there, it was very quiet. It was farmland and lots of open countryside.

Why there? - Honestly? The French always believed that Britain's soldiers could be doing more to try and win the war. The River Somme was where the two armies met, and so they picked it because they would be close by and they could keep an eye on them!

The Western Front

The Allies might have had lots of plans for the Western Front in 1916, but before they could carry any of them out, the Germans attacked. The Battle of Verdun was fought between February and December 1916. It was the longest battle of the First World War.

Verdun, a fortified town on the River Meuse, was as symbolic a place for France as Ypres was for Belgium. Have you heard of Atilla the Hun? He tried to take Verdun in the 5th Century! Like important border towns in Belgium, it was surrounded by forts Two that would become very famous were Fort Vaux (make rhyme with sew) and the biggest, Fort Douaumont (Doo-ow-mon).

The Germans attacked on 21st February. General Falkenhayn believed that if his armies caused enough French casualties, they could be beaten, even in trench warfare. We believe now that he thought the French would try to hold on to Verdun for all they were worth, and that the British would start a new offensive to help draw attention away.

Verdun Part One: 21st February –1st March

General Joffre knew about the possibility of a German attack, but did not believe that it would be a big offensive. He thought it would be a distraction because the area was not worth a lot to an army. He was wrong.

This photo shows the Verdun front in March 1916. February is an early start for an offensive, as you can see by the snow everywhere!

On the first day of the battle, the Germans carried out a ten-hour artillery bombardment. This means that for all that time, they fired shells at the French positions. We think they fired about a million shells at that time. Then, their soldiers went forward, some of them with flame throwers.

Fort Douaumont was captured by German soldiers, and a French counter-attack failed.

By 27th February, the ground had begun to thaw, and where it had been icy and firm, it turned into thick mud. More French troops arrived, the German guns couldn't move and the battle slowed down and then stopped. In places, the German soldiers had moved forward, or advanced, up to two miles. That's a lot in the world of trench warfare!

French troops on the street in Verdun during the battle.

The Germans also used Stormtroopers, or Sturmtruppen. This was a new idea. Stormtroopers were specially trained. Instead of attacking the enemy trenches and trying to make sure that they kept them by clearing all French troops out of the way, they stormed through and got as far as they could. Then other, normal soldiers would follow them to do the clearing up, which we call consolidation.

In this 1916 photo German artillerymen are working out where to send their shells.

Verdun Part Two: 6th March –15th April

After the first part of the battle, General Falkenhayn did not know whether to carry on and put more soldiers into the battle or call it quits. In the end, the Germans decided to carry on. They planned to make two attacks; one on 6th March and another three days later. Fighting was fierce again, and many men were killed on both sides. It took a week for the Germans to get as far as they had planned for the first day. So they had a bit of success, but it cost a lot.

Just like in other battles on the Western Front, wherever the French Army was, you would find troops from French colonies. In this photo you can see Moroccan soldiers at Verdun.

By the end of March, Germany had lost more than 80,000 men at Verdun, and again, they thought about giving up on their offensive. Was it really worth getting involved in another drawn out battle where there could be no winner? What do you think?

Verdun Part Three: 16th April –1st July

And yet still, the commanders of the 5th Army Corps wanted to continue. It was very hard for them to make the German positions safe, and so for them, the only solution was to carry on attacking. If not, the commanders reported to Falkenhayen, they might as well go all the way back to where they were before 21st February.

The Germans sent more men to Verdun, including all the way from the Eastern Front, and attacked again in a big way. But progress was still very slow. The French were determined to stand their ground and casualties were very high. The German troops tried to change their approach, but nothing seemed to work. By the middle of May, the Germans were only carrying out little attacks, if the French attacked them first, or if there was something they could capture that would help them in future, like high ground.

By this time, a new French General had arrived called Robert Nivelle, and he ordered his men to retake Fort Douaumont. A full-scale attack began on 22nd May, but despite another 10,000 casualties on both sides, the fort stayed in German hands. To make things worse, the Germans then captured Fort Vaux. The French were forced back to what they called 'the Line of Panic'!

By June, French morale was very low. In some regiments, men were refusing to follow orders. On 23rd June, General Nivelle issued an order that said: *Vous ne les laisserez pas passer, mes camarades* ('You will not let them pass, my comrades'). Fleury changed hands sixteen times in seven weeks, and by the end of June, everyone was so exhausted that they simply stopped fighting.

This photo shows a wounded man being sent away from the battlefield at Verdun.

In this photo you can see men of the French 164th Infantry Regiment in a trench at Verdun.

German soldiers on the march.

In this photo you can see a German bombardment in action.

Because of the Battle of Verdun, the French were not able to take a big part in the summer offensive on the Somme, and so for the first time, most of the work would be done by British soldiers. French soldiers would do their attacking, much less than originally intended, south of the river Somme.

For weeks, the British Army had been getting ready. It took a lot of work to get the area ready for such a big battle. The Allies had to build roads, move in supplies of food, water, shells. They had to move soldiers here too, and train them so that they were ready to attack in the summer.

These are some of the British Soldiers who took part on 1st July

These are some of the milions of shell cases from the Battle of the Somme.

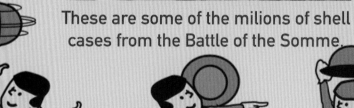

This photo was taken to show what going 'over the top' might have looked like.

The Germans had had a lot of time to make this positon strong too. They did not just have one system of trenches full of men ready to defend the Somme, but three. Also, any time their systems passed through a town or village, they had turned it into a mini fortress.

The Somme

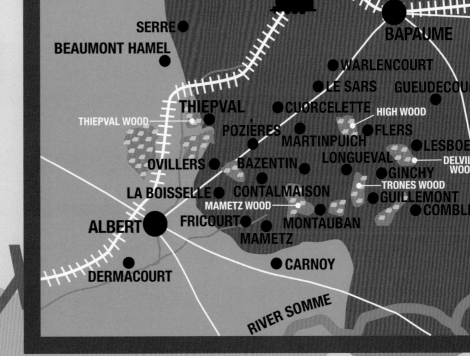

SOMME

GOMMECOURT

SERRE

BEAUMONT HAMEL

BAPAUME

WARLENCOURT

LE SARS   GUEUDECOURT

THIEPVAL   CUORCELETTE

THIEPVAL WOOD   HIGH WOOD

POZIÈRES   FLERS

MARTINPUICH

OVILLERS   BAZENTIN   LONGUEVAL   LESBOEUFS

DELVILLE WOOD

GINCHY

LA BOISSELLE   CONTALMAISON   TRONES WOOD

MAMETZ WOOD   GUILLEMONT

ALBERT   FRICOURT   MONTAUBAN   COMBLES

MAMETZ

CARNOY

DERMACOURT

RIVER SOMME

The Battle of the Somme was supposed to end the First World War. Using all of the new soldiers, and all of the new shells and equipment, there was a very daring plan that, if successful, would see the German Army broken on the Western Front and the Allies, led by the British, chasing them all the way home. Just like at Verdun, an artillery bombardment before the first day of the battle fired tens of thousands of shells, to try and destroy as much of the German lines as possible before men went 'over the top' of their trenches and into battle. The fighting finally began on 1st July 1916.

But the plan failed. Although the fighting was successful around Montauban in the south, at the other end of the battlefield, the soldiers got nowhere. 1st July 1916 is still the worst day in the history of the British Army. There were about 60,000 casualties, and of those 19,000 men died in the opening of the Somme offensive. The deaths were made worse by 'Pals Battalions'. These were big groups of men in some towns and cities who all signed up to serve together. When their battalions were destroyed on 1st July, it meant that lots of places lost a lot of their young men on one day. Accrington is one example of a town badly hit, along with the likes of Sheffield, Bradford, Barnsley and Leeds.

There are lots of reasons why things went so badly wrong on 1st July. Here are some of the most important:

- The Allies fired a lot of shells, but the battlefield was so big that it still wasn't enough to flatten everything ready for the infantry attack. Infantry is what we call soldiers who move on foot, unlike the cavalry on horses.

- The German positions were VERY strong. They had a lot time to prepare the area.

- The Allies used lots and lots of men. But, one machine gun can kill a lot of men. And on 1st July the Germans had a lot of machine guns.

- The plan was just too big. The soldiers were asked to do too much, too quickly, and even if they did really well on 1st July, it was never going to be possible to achieve all of their objectives.

Sir Douglas Haig took over the British armies on the Western Front as Commander in Chief before the Battle of the Somme. He was a hard working, serious man and a former cavalry officer. He had long thought war was coming for Britain before 1914, and had worked hard to help the army prepare.

But what could the Allies do? They could not pack up and go home. For the rest of the summer, the fighting was dominated by a lot of woods that needed to be captured. The trees were all burnt and cut down by fire very quickly, but the mess left behind provided lots of places to hide, so it was very difficult to completely capture them. You can see them all on the map. Trônes Wood and High Wood were infamous, but there were two that were even worse and impacted certain areas very badly.

Attempts to capture Mametz Wood completey destroyed the Welsh Division in July. Thousands and thousands of men died, and the division would not be ready to fight again until 1917. Delville Wood was perhaps the worst of all, and there is now a memorial there for South African soldiers. This is because when they arrived to try and take it, more than 3,300 men went in. By the time they came out again, there were only 765 soldiers left able to fight. As they marched past their commanding officer, he cried.

This photo shows what was left of the trees in Delville Wood by September 1916.

These are British machine-gunners with their gun. Can you see how much better gas masks had got already?

By 1916 most of the Indian troops had left the Western Front, but some cavalry took part in the Battle of the Somme.

This photo shows French soldiers outside a ruined restaurant at Herbiecourt.

The Battle of the Somme had become a battle of attrition. This means that rather than one big fight with a grand ending, just like at Verdun it had become a series of little fights with both sides gradually chipping away at each other and not getting very far. Think of it like cricket. Instead of a quick 20-20 fixture, it had turned into a very long and uninspiring test match. And yet the Allies were gradually moving forward. If they stopped, the Germans would be going nowhere, and so the only thing to do was carry on. They did decide, though, that they should stop, get ready properly and carry out a significant attack in September, instead of wasting resources. That's men and equipment.

The fighting that took place in the First World War completely destroyed whole areas of France. Villages ceased to exist, roads were destroyed. The landscape was covered in shell-holes as far as the eye could see. Soldiers on the Somme sometimes found it very hard to get around because there were no features such as buildings and trees left to show you where you were. They said that the Somme looked like the surface of the moon.

These photos show you how much damage was done to villages and homes on the Somme. The picture above is of Guillemont High Street!

Troops moving through the ruins of Contalmaison.

The Allies once again attacked on 15th September at the Battle of Flers-Courcelette. This is named after two places on the battlefield, but it was still part of the Somme offensive. This would be the last time that the British attacked on the Somme in 1916 and still hoped to win the war. Once again it was costly and many, many soldiers were killed. And once again it proved too big a task to try and completely defeat the German Army.

In this photo you can see men attacking near the village of Ginchy.

But even if the battle was not important in terms of the result, it has become very famous for one reason. It was the first day in the history of the world that tanks were used in battle.

Tanks, or landships, had been coming for a while. The idea of them was championed in the navy by Winston Churchill, but the army was working on them too. By 1916, hundreds had been built, tested and taken to the Western Front. They were transferred in secret by trains. To get them into position ready for the fighting in September, they were moved at night. Aeroplanes flew backwards and forwards to mask the sound of the rumbling engines. Men swept the ground so that the Germans wouldn't see any tracks. In the daytime they were hidden under big sheets of canvas or by branches.

Everyone was determined that they would be a big surprise for the Germans,

Germany just hadn't thought of tanks, and efforts to keep them secret were very successful. The sight of them was a huge shock. German soldiers ran away screaming in some cases. What were these terrible monsters coming towards them breathing fire and crushing everything in their path!?

Tanks were a completely new invention and did not make a huge difference to the battle, but they were clearly going to completely change warfare and they had certainly made their presence known!

The first tanks were called the Mark I. The wheels were supposed to make balancing easier!

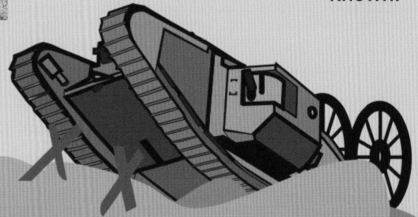

After Flers-Courcelette the British Army knew that the war would not be finished in 1916. But the problem now was making sure that the Allied troops held the safest positions possible for the winter. Not only that, but the men in charge wanted to get themselves good 'jumping off points' for the spring. They wanted the best start possible when the fighting began again. For this reason, fighting continued on the Somme long after the weather started to worsen at the end of the year.

More attacks were made at Thiepval, where the troops had not really gone anywhere at all since 1st July. Attention after that was focused on the River Ancre. The last battle began on 13th November, and during the Battle of the Ancre troops advanced in blizzards. Finally places like Beaucourt and Beamount Hamel were captured.

This picture shows you some of the trouble that men were having trying to keep the battle on the Somme going by October and November. Can you see how wet it is?

In this photo you can see just how much mud men had to deal with on the Somme,

By now the battlefield was in a disgusting state. It was time to put an end to the offensive. The German army was exhausted and battered but not defeated, The Allied leaders had already started to think about how they would start again in the spring.

Verdun Part Four: 1st July – 17 December

Meanwhile, at Verdun, Falkenhayn was replaced with two men: Paul von Hindenburg and Erich Ludendorff. They would become very powerful in Germany,

In October the French began the First Offensive Battle of Verdun, when they decided to fight and try to take Fort Douaumont back. They fired nearly a million shells, including huge ones from guns that could only be moved about and fired from trains! The fort was recaptured on 24th October by French marines and by colonial troops from North Africa.

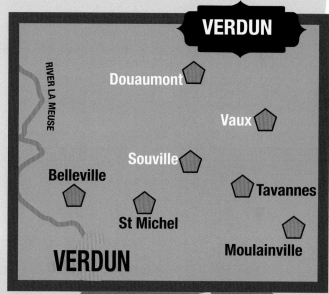

VERDUN

RIVER LA MEUSE

Douaumont

Vaux

Souville

Belleville

Tavannes

St Michel

Moulainville

VERDUN

This photo shows a French railway gun. These guns were meant for ships. This one was named Simone.

139

In December there was a Second Offensive Battle of Verdun. This time the French soldiers attacked on 15th December after firing more than a million shells in less than a week. The German Army in front of them collapsed and the French were now taking back ground they had lost all the way back in February. Thousands of German soldiers were captured and became prisoners of war. In fact, when German officers complained to the French General in charge, General Mangin, about being uncomfortable, he is said to have joked: 'We do regret it, gentlemen, but then we did not expect so many of you!'

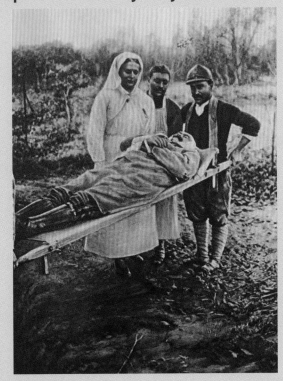

This photo shows French soldiers lining up to get soup after a spell in the trenches at Verdun.

This photo shows the body of General Ancelin being taken away from Fort Douaumont. He was killed on 24th October 1916.

Verdun

GERMAN
340,000 MEN
= 10,000

FRENCH
350,000 MEN
= 10,000

Of all the battles of the First World War, France and Germany remember Verdun. The Germans called it the 'bone grinder', or 'the world's blood pump'. It is very difficult to try and work out how many men were casualties but one guess is that about 340,000 Germans and 350,000 Frenchmen were killed, wounded, or taken prisoner. The battle had lasted for 302 days.

The Battle of the Somme lasted nearly 150 days too. More than 350,000 British soldiers were casualties, 200,000 Frenchmen and about half a million Germans. Imperial British troops also paid a heavy price for the fighting.

The Somme

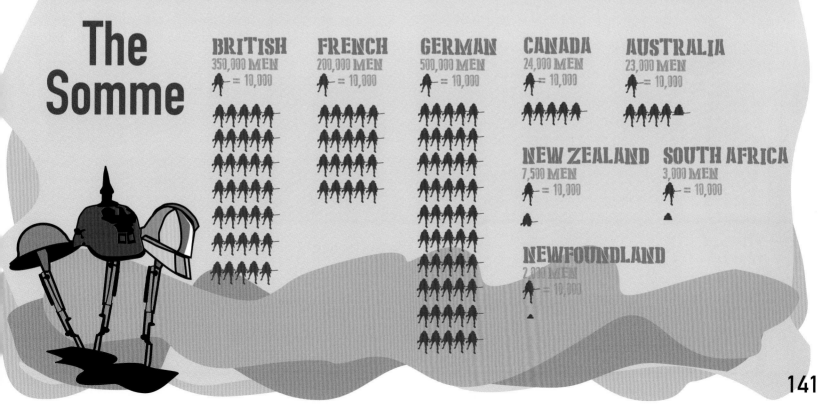

BRITISH
350,000 MEN
= 10,000

FRENCH
200,000 MEN
= 10,000

GERMAN
500,000 MEN
= 10,000

CANADA
24,000 MEN
= 10,000

AUSTRALIA
23,000 MEN
= 10,000

NEW ZEALAND
7,500 MEN
= 10,000

SOUTH AFRICA
3,000 MEN
= 10,000

NEWFOUNDLAND
2,000 MEN
= 10,000

Trench Life

What did men eat in the trenches?

It really depended on what country you were from. If you were British, you would eat a lot of tinned 'bully' beef. The French ate something similar but called it 'monkey' as a joke. Unidentified meat was common. If you were German you would grow used to 'shrapnel soup' or schrapellsuppe. It was a pea soup and the name gives you some idea of how hard the peas were! The Austro-Hungarians equally hated 'barbed wire' which was a feast of dry vegetables. Bread made up a large part of a soldier's diet, but as the war went on food was in short supply. Austro-Hungarian soldiers were given bread that had been 'stretched' further with sawdust, or even sand!

These French colonial soldiers are getting coffee ready for everyone.

You'd ask people to send you treats whenever possible. This French soldier has got hold of Christmas pudding!

Where do you go to the toilet in the trenches?!

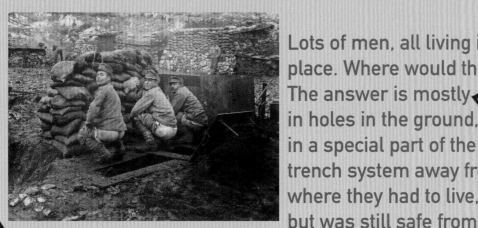

Lots of men, all living in one place. Where would they 'go'? The answer is mostly in holes in the ground, in a special part of the trench system away from where they had to live, but was still safe from the enemy. If they were lucky, a pole would be put across the hole to sit on!

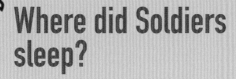

Where did Soldiers sleep?

There is a simple answer to this. A soldier will learn to sleep anywhere you let him! This big group is having a nap in a field!

You can see from this photo how happy this soldier is to be 'on leave'.

Yes! Usually they were allowed home for a week or two. They might have to wait a long time for their turn, and it wouldn't happen if there was a lot of fighting going on, but soldiers really looked forward to it.

Did soldiers get a holiday?

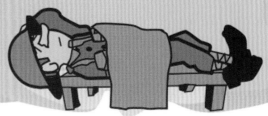

143

Soldiers only fought for a small part of their time. The rest of the war was very boring, and so it was important to keep them busy when you could! There were sports days and events. You can see Austro-Hungarian soldiers in these photos playing football and doing gymnastics.

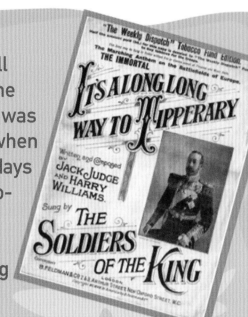

Plays and musical events were popular too. In this photo you can see Russian soldiers who are taking part in a masked play.

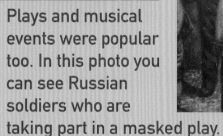

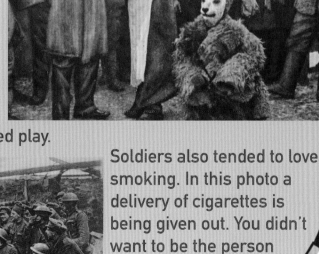

Soldiers also tended to love smoking. In this photo a delivery of cigarettes is being given out. You didn't want to be the person to come between a Tommy and his 'fags'.

It was very, very important to keep soldiers healthy. If all of them were sick, who would do the fighting? Trench warfare caused a lot of particular problems because men lived in very dirty conditions, with few chances to get clean.

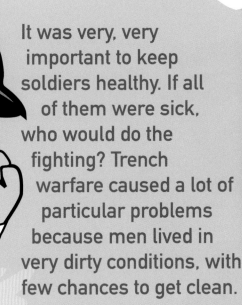

Trench foot was a very common problem. Men's feet could get wet, and stay wet for far too long. Like when your fingers go wrinkly from being in the bath! Add dirt, and imagine keeping wet socks on for days, maybe weeks on end! The photo above shows officers inspecting feet. You could get into trouble for not looking after your feet properly. There were things you could do to try and stop the water rotting the skin. Rubbing whale oil was one solution, or Vaseline.

Regular inspections by doctors helped keep men healthy. In this photo, a doctor in Salonika is doing check ups on some Indian troops.

Problems with lice and creepy crawlies were constant in the trenches. Clothes were fumigated, but getting eggs out of the clothing and stopping the lice coming back was difficult. These French soldiers are trying to delouse their uniforms by hand.

145

Shell Shock

We now know that war can damage someone's mind as much as their body. People's mental health can be badly hurt by the things that they are forced to see and do. The First World War was the first time that people began to pay proper attention to this idea.

On this page are pictures of British, German and French soldiers. You can see that something is wrong, can't you?

At the beginning of the war men started reporting headaches, being unable to sleep, pains in their ears and dizziness.

It was called shell shock at first. People thought it was caused by the shock waves of having shells go off nearby. Mental health cases were also called war neurosis, or neurasthenia, or just marked as 'debility'. In Germany they called it 'kriegszitterer' or war tremors.

It caused many, many different types of emotional and physical symptoms.

Sometimes, mental health issues could be so severe that they caused physical problems.

The problem was so widespread, amongst all nations, that special hospitals had to be opened just to deal with cases of shell shock. You might have heard of the famous hospital at Craiglockhart in Scotland.

Despite this, understanding mental health and war was still very new, and often men suffering from what we now might call PTSD, were accused of being cowards. In some cases, they were even executed for crimes like running away.

Cases of shell shock continued to grow and grow during the war. In the 1920s there were still nearly 70,000 men being treated for mental incapacity caused by the war. In France, there were still men being treated in hospital for mental health issues caused by the First World War in the 1960s.

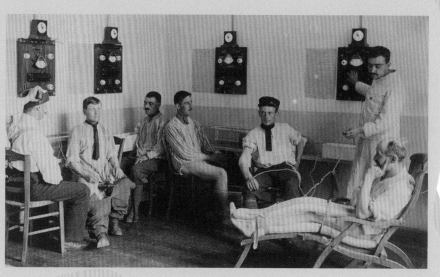

Lots of different things were tried to help men who were suffering from shell shock. This photo shows a hospital in France in 1915, where they are using electrical therapy.

Prisoners of War

We keep talking about casualties, and these numbers always include men who are captured. If you capture the enemy, letting him go is a bad idea. He'll go straight back to the other side and fight again. He might even be able to provide his superior officers with information that will help the enemy to defeat you.

But equally, you shouldn't hurt him either. If you did that, what do you think would then happen to your friends if they were captured?

And so, really, the answer is that you treated your prisoners the way you would like to be treated if you were captured. You fed them, you provided at least some medical care, and you let them do things like write or receive letters or packages from home.

The experience varied hugely, but if you were an officer held prisoner by the Dutch, for instance, you might even be allowed to go home on leave as long as you gave your word of honour that you would come back after your holiday!

Above you can see Bulgarian soldiers who have just been caught by the French. During the battle you would be taken to a 'cage', a rough camp like the one below, for Ottoman soldiers at Gallipoli.

There could lot of marching and a lot of waiting around. These Ottoman soldiers are under an Indian guard in Mesopotamia.

These Germans prisoners from Ypres have arrived at Southend. You will often see that prisoners look quite happy! Often they had had enough of the war.

These Russian prisoners were captured by the Central Powers in 1916.

There were camps for civilians who were in the wrong country when war began. You didn't want them to go home and then join the army to fight you!

These British men are being held at Ruhleben, a racecourse near Berlin.

149

In this photo you can see German prisoners passing the time by playing cards.

It was common to have prisoners dig graves. These Germans are working for the French,

Being a prisoner of war could be boring, there wasn't always a lot, to do. But you were allowed to put your prisoners to work, either on the battlefields (but not armed, as you don't want to give your enemy a rifle, he might use it on you. and you can't ask them to shoot at their own men) or you could send them to your country.

It was very common for prisoners to do agricultural work. Here you can see British soldiers near Döberitz and Germans with their plough. It was a waste to have healthy men doing nothing when food became more and more scarce during the war and farms needed tending.

In this photo a British soldier is giving a German prisoner a haircut!

However nicely you treated your prisoners, people still wanted to escape. In this photo, you can see that the French camp requires the German prisoners hand in their shoes at the end of the day It makes it harder to run away!

However much we'd like to think that all prisoners were well looked after, unfortunately it wasn't the case. Sometimes, it couldn't be helped. Some countries had hundreds of thousands of prisoners to take care of, and not enough food to feed even their own people. The Red Cross and the Red Crescent and other organisations did help. Neutral countries were also allowed into prisoner camps to check conditions. Sometimes, when prisoners were not treated well it caused a political scandal. This happened with British officers in Germany and in Britain when it came to how to treat the captured crews of U-Boats. Of course, sometimes, people just didn't want to take care of prisoners properly, and on some fronts, such as in Mesopotamia, people didn't play by the European rules of war.

This photo shows German prisoners at work for the New Zealanders having their health checked.

Mesopotamia

Mes-o-po-ta-mia sounds like a terrifying and complicated word, but it's just very old. It means 'the land between two rivers'. This makes perfect sense because its in West Asia, between the River Euphrates (Yoo-fray-tees) and the River Tigris. Nowadays, it makes up parts of Iraq, and bits of Kuwait, Iran, Syria and Turkey. In 1914, it was part of the Ottoman Empire, but the control that they held over the region was loose. Using German money, for years the Turks had been building a special railway that would go from Berlin all the way to Baghdad, but by the time of the First World War, it still wasn't finished. Most of the time, Turkey was happy to run Mesopotamia by proxy. This means that they didn't have to be there, and local, friendly people controlled it for them.

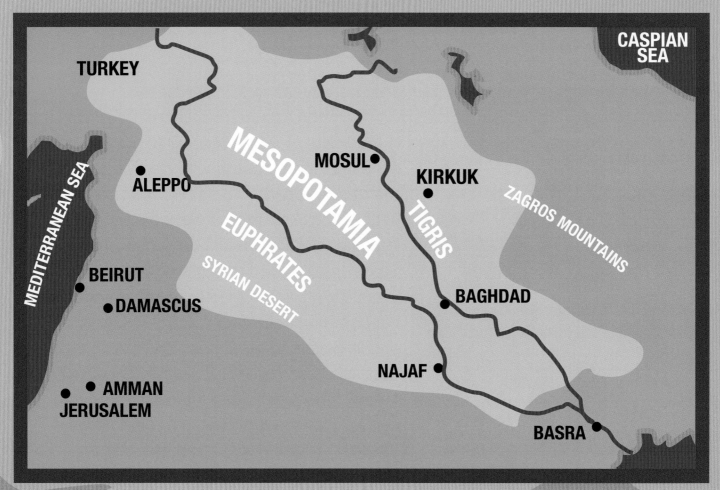

Mesopotamia is all swamps and deserts and because of the intense heat and a lack of roads, it made sense that, as much as possible, armies would stick close to the rivers. There was an endless supply of water, a quick way to move supplies and help the wounded. It also meant that the Royal Navy could help with the campaign. As a General, you'd have to be mad to move away from the rivers.

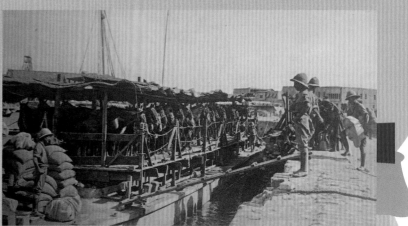

It might have been mostly desert, but Mesopotamia experienced floods too, when the snow melted in the mountains to the north. In this photo a British soldier is helping a local family leave their home.

Everything was easier if you could transport things by river. These horses are going to be sailed up the Tigris.

The Royal Navy was reliant on the Anglo-Persian Oil Company for the oil they needed for ships. At the very beginning of the war, Britain sent troops to Abadan, to protect one of the very first oil refineries in the world. This meant landing troops at the Shatt al-Arab. This is the name for the place where both the Tigris and the Euphrates come together and reach the sea. This was not an area where the Ottoman Empire had lots of troops hanging around. There weren't any large numbers of soldiers for many hundreds of miles. The closest big units were in Baghdad, and so there was no strong opposition to the British/Indian arrival.

This photo shows some of the few Turkish soldiers who were in Mesopotamia when the British and Indian troops arrived. They are being kept on a prison ship.

Most of the troops that the British Empire sent to Mesopotamia were from India. In fact, Indians had mostly been removed from the Western Front after 1915, and moved to warmer climates, or closer to home. The British Indian Army did have white soldiers, and a lot of white officers, but most of the troops were Indians.

But what do we mean when we say India in 1916? We mean everything that is now India, Pakistan, Bangladesh, Burma and parts of Nepal. That's millions of people, with different religions, beliefs and ethnic backgrounds.

More than a million Indians fought in the First World War. Of those 74,000 were killed.

The war had a huge effect on the future of the country and how Indians saw the Empire. Quite rightly, many people, white and Indian, thought that the country deserved some kind of recognition in how they were treated, and how much power they had, for all that they had done for Britain. Does that sound fair to you?

The Indian Army was made up of lots of different religions including men who were Hindus, Sikhs, Muslims, Christians and Jewish.

An age-old caste system which divided people primarily of the Hindu faith into upper and lower segments of the society was integrated into the structure of the Indian Army.

The British had to take caste, religion, customs and traditions into careful consideration and treat them with care in the army. For example, soldiers of different faiths needed to be catered for by setting up different faith-specific kitchens.

Most of the campaign would be run by the British government in India, not by the War Office in London. Another reason for carrying out a campaign in Mesopotamia was prestige. This means that people thought it would make Britain look good in India if they conquered Mesopotamia. It would make British India look powerful and successful. Does prestige sound like a good excuse to go to war to you?

For this reason, the force that landed in Mesopotamia did not just stop to look after the Royal Navy's oil supply. They began to move inland. First they had to beat the Ottoman troops at the fortress of Fao. There were only 350 Turkish soldiers, so it was not difficult. After that, the whole division went ashore and captured the city of Basra on 22nd November 1914. The Ottoman troops left the city and began retreating up the Tigris, but the British and Indians did not stop there. At the Battle of Qurna they captured 1,000 men and the local Turkish commander. This meant that the oil was safe and so was Basra. The nearest Turkish troops were nearly 300 miles away and did not look too interested in coming down to force them out again.

In these photographs you can see what both Turkish foot soldiers and cavalry looked like.

In a desert campaign, nothing is more important than water. Above you can see men filling cans for drinking.

This photo shows soldiers having a bath in the River Tigris.

Above you can see a Turkish mine. It was floating in the Tigris ready to destroy ships coming up the river.

The Turks were far more interested in other campaigns, like Gallipoli, or events in Palestine. But at the beginning of 1915, Süleyman Askerî Bey took over the Ottoman forces in the Iraq area. He was determined to take back Basra and the Shatt al-Arab. He moved south, and in the middle of April attacked the British camp at Shaiba. The British Indian troops pushed back, and eventually Bey was forced to retreat 75 miles.

The British were so pleased with their progress so far, that they ordered an advance up the Tigris. Things went well, and the government in London was so pleased that they began to encourage General Townshend, commanding the troops advancing along the river, to take Baghdad.

But the Turks were beginning to take this campaign seriously. They shuffled their men, and decided that they would put a German, General Colmar von der Goltz, in charge. He was 72 years old, but had written books on how to campaign, and had worked for many years in the Ottoman Empire as a military advisor.

While they waited for him to arrive, however, Townshend and his men continued to move up the river and fought the Battle of Ctesiphon (Cesi-phon) with its famous arch, 25 miles south of Baghdad. This time the Turks got the upper hand and the British were forced to retreat. Townshend fell back, but calmly, to the town of Kut-al-Amara and made his position in the town as safe as possible. The Ottoman forces surrounded the town and a siege began.

In this photo you can see a roll call for an Indian unit. Soldiers would be very familiar with this, as you always needed to check everyone was there before you moved on.

The war flowed back and forth past the famous arch of Ctesiphon. It is the only part left of an ancient city and is more than 1,500 years old! It was part of a palace, and probably spanned the top of the throne room. Luckily, it was not damaged by the war, but is in need of a lot of restoration to preserve it.

The Siege of Kut began on 7th December 1915. Von Der Goltz arrived and directed the Ottoman defences, which were built up to make sure that no more British Indian troops could come up and help Townshend and his men. Slowly, they began to run out of supplies.

General Charles Townshend was an experienced officer who had had a successful career. The Siege of Kut and the failure of his campaign in Mesopotamia ruined him. His reaction to the suffering of his men, however, was not good and meant that he did not attract much sympathy. After the war he went to live in France, but he never held a command again.

This photo shows General Townshend in his office whilst the Siege of Kut was in progress,

This photo shows you some abandoned defences alongside the River Tigris.

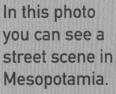

In this photo you can see a street scene in Mesopotamia.

In the photo above, you can see a British camp in Mesopotamia. This theatre of war was very different to the Western Front!

Meanwhile, the British decided to send a relief force to save them. None of the attempts were successful, and General Aylmer, who was in charge of the relief effort, failed at the Battle of Sheikh Sa'ad, the Battle of the Wadi, the Battle of Hanna and the Battle of Dujaila Redoubt. Lots of men were killed in these attempts, and because planning had not been properly done, a lot of these deaths could have been prevented. For example, there were no proper arrangements to take wounded men from the battlefield and help them. Lots, both white men and Indians, lay where they were until they died with no medical attention. This would cause outrage in India and in London.

This photograph shows Indian troops on the move near Kut.

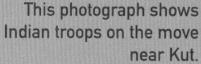

Meanwhile in Kut, some supplies were dropped from the air, but it wasn't nearly enough. It became clear that if Townshend did not surrender, his men would starve. Added to that, they did not have enough medicines and disease was also beginning to spread throughout the men.

One of the last attempts to supply the men in Kut was made by a paddle steamer called HMS *Julnar*. She had been taken for navy service, and on 24th April 1916, with a crew of brave volunteers, she tried to outrun the Turkish guns on the River Tigris and take supplies to the men in Kut.

Carrying more than 250 tons of supplies, Julnar was spotted by the Ottoman defenders and shelled. The two men in command, Lieutenant Humphrey Firman and Lieutenant-Commander Charles Cowley, were awarded the Victoria Cross for their bravery in trying to relieve the suffering of those at Kut. This was the last hope for the thousands of men inside Kut, and it had failed. The mission can be called a 'forlorn hope'. This means that you know you will probably fail when you volunteer. Do you think you would have volunteered?

In these photos you can see what the lack of supplies at Kut did to soldiers.

This photo shows Townshend with his captors, can you see he isn't looking at the camera? Why do you think that might be?

On 29th April, Townshend surrendered. It was a humiliating defeat for Great Britain, and it was happening just a few months after the evacuation of Gallipoli too. The Government in London and in India was determined to try and defeat the Ottomans in Mesopotamia, but for now, more than 13,000 British and Indians still inside the town became prisoners of the Turks. They were forced to do a 'death march' all the way to Anatolia, This means that they were expected to walk from Iraq to Turkey. They were not given proper food and water and many were already very sick. Many were beaten and by the end of the war, only 20% of the men who had survived Kut were still alive. The Turks treated the Indian muslim soldiers better, and some of them even joined the Ottoman forces later in the war.

Eastern Front

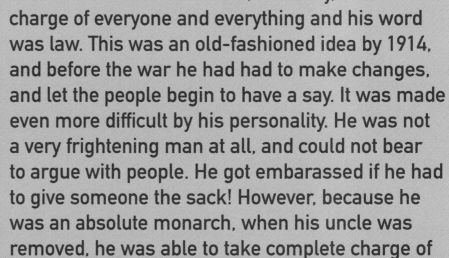

LAKE NAROCH

Until the end of 1915, the Russian Armies had been commanded by Grand Duke Nicholas Nicolaevich, the Tsar's uncle. He was an experienced General and led Russia through the first part of the war. But with the terrible defeat suffered during the Gorlice-Tarnow Offensive, much like in other countries taking part in bloody and terrifying battles, a change was made.

Russia was an autocracy. The monarchy was absolute, which means that Tsar Nicholas II, in theory, was in charge of everyone and everything and his word was law. This was an old-fashioned idea by 1914, and before the war he had had to make changes, and let the people begin to have a say. It was made even more difficult by his personality. He was not a very frightening man at all, and could not bear to argue with people. He got embarassed if he had to give someone the sack! However, because he was an absolute monarch, when his uncle was removed, he was able to take complete charge of his own armies in September 1915. In Britain, if the war went wrong, George V would not be blamed by the people, because he was not involved in the decision making. This is called a constitutional monarchy, where the monarch reigns over the country, but does not rule the people and tell them what they have to do. This made the British king safe. It would not be the same for Nicholas II in Russia, because his fate was now tied to the war. There would be nowhere to hide if it all went wrong.

Nicholas II and George V were cousins. Their mothers were sisters. They looked alike, and they had similar personalities too, but what was expected of them in each of their countries was very different.

In this photo you can see Nicholas II inspecting a Russian artillery unit.

The Russians were asked to attack the enemy by the French, who were struggling at Verdun, at the beginning of 1916. They decided to carry out an offensive at Lake Naroch, because they outnumbered the Germans there.

The attack began on 18th March. Unfortunately, the preparation by the Russian Army was lacking. They had failed to prepare the way for the infantry with their artillery barrage. The Russians ended up making a lot of direct attacks right at the Germans and suffered very heavy casualties. The weather was also very bad. First it was cold and then suddenly it got warmer and rained and the battlefield turned into a swamp. They seized ground, but could not hold onto it.

They were suffering all of the same issues on the Eastern Front that the Allies would encounter on the Somme in a few weeks time. They tried to kick-start the offensive with a second attack at Riga on 21st March, but this was a failure too. Estimates are very different, but Russia might have suffered 100,000 casualties, 12,000 of them from hypothermia alone. Germany suffered another 20-40,000.

This photo shows German soldiers taken prisoner during the Lake Naroch offensive.

Millions of men were taken prisoner on the Eastern Front in the First World War. It was very important to talk to them to try and get information about the enemy, especially the officers, because they always know more about what is going on. In this photo, Russian officers are interviewing Austro-Hungarian officer prisoners.

Fortunes would soon be reversed thanks to the Brusilov Offensive. In Russia this is called 'Brusilov's Breakthrough' or the June Advance.

General Brusilov wanted to start a massive offensive against Austria-Hungary in Galicia, an area which is now in the Ukraine. He thought he could take the pressure off of Britain and France, and Italy. Russian soldiers outnumbered the enemy in this area, and so he even hoped that he would be able to finish the Austro-Hungarian army off and knock them out of the war completely.

This plan was HUGE. On 1st July 1916, on the Somme, the main British force was trying to take about 16 miles of the German front line. For the Brusilov Offensive, the line would be 300 miles long! That's about the same distance as London to Newcastle, or a bit longer than Los Angeles to Las Vegas!

The Russians rushed to get four armies ready because of the Battle of Verdun. They made a huge effort to hide what they were up to, with false radio traffic, false orders being carried by men who were captured on purpose. They dug trenches in secret to use during the battle, and even used dummy artillery to pretend to be in places they weren't!

How do you feed an army this big? Here you can see mobile kitchens being moved by river in Galicia.

These cows are all on their way to the Russian Army in Galicia.

The battle began on 4th June 1916. This time, instead of wasting shells like they did earlier in the year, the Russian guns were accurate and fired for much less time. This was a huge advance in using artillery. The attack was a big success.

Here you can see Russian soldiers hiding from shells in long grass on the battlefield.

In this photo you can see a bomb-proof telephone post built by the Austro-Hungarian Army.

This photo shows Russian soldiers relaxing in a captured Austro-Hungarian trench in June 1916.

Here you can see both soldiers and local villagers watching fighting during the Brusilov Offensive.

SIXTEEN MILES

At the time of the First World War, Poland was partitioned into sections 'belonging' to Germany, Austria-Hungary and Russia. This meant that Polish men could find themselves fighting each other in battle. In the Austro-Hungarian empire, the Polish Legions, led by Józef Piłsudski, had been created and they would find themselves in the opening stages of the Brusilov Offensive. They had been in the area around Kostiuchnówka since the end of 1915, and had captured the town on 27th September. Since then it had been very difficult for these Austro-Hungarian troops to hold on.

Józef Piłsudski formed the Polish Legions because he thought it was the best way to try and win independence for Poland.

This photo shows German troops in a recaptured trench at the beginning of July.

The Russian advance of June 1916 would smash right into men of the Polish Legions at the Battle of Kostiuchnówka. They were only about 6-8,000 of them, facing more than 25,000 Russians. It would be the most savage fight that the Polish legionnaires took part in during the First World War.

When the Russians arrived on 6th June, the Poles dug in. More and more Russian reinforcements were fed into the fight, but despite this, the Polish force carried out a counter-attack, surprising the enemy.

In this photo you can see men of the Polish legions learning how to use their rifles.

However, on 4th July the Russians came again. The Polish troops were outnumbered 10 to 1, but they still managed to force Brusilov's men to retreat. But Hungarians along the Central Powers' front nearby had begun retreating. When your neighbour does this, it usually means that you have to follow, or risk being cut off and surrounded. By July 6th, the Austro-Hungarian forces were falling back along the whole of their front line, and nearly half the Poles had become casualties.

The Russians were moving so fast that the Archduke Josef Ferdinand, who was commanding the 4th Austro-Hungarian Army in the region, only just managed to get away before being captured. It was becoming the biggest disaster of the war so far for Austria-Hungary, even though Germany sent reinforcements to help. The Russians had taken more than 200,000 prisoners. In fact, they now risked going too far, and not being able to supply and reinforce their men!

This photo shows Russian troops during the Brusilov Offensive.

And this one shows Austro-Hungarian soldiers at work.

In this photo you can see men from a Hungarian battalion moving across the front near the Dniester River.

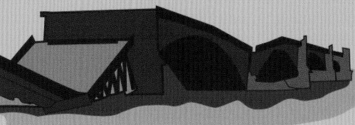

In places, the Austro-Hungarians did try and fight back. An attack at the end of July managed to hold the Russians up, but then on 28th July, Brusilov began attacking again. He found it hard to supply his men, but by the 20th September they had reached the Carpathian mountains.

Brusilov was a hero. He had managed to force the Germans to transfer soldiers away from the Western Front, where the battles of the Somme and Verdun were raging. Austria-Hungary was no longer able to get by without German help if it wanted to fight offensives. Brusilov had also done brilliant work at advancing tactics for this new, industrial warfare. He had looked for particular weak points in the Austrian line and used them to cause chaos, then sent his men in to exploit them.

Alexei Brusilov earned the nickaname 'The Iron General'. He had been serving in Galicia since the beginning of the war, with quite a lot of success.

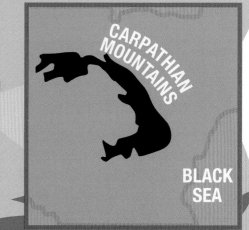

CARPATHIAN MOUNTAINS

BLACK SEA

It makes sense to do everything you can to hold up an advancing army. The Austro-Hungarians set fire to buildings and crops to cause as much smoke as possible to hide what they were doing.

In this photo you can see Russians trying to mend a bridge that has been blown up by the enemy.

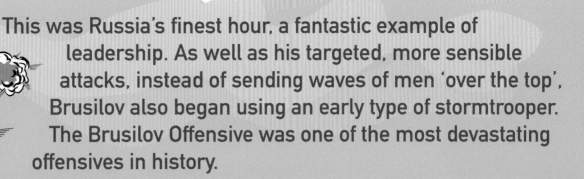

This was Russia's finest hour, a fantastic example of leadership. As well as his targeted, more sensible attacks, instead of sending waves of men 'over the top', Brusilov also began using an early type of stormtrooper. The Brusilov Offensive was one of the most devastating offensives in history.

BUT, such a huge battle came at a huge cost. During the offensive, Russia might have suffered as many as a million casualties. The same goes for Austria-Hungary. Germany suffered up to 300,000. The Brusilov Offensive left the Russian Army in a terrible state. It had taken too much out of them, both in terms of men and morale. The war was not won, and they would never be able to repeat this effort.

This photo shows wounded soldiers being taken away from the battlefield.

In this photo you can see Russian soldiers marching through Lutsk.

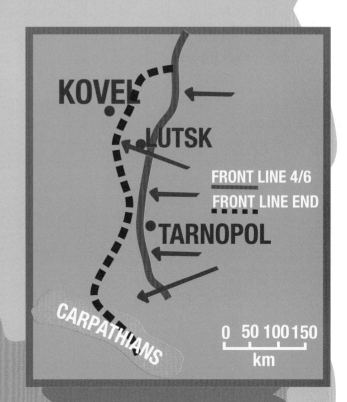

KOVEL

LUTSK

FRONT LINE 4/6
FRONT LINE END

TARNOPOL

CARPATHIANS

0 50 100 150
km

Until 1916, Romania had remained neutral, and in fact, King Carol preferred Germany. However, his politicians favoured the Allies, and the early success of the Brusilov Offensive convinced them to enter the war on the side of the Allies on 27th August 1916.

Everyone wanted to be friends with Romania, because she had the only oilfields in Europe. The Allies were thrilled when Romania joined them because not only would the Germans now be denied the petrol they had been buying from them, but they would also have their rail links to Turkey cut, because the lines went through Romania.

This photo shows Romanian troops on the march.

CARPATHIAN MOUNTAINS
TRANSYLVANIA
ROMANIA
KURT BUNAR
BAZARGIC
BRASOV TURTUCAIA
DANUBE
CONSTANTA
BUCHAREST
BLACK SEA

Things started very well for the Romanians. They overwhelmed the Austro-Hungrian forces in The Battle of Transylvania (yes, where Count Dracula is from!) This was part of Hungary at the time, but Romania really, really wanted it. On 27th August 1916, three Romanian armies attacked across the Carpathians and entered Transylvania, which was part of the Austro-Hungarian Empire.

By mid-September, however, the Germans had managed to send help. General Falkenhayn might have been fired from the Western Front because of his failure at Verdun, but he was put in charge of the Austro-Hungarian troops in Transylvania, and managed to stop the Romanian advance. It was also becoming clear that the Romanians had made a lot of mistakes, and that they were not properly equipped or trained to fight this kind of war. They had also got so excited about taking Transylvania, that they ignored the fact that the Bulgarians had forces nearby and that they were the enemy!

Bulgarian troops had crossed into Romania in the south at the beginning of September too. Russian troops, with some Serbian volunteers, arrived straight away to try and help, but at the Battle of Bazargic, German, Ottoman and Bulgarian troops defeated them.

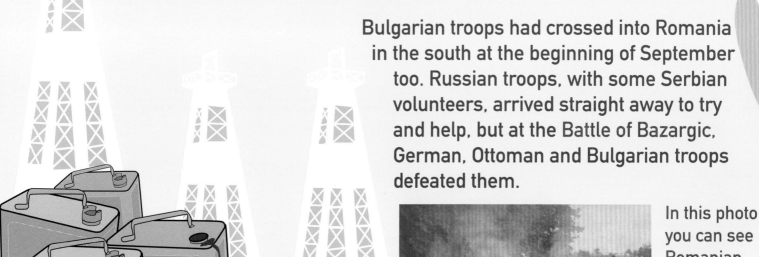

In this photo you can see Romanian soldiers stopping by the road for their dinner.

Soon the Central Powers were ready to fight back. They were led by German General August von Mackensen who drew together German, Bulgarian and Ottoman soldiers. Bulgaria started the counter-attack on 1st September, aiming for Constanța. The Battle of Turtucaia was fought over a fortress that dated back to Roman times. After five days, the Romanians defending it surrendered.

In mid-September, the Romanians decided to stop attacking in Transylvania and instead try to destroy von Mackensen's armies. The plan was called the Flămânda Offensive and it was here that the Romanians would cross the River Danube. Elsewhere, a joint Romanian and Russia attack would fight towards Kurtbunar. The Romanians did manage to cross the river, and on 1st October the joint forces only managed to make a little dent in the Central Powers' position. They did not manage to break the enemy at Dobruja, and then a storm destroyed the crossing they had built over the Danube. The operation was cancelled.

In this photo Romanian troops are observing from their position. The machine-gun they are using is French. It was very common for allies to share weapons.

This photo shows Bulgarian soldiers marching through a Romanian town in 1916.

After they had managed to stop the Romanian advance into Transylvania, General Falkenhayn forced the Romanian troops back towards the Carpathian mountains. On 4th October the Romanians attacked German forces at Brasov, but with no success. By 25th October, up and down the line the Romanians were back where they had started in August.

ALPEN KORPS

One of the units that helped push them back was the Alpenkorps. This was a special German unit of mountain troops.

In this photo you can see a Romanian defensive position. It was captured by members of the Alpenkorps in 1916.

This photo shows members of the Alpenkorps in the Turnu Roșu Pass in the Carpathian mountains.

Serving with the elite Alpenkorps on the Romanian front was the future Field Marshal Erwin Rommel. He would be one of Germany's best known generals in the Second World War.

By the end of November, winter had arrived on the battlefield, and the Romanian armies were being forced back through the Carpathians.

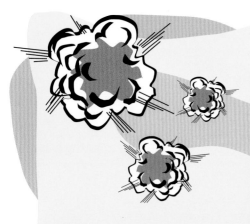

The Russians had been trying to stop General Mackensen's men further south, but on 19th October the German sent his men forward in another offensive. The mix of Bulgarian, Ottoman and German troops defeated the Romanians and the Russians, and forced the Allies to retreat from Consanta. The Russians were running out of supplies, and morale was low. But things only got worse. On 23rd November, Mackensen sent his best troops off to take Bucharest, the Romanian capital. The Romanians desperately tried to defend it, but they needed the Russians to play their part in a daring plan and they refused. The government and the King, with his court, left the capital on 6th December and German cavalry occupied the city. More than 150,000 Romanian soldiers were taken prisoner. By the time the German-led advance was stopped in January 1917, Romania's army had suffered nearly half a million casualties. It is estimated that about 60,000 German, Austro-Hungarian, Bulgarian and Turkish losses were suffered. Two-thirds of Romania was now in enemy hands.

In this photo you can see German cavalry riding through the streets of Bucharest in November 1916.

The First World War really was a global conflict, and for that reason, we need to look at what took place in Africa during the years 1914–18. All of the major European powers had colonies or dominions on the continent. You can see how it was divided up on the map.

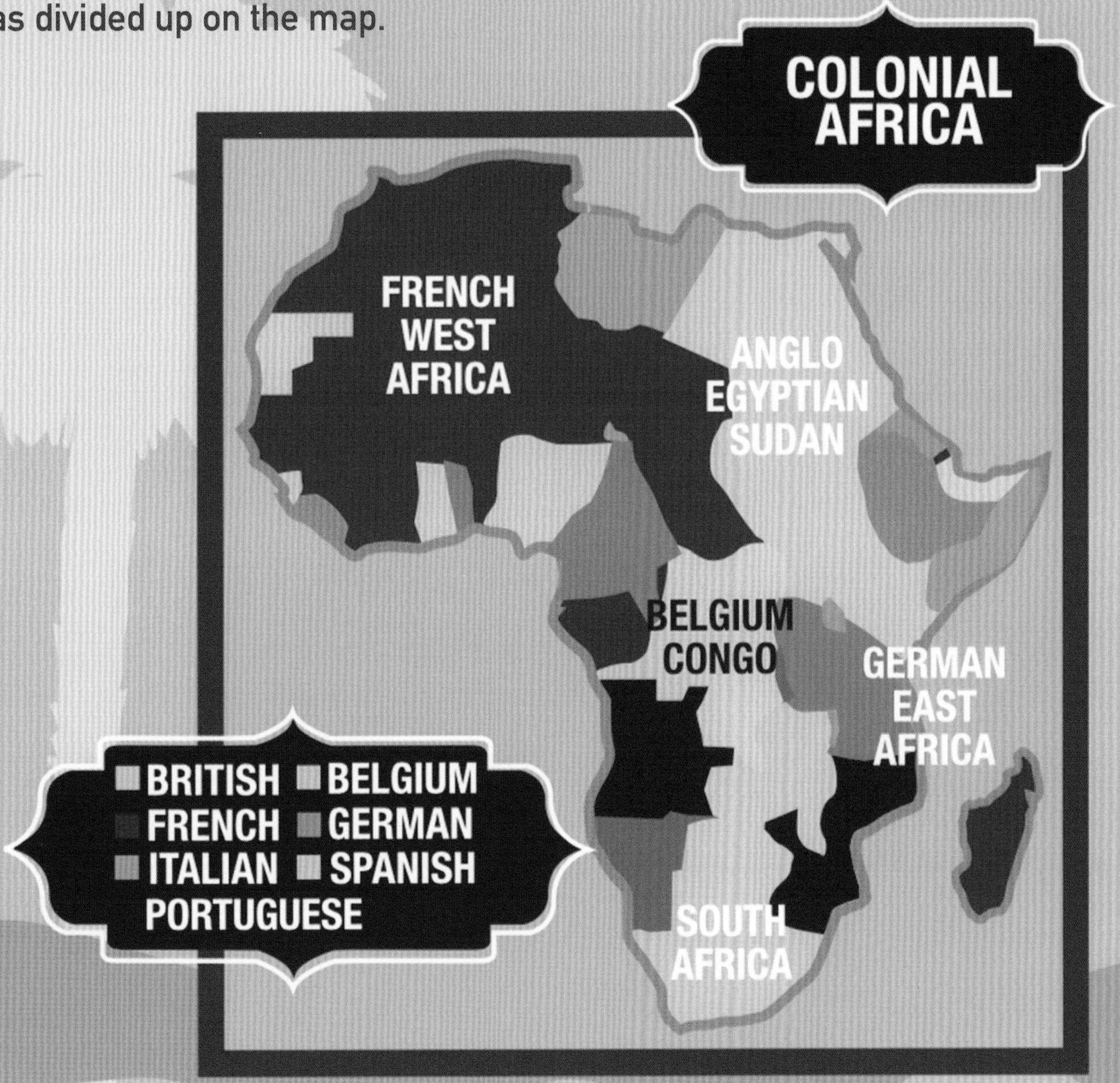

Africa

COLONIAL AFRICA

FRENCH WEST AFRICA

ANGLO EGYPTIAN SUDAN

BELGIUM CONGO

GERMAN EAST AFRICA

SOUTH AFRICA

- BRITISH
- BELGIUM
- FRENCH
- GERMAN
- ITALIAN
- SPANISH
- PORTUGUESE

However in many cases these African 'possessions' were quite new and not very well defended. Empires had something to gain if they started grabbing at each other's colonies, but that could get very messy. In fact, the countries with a presence in Africa had long ago agreed that if they found themselves at war at home in Europe, they would have their colonies in Africa remain neutral. But despite the agreement, it would not be long before European powers began meddling in each other's affairs in Africa.

All of the European powers fighting each other in Africa relied on recruiting local men to do battle. These men are working as bush skirmishers for the British. But war does not just kill the people fighting. There are consequences for other people too. As well as men killed whilst fighting, thousands of African men left their homes, which meant that farming was neglected and people went hungry. Disease would kill thousands more by the end of the war. One guess is that more than a million people died because of the war just in East Africa.

One thing that the imperial powers could do to each other was to undermine the presence of their enemies in Africa. For example, in Morocco, the Germans decided to make friends with men who had been pushed from power by the French, and support them. The French fought against the Zaian Confederation, which was a collection of the Berber people, long after the war ended in Europe.

This photo shows the French arriving in Morocco in 1912 to establish a protectorate. This is a back-door way of taking over a country without calling it a colony, and implies you are doing it for the good of the country in question!

In this photo you can see German prisoners of war being put to work by the French in Morocco.

The Zaian War finally ended in 1921, with victory for France, who massively outnumbered the Zaian Confederation. This photo shows the surrender of the Berbers. By 1921, there were nearly 100,000 French soldiers in Morocco.

Britain had fought a war in South Africa as recently as 1902, and though it was finished, there was still a lot of bad feeling against Britain amongst the Boers. At the beginning of the war, the British government asked South Africa's leaders to carry out an attack on their neighbouring German colony. The South African government said yes, but some important men were opposed to this. One of them was General Beyers, who commanded South Africa's defence force. Another was a senator, General Koos de la Rey. To the authorities, it looked like these two men were attempting to start a rebellion. They claimed that they were discussing resignations of officers. Unfortunately, on the way to the meeting a policeman shot at De La Rey's car, apparently thinking that it belonged to a dangerous criminal gang they were looking for. The Senator was killed, and some claimed it was a government assasination.

WHAT IS A BOER?
Before the First World War, lots of white people had settled in what is now South Africa. Many came from Britain. However, many were of Dutch or German origin and they were called Boers. The word just means 'farmer', as traditionally, that was what they did when they arrived in Africa.

This photo shows a Commando unit with their armoured train during the rebellion.

In this photo, you can see Loyalist men escorting three captured rebel leaders back to Pretoria.

Lieutenant Colonel Maritz was commanding South African troops on the border of German South West Africa and he decided to side with the Germans. Then he announced that 'the former South African Republic and Orange Free State as well as the Cape Province and Natal are proclaimed free from British control and independent, and every White inhabitant of the mentioned areas, of whatever nationality, are hereby called upon to take their weapons in their hands and realise the long-cherished ideal of a Free and Independent South Africa'. He, Beyers and three others claimed that they would lead this new government.

They began seizing towns, and some 12,000 rebels joined their various forces. The Government of South Africa declared martial law on 12th October 1914, and troops belonging to General Louis Botha, the Prime Minister, and to Jan Smuts, both of whom had fought against the British a decade before, destroyed the rebellion.

Lots of Africans also took the war in Europe as an opportunity to fight against imperial rule. 20,000 men joined together to fight the French in French West Africa (which is now Burkina Faso and Mali.) The Tuareg rebelled in what is now Niger, and British Somaliland was threatened by the continued opposition of Sayyid Mohammed Abdille Hassan.

In this photo you can see an example of what Tuareg warriors looked like.

Hassan was nicknamed 'the Mad Mullah' by the British. He was Somali, and fought against colonial rule for twenty years, including during the First World War. He led the Dervish movement. The photo below shows you what his warriors looked like.

Ag Mohammed Wau Teguidda Kaocen was a Tuareg noble who led the Kaocen Revolt against French Rule in the Air Mountains.

The Ottoman Empire had made a loud cry to the muslim world to declare a Jihad (Jee-had) on Great Britain. They hoped it would ruin British interests in India, Africa, all over the world. Throughout the war, in Ethiopia and Somaliland, Britain would remain worried about the idea of an African jihad, but it never came to pass on the scale they feared. Even though the world-wide Jihad never materialised, there were some instances of Islamic opposition to Britain. A few Indian muslim troops in East Africa rebelled in 1916. In some units men gave themselves self-inflicted wounds so that they could not fight and others deserted, or ran away.

WHAT IS JIHAD?

This Arabic word might not mean what you think it does. It just means 'struggling'. It means struggling towards the path that God would want you to take, and doing right by him. Now, this can be an internal stuggle, where you try to be a good person and not do bad things. But you do find times in history like this one, where Turkey wanted to call Muslims to war against Britain. This idea of Jihad is 'by the sword', so fighting for God. We've seen this a lot in recent years, because the word has been used by terrorists and other violent groups to justify killing non-Muslims. This has nothing to do with Islam, and what it tells people about how they should behave. This is an example of fundamentalism, which is when people with extreme views (you can call them extremists) twist an idea for their own use. They do this to try and justify their behaviour. All you need to remember is that the word Jihad does not automatically mean trying to hurt other people. A lot of places where it appears in the *Quoran*, Islam's holy book, it has no violent or military meaning at all. Think of it like the word 'crusade'. Yes, you can be talking about Christian holy wars, but you could also say, 'my mum has gone on a crusade to make me keep my bedroom tidy'. There's nothing religious about that!

WEST AFRICA

Of course, the imperial powers saw the advantages of attacking each others' colonies. In West Africa, in August 1914, separate groups of French and British troops invaded the German colony of Togoland. This attack began as early as 6th August, just two days into the war.

The British force was formed from the West African Frontier Force, which existed to protect the British colonies in West Africa of Nigeria, Gold Coast, Sierra Leone and Gambia. Led by white officers, the soldiers were primarily African. The French, too, sent Senagalese 'Tirailleurs'. This word just means rifleman, or a sharpshooter. By this time, although they were named Senegalese because of their origins, the men were from different parts of Africa.

This photo shows African troops fighting for Germany in the First World War. We've already looked at outdated views on race. You can see them in this picture, where black soldiers are under the command of a white officer.

This photo shows German native prisoners being guarded by men working for the British.

In this picture you can see a British post in the Cameroons.

The campaign went badly for Germany, and by the end of August Togoland had surrendered to the Allies. By this time, the Allies were also beginning to attack Kamerun. British, French and Belgian troops, as well as soldiers sent from the West Indies, would fight here, and it would take a lot longer to seize this colony from Germany.

Kamerun was a large colony, made up modern day Cameroon, along with parts of Nigeria, Chad, Gabon, the Republic of Congo and the Central African Republic. At the beginning of the war, Europeans had still not explored a lot of it.

The first battle between British and German troops in Kamerun happened at the Battle of Tepe on 25th August. At the end of this small fight, the Germans withdrew. By 1915 they had fallen back to the mountainous country inland and in 1916 they finally surrendered. In all of these West African cases, the German colonies were divided between Britain and France after the war.

Jan Smuts

Germany also had a colony in the southern part of Africa. After the Maritz Rebellion was defeated, this was attacked by South African troops, with the dominion acting on Britain's behalf. The South Africans were defeated at the Battle of Sandfontein, close to their own border with the German colony. By February 1915, however, they were much better organised. The South African force was divided into two parts both commanded by national heroes. General Smuts took charge of one, and General Botha the other.

SOUTH WEST AFRICA

Botha took command of the northern force at Swakopmund, and began his invasion in March. Things went well, and he entered Windhoek, which is now the capital of Namibia, on 5th May 1915. The German surrender was rejected and fighting continued until July, when after a final stand at Otavi, the German troops surrendered on 9th July.

Louis Botha

The fighting in Africa could take place across huge areas. For this reason, if there was a railway nearby it could be very useful. This engine is so important that for the first time, South Africans have tried floating one across the Orange River!

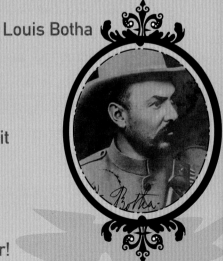

This photo shows local German volunteers as part of a mounted camel unit.

In this photo South African soldiers ride a train on a captured German railway line.

The soldiers in this photo are from the Transvaal. Most of them are from a Scottish background.

In this photo you can see General Botha's men riding over sand dunes.

In the meantime, Smuts also invaded. As he moved north, the Germans in the south were forced to run north towards Botha's men. Faced with certain defeat, they too surrendered.

Even before the declaration of war between Germany and Portugal in March 1916, their troops had clashed on the border between German South West Africa and Portuguese Angola. The Germans were actually on top, until defeat at the hands of Botha and Smuts restored Portuguese control.

In this photo the German Governor signs a surrender of the colony in front of General Botha.

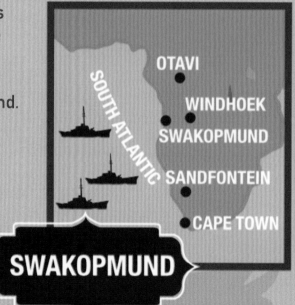

OTAVI

WINDHOEK

SWAKOPMUND

SANDFONTEIN

CAPE TOWN

SOUTH ATLANTIC

SWAKOPMUND

The East African campaigns of the First World War were fought in the countries we now know as Tanzania, Mozambique, Kenya, Uganda, Zambia, Rwanda, Burundi and the Democratic Republic of Congo. In 1914, the imperial powers who claimed these territories were Britain, Germany, Portugal and Belgium. This was by far the longest of the African campaigns in 1914–18, because Germany wanted to force the Allies to send troops to fight here when they were needed in places like on the Western Front.

These photos show colonial life in Africa before the First World War. You can see things like the building of the Uganda Railway, a new police force in German East Africa

and a modern street scene in Mombasa, Kenya. But what else do these photographs tell you about Imperialism?

German East Africa was made up of areas that are now Rwanda, Burundi and Tanzania. It had a protection force of 260 Europeans, and about 2,500 Africans. There were also about 2,500 white settlers who made up a reserve that they could call on. This was the largest force anywhere in the German colonies. At the beginning of the war, none of the imperial powers involved really wanted to carry out an exhausting invasion and had planned to stay neutral. However, these plans did not last long.

You can see how different the war was in Africa in these photos. Above, British troops are on the march near Mount Kilimanjaro. On the left men from Rhodesia are crossing the Lusemfwa River in Zambia.

Paul von Lettow-Vorbeck was 44 when the war began. He had previously served in China and also in German South West Africa. He therefore had a lot of experience in Africa that would be useful in the First World War. He had been in German East Africa since April 1914, commanding the Schutztruppe, or protection force.

German and Aksaris crossed the border into British territory in August 1914 and started raiding. By September they were probing deeper into Kenya and Uganda. The British obviously wanted this to stop. There was some skirmishing on the slopes of Mount Kilimanjaro, and a bigger force made for Tanga, which is now in Tanzania. In total the British had sent 12,000 troops from India, and had local volunteers too, but although they massively outnumbered the Germans, they were badly beaten. Not only were they defeated, but when they ran away, the enemy was able to capture their modern equipment, medical supplies, tents, blankets, food and even machine guns.

Askari means 'soldier', or 'warrior' in Swahili, which is a language used in East Africa. Askaris could be found both in the British King's African Rifles and in the German Schutzruppe.

Above you can see the Askaris ready to go to Longido.

This photo shows German colonial troops.

192

German ships had control of Lake Tanganyika, but in 1915, the British transported two motorboats, HMS *Mimi* and HMS *Toutou*, 3,000 miles by land to the British shore of the lake. One by one, with two Belgian ships also commanded by a Royal Navy officer, they began to dismantle the little German fleet. The *Kingani* was captured on Boxing Day and put into Allied service as HMS *Fifi*. Another ship was sunk, and in February 1916 the *Wami* was run ashore and burned. It was later put back in the water in British service.

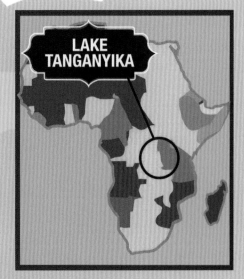

By 1916, Britain had decided to go on the offensive in East Africa. Eventually, General Smuts was given the job of defeating the Germans. He had a big army that included 13,000 South Africans, 7,000 Indians and thousands of African soldiers and camp followers to do jobs like moving the equipment. Altogether there were nearly 75,000 men. There was also the Belgian force and a group of Portuguese military units from Mozambique. The Germans had just under 14,000 men.

In this photo General Smuts is meeting colonial troops.

This photo shows African soldiers digging a defensive position near Lake Tanganyika.

This photo shows soldiers climbing through the East African bush in 1916.

In this photo you can see Indian soldiers building a railway line.

Smuts decided to attack from different directions. The main attack came from British East Africa to the north. At the same time, two groups of men also came from the Belgian Congo in the West, crossing Lake Victoria. Finally, more men were coming from Lake Nyasa in the southeast. None of these forces managed to catch General Lettow-Vorbeck, and disease was a terrible problem. Whenever the Allied forces got close, the Germans would retreat. They ended up trapped in the southern part of German East Africa. Smuts replaced his troops with thousands of Askari. As the campaign went on, more and more of the British force was made up of African soldiers.

British offensives continued into 1917, but then it was Germany's turn. On 23rd November the Schutztruppe crossed into Portuguese Mozambique to steal supplies. Thanks to fights like the Battle of Ngomano the Schutztruppe managed to keep going for longer, but there were close shaves at places like Lioma and Pere Hills. Lettow-Vorbeck went back to East Africa and then in August crossed into Northern Rhodesia, which was British. They were still fighting when the Armistice was signed in Europe, ending the war. The Germans took Kasama on 13th November but then heard that they had lost the war. They formally surrendered on 25th November 1918.

This photo shows an African artist's interpretation of the surrender of General Lettow-Vorbeck. Why do you think they wanted to recreate this moment?

Nearly a million people participated in the First World War in Africa. All sides conscripted thousands of Africans to carry food and supplies. Africa is huge, and things need to travel a long way! A lot of the time they had to rely on people carrying things by hand, because the roads and railways were few. More than 7,000 African civilians from Uganda alone were conscripted by the British to form the Congo Carrier Section to supply the Belgians. This was because the Belgian government left its men to feed themselves, and so if there was not a huge operation by the British to bring them what they needed, they would steal what they needed from civilians. This could lead to disorder, a complete breakdown of food available to feed the population and even famine.

The situation in German East Africa showed what happened when the system did not work. Carriers were not paid properly and food was taken from civilians. This and heavy rains in 1917 caused a famine. One historian estimates that this led to another 300,000 civilian deaths in German East Africa. The flu pandemic also badly affected Africa. For example, more than 10% of the whole adult, male population in Kenya eventually died as a result of the war and its impact.

This photo shows carriers on the road in East Africa. More than 600,000 Africans served in the First World War. That's about 60% of nearly a million people that took part in the war in some way on the continent.

Famine is a lack of food on a big, big scale. War is one of the top causes of famine, but when it is combined with other causes, like crop failures or disease, all of which hurt Africa in the First World War, it can be even more devastating.

Britain and Italy would also fight the Senussi, a religious order from Libya and Egypt, from 1915 until 1917. Germany had tried to make friends with the Senussi, but when the Islamic Ottoman Empire joined the war, they managed to convince their fellow muslims to declare a jihad, against the Allies and attack Egypt from the west.

Fighting against the British took place along the Egyptian coast, right on the edge of Africa, and further inland, moving from oasis to oasis to stay close to water. It was a very different type of war, with troops travelling huge distances in the desert. Men from Britain, India, South Africa, Australia and New Zealand all took part in the campaign against the Senussi.

NORTH AFRICA

This photo shows Bedouin prisoners captured by the British.

The Ottomans had hoped that the Senussi attacking from the west would help them in attacking the Suez Canal from the east. Really, the Grand Senussi understood that Britain was much less of an enemy to his ambition than France, who had lots of colonial power in North Africa, or Italy, who had claimed Libya. Peace was agreed between Britain and the Senussi in April 1917, and soon afterwards another with the Italians, and war in the Western Desert came to an end.

This photo shows the burning of a Beduoin camp. It was very difficult in some circumstances to know whether the local population was on your side, or spying for the enemy.

In this photo you can see men of the Dorset Yeomanry who have survived the Battle of Agagia on 26th February 1916. The Dorsets carried out a cavalry charge and cut off the retreating Senussi. They chased them into the desert, and captured their baggage train, but more than 30 men were killed.

Italy

After four failed attempts on the Isonzo in 1915, it's not really surprising that General Cadorna decided that he was going to try again as soon as the spring came. This next battle was not really a big effort though. The Fifth Battle of the Isonzo started on the 9th March 1916. It was the smallest of the battles along the river, the weather was terrible and by the 15th it was all but over. With promises of more supplies and equipment from their allies, Italy planned to begin all over again in the summer.

5

ISONZO

In this picture, you can see Italian soldiers in their trenches during the Fifth Battle of the Isonzo

Before Cadorna could attack on the Isonzo, the Austro-Hungarians launched the **Trentino Offensive** on the 15th May 1916. This is also known as the "Strafexpedition" (Punitive Expedition)". In Italy, they call it the **Battaglia degli Altipiani** (Battle of Asiago). This is near Vicenza, and not that far from Venice. The Austro-Hungarians attacked on a front more than thirty miles long. They broke through the middle of the Italian line, and it looked like disaster for Cadorna and his men. The Italian general quickly sent reinforcements. The Austro-Hungarians kept trying, but when the Brusilov Offensive was launched in the east on the 4th June, they couldn't fight on both fronts at once. Things were so bad for Austria-Hungary in that battle on the Eastern Front, that they sent men there instead.

This photo shows a statue of a famous local nun, Giovanna Maria Bonomo, that has survived the destruction of the Asiago offensive.

In this photo you can see a very big Austro-Hungarian gun in action during the battle!

The **Sixth Battle of the Isonzo** was the most successful of all the Italian attempts on the river. The Austro-Hungarians had taken men away from the Isonzo to fight the Asiago offensive and to help face Brusilov's advance in Galicia. Cadorna decided that he was going to attack again and this time he was determined to take the town of Gorizia.

The battle started on the 6th August, with a very heavy bombardment. In under an hour the Italians got to the top of Mount Sabotino. At the same time, they were attacking Mount San Michele. Again they got to the top quickly. Having these two high points, the Austro-Hungarian defences around Gorizia collapsed. The first Italian troops entered the city and finally they crossed the Isonzo River. Cadorna called the attack off on the 17th August. The Austro-Hungarians still held lots of high ground to the north and east of the town, and so they hadn't been completely defeated. They could see everything that was going on inside Gorizia.

In this photo, you can see Italian soldiers examining a captured Austro-Hungarian machine gun during the Seventh Battle of the Isonzo.

The **Seventh Battle of the Isonzo** happened in September. It was short, only lasting for three days. It may seem silly how many times Italy attacked in this same spot, but they were managing to gradually chip away at the enemy. It was becoming clear that the Austro-Hungarians would need German help here too.

In the first picture Austro-Hungarians guard Italian prisoners after the Eighth Battle of the Isonzo. In the second, you can see Italian soldiers leaving their trenches during the Ninth battle.

9
ISONZO

8
ISONZO

The **Eighth Battle of the Isonzo** only lasted two days. It was really just a case of Cadorna's Italian troops carrying on from the seventh battle. On the 12th October, the battle was called off, to give the army a chance to recover. However, the **Ninth Battle of the Isonzo** began just a few weeks later on the 1st November. Once again it only lasted a few days and again it was unsuccessful. In the seventh, eighth and ninth battles, the Italians had suffered 75,000 casualties, so it was not only the Austro-Hungarians who were getting worn out. There was now a long break while both sides recovered their strength.

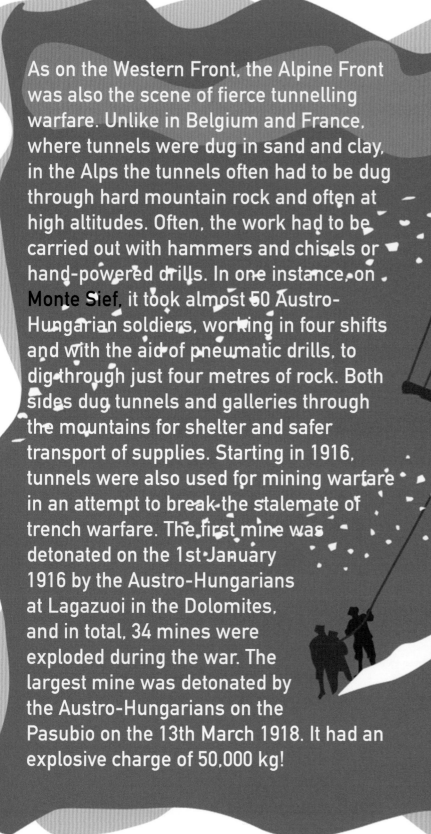

As on the Western Front, the Alpine Front was also the scene of fierce tunnelling warfare. Unlike in Belgium and France, where tunnels were dug in sand and clay, in the Alps the tunnels often had to be dug through hard mountain rock and often at high altitudes. Often, the work had to be carried out with hammers and chisels or hand-powered drills. In one instance, on **Monte Sief**, it took almost 50 Austro-Hungarian soldiers, working in four shifts and with the aid of pneumatic drills, to dig through just four metres of rock. Both sides dug tunnels and galleries through the mountains for shelter and safer transport of supplies. Starting in 1916, tunnels were also used for mining warfare in an attempt to break the stalemate of trench warfare. The first mine was detonated on the 1st January 1916 by the Austro-Hungarians at Lagazuoi in the Dolomites, and in total, 34 mines were exploded during the war. The largest mine was detonated by the Austro-Hungarians on the Pasubio on the 13th March 1918. It had an explosive charge of 50,000 kg!

This photo gives you some idea of what it was like to work underground on the Italian Front. These Austro-Hungarian soldiers are digging a tunnel

Another danger on the Alpine Front, was avalanches! This was especially the case in December 1916, when the combination of heavy snowfall and a sudden thaw created the perfect conditions for them. We think that 10,000 soldiers on both sides lost their lives as a result of avalanches that month, which is the highest number of deaths caused by snow/ice in history. The worst day was the 13th December when, before dawn, 200,000 tons of snow plunged down Mount Marmolada, directly onto the wooden barracks of an Austro-Hungarian battalion of mountain troops. Of the more than 300 soldiers sleeping in the barracks, only a handful were rescued. Some 270 were buried alive but only 40 bodies were recovered. Later that same day, another avalanche hit an Italian barrack causing further deaths. Although this happened on a Wednesday, the event became known in Austria-Hungary as 'White Friday'. In Italy it was known as 'The Black Santa Lucia' as it happened on Saint Lucy's Day. Even today, more than 100 years later, the bodies of soldiers who fell victim to avalanches are still found in the Alps when the snow thaws.

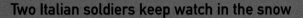
Two Italian soldiers keep watch in the snow

Salonika

On the Macedonian front, the Allies decided to attack the Bulgarian forces at Lake Doiran. A combined force of British and French troops, nearly 50,000 men, began their offensive on the 9th August. All of their attacks were beaten back by the Bulgarian defenders.

Conditions were very different here. It was very hot in summer with mosquitoes plaguing the troops on both sides. It was so bad in some places that both sides withdrew from the front line when it was in a valley, up into the hills to escape them. At one point there was a no-man's-land between the opposing forces of twelve miles. The mosquitoes brought the deadly disease malaria with them, which killed lots of men or made them sick. Then in winter the temperatures got very cold and men suffered from exposure and frostbite. These extremes meant that fighting was limited to the easier conditions of spring and autumn.

FRANCE

BRITISH

BULGARIAN

ROMANIAN

This photo shows Bulgarian troops waiting to go into battle.

Meanwhile, nearly 100 miles to the southwest, the Bulgarians were planning. They wanted to launch two attacks, one on each end of the Allied line. The Bulgarian First Army, commanded by General Buyadzhiev, was to attack and take the city of Florina and the Chegan mountain range, while the Second Army, commanded by General Todorov, would attack into northeastern Greece. First Army's attack, known as the Chegan Offensive or the Battle of Florina, began on 17th August, and while Florina was captured soon after, the Bulgarians were too thinly spread and lacked artillery. They were soon stopped by the Serbian defenders, and could not take the mountain range. On the 27th August, it was over and the Bulgarians were forced to dig in.

In these pictures you can see General Boyadzhiev and Bulgarian troops going into battle on the Salonika front. Look at how hilly it is!

BULGARIAN

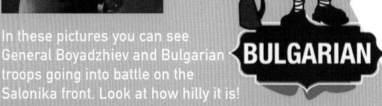

SERBIA

Things went better for the Second Army. General Todorov's attack, known as the Struma Operation, began on 18th August on a long front defended by French and Greek troops. But wasn't Greece still neutral? Yes. So what was going on? Well for a start, King Constantine did not want to get involved, but his Prime Minister, a man named Venizelos, preferred the Allies. People disagreed on who to side with all over the country. This caused the National Schism (say 'shizzem'), This just means a big, serious disagreement. This situation would not be fixed in 1916.

The photo on the right shows Greek troops on the march at Salonika.

Below you can see just how many different nations came to be represented at Salonika. From left to right, you can see soldiers from Indochina, France, Senegal, Britain, Russia, Italy, Serbia, Greece and India.

GREEK

King Constantine

Eleftherios Venizelos

207

The ridiculous thing was, that because of all the arguing going on between Greek politicians and the King, the Greek soldiers were ordered to do absolutely nothing to stop the Bulgarian Second Army's invasion of their country. Bulgarian soldiers got miles and miles into Greek territory, and took an area bigger than Dubai. Or in England, bigger than the whole county of Suffolk! Nearly 7,000 Greek officers and men were sent to Germany as prisoners. It was a great victory for Bulgaria, but because of the failure of the Chegan Offensive, it proved to have little effect. In Greece, however, some men were furious. General Nikolaos Christodoulou refused to obey orders, and with his men he joined the Movement of National Defence in Thessaloniki. This was a second, rival government led by Venizelos, so the situation in Greece was getting worse and worse. Both were trying to run Greece at the same time!

This photo shows the men who led the Movement of National Defence because they were so angry that the Greek Army was not allowed to defend their country. Venizelos is in the middle.

WITHOUT PREJUDICE.

Ferdie. "I HOPE I DON'T INTRUDE?"
Tino. "OH, NO! MAKE YOURSELF AT HOME. THIS IS LIBERTY HALL."

This is a British cartoon from the war. It makes fun of King Constantine for letting Bulgaria invade his country. You can see the Tsar of Bulgaria climbing in through his window!

FRANCE

BULGARIAN

GREEK

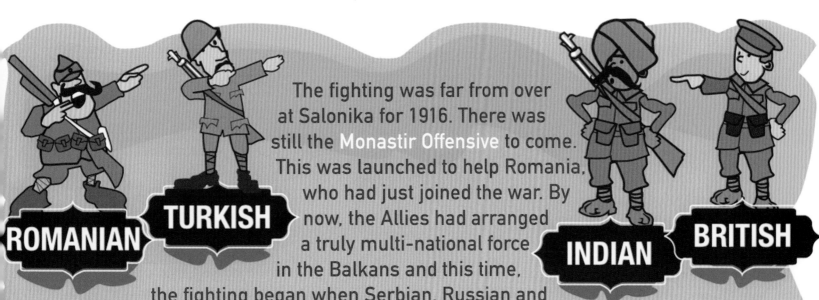

ROMANIAN

TURKISH

INDIAN

BRITISH

The fighting was far from over at Salonika for 1916. There was still the Monastir Offensive to come. This was launched to help Romania, who had just joined the war. By now, the Allies had arranged a truly multi-national force in the Balkans and this time, the fighting began when Serbian, Russian and French troops attacked the Bulgarians. The first battle lasted for three days, and was a victory for the Allies. On the 12th September, Serbian soldiers attacked Gornichevo. Two days later, the Bulgarians had been forced into a retreat. They even left their guns!

The beginning of the offensive also saw the Battle of Kaymakchalan, which was another fight between Serbia and Bulgaria. It was fought from the 12th to the 30th September, and the Serbs captured the peak of Prophet Elijah. It was a very costly battle. Serbian casualties numbered 10,000 and the Bulgarians lost lots of men too.

RUSSIAN

FRANCE

ITALIAN

SERBIA

GERMAN

BULGARIAN

SERBIA

This photo shows Serbian troops in a front line trench during the Battle of Kaymakchalan

Here you can see French soldiers who have just arrived at Salonika

BRITISH

FRANCE

There was now a pause, and even more countries arrived in the Balkans! Ottoman soldiers would come to help Bulgaria, along with Germans. The Battle of the Crna Bend (say 'cerna', it means 'red' in Serbian!) lasted for two months (October and November). The Serbians first tried to cross the Red River on the 5th October. By the middle of the month the Bulgarians were fiercely still clinging to their positions. On one night the Serbs made EIGHT attacks and all of them were forced back! In the end, the Allies did gain some ground, but it was not of much strategic use. This means it was not useful in terms of planning future strategy needed to win battles. It also was not enough to keep Romania safe from being attacked by the Central Powers.

BULGARIAN

TURKISH

GERMAN

RUSSIAN

The War at Sea

There were naval clashes and actions all over the world during the war. The defence of the Suez Canal was supported by ships like *Ocean* and *Swiftsure*. Ships from the Italian Navy also led a brave evacuation of what was left of the Serbian Army from Albania. There were also scraps between gunboats in East Africa, and the German ship *Königsberg* was sunk in the Rufiji River.

YARMOUTH
LOWESTOFT

In the spring, the German Navy carried out another raid using ships on Britain's east coast. This time Lowestoft and Yarmouth were hit. A new Admiral, Reinhard Scheer, had become the commander of the German High Seas Fleet in February 1916. He thought that if he did aggressive things like this, he could lure the British out into open water and have a big battle on his terms. Lowestoft and Yarmouth also both had military significance, and damaging operations there would stop Britain from policing U-boats and keeping the seas free of mines.

On the 24th April 1916, 200 houses were hit by shells. As well as several naval casualties, three civilians were killed at Lowestoft and 19 wounded. Throughout the world, people were shocked and the raid did a lot of damage to Germany's image.

In this photo you can see a policeman at Lowestoft picking through the ruins of a bedroom in a convalescent home. When Germany claimed that the raid was carried out on military targets, they were criticised heavily.

Admiral Scheer

Only once did Britain and Germany's navies clash in a BIG battle in the First World War, and this was at the Battle of Jutland. Jutland is a part of Denmark, and the battle happened in the water nearby. Germans call the Battle 'Skagerrakschlacht'. Skagerrak is a name for the stretch of water that runs between Norway, Sweden and Denmark, where the battle took place.

Understandably, both countries were a bit reluctant to see their expensive ships smashed to pieces. The British Grand Fleet lived mainly at harbours like Rosyth, which is on the Firth of Forth and at Scapa Flow, which is in the Orkney Islands, north of the Scottish mainland. The German High Seas Fleet used bases at Kiel, Wilhelmshaven, Danzig and Cuxhaven.

Because he could not take on the whole Grand Fleet face to face, as he would lose, Scheer's plan was to lure out part of the fleet and destroy it. He would use a fast group of ships under the command of Vice-Admiral Hipper to trap Vice-Admiral Beatty's battlecruisers. Unfortunately for the Germans, the Russians had captured a codebook from one of their ships and at Room 40 the Royal Navy found out that the enemy was planning a big fleet action. On the 30th May the Grand Fleet set sail to join with Beatty, just in case.

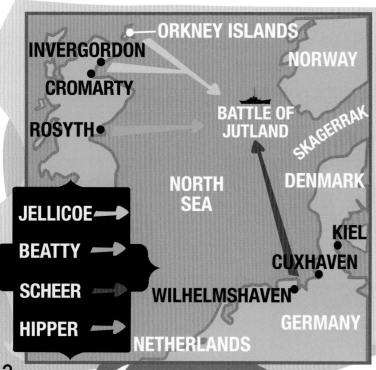

ORKNEY ISLANDS
INVERGORDON
NORWAY
CROMARTY
ROSYTH
BATTLE OF JUTLAND
SKAGERRAK
NORTH SEA
DENMARK
JELLICOE →
BEATTY →
KIEL
SCHEER →
CUXHAVEN
HIPPER →
WILHELMSHAVEN
GERMANY
NETHERLANDS

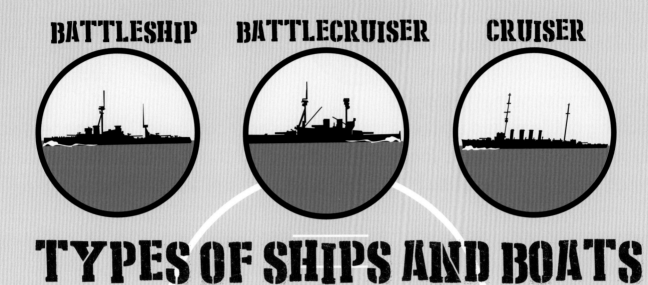

BATTLESHIP   BATTLECRUISER   CRUISER

TYPES OF SHIPS AND BOATS

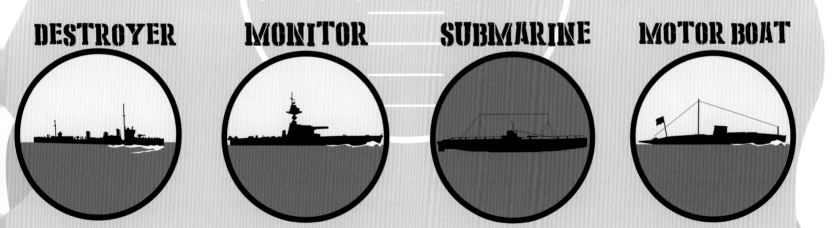

DESTROYER   MONITOR   SUBMARINE   MOTOR BOAT

WOULD YOU BE ABLE TO TELL THE DIFFERENCE?

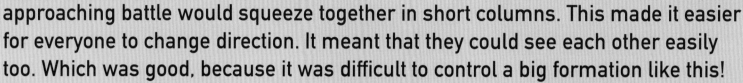

So what did a naval battle look like in 1916? It was all about what they called concentration of force. This meant that the ships approaching battle would squeeze together in short columns. This made it easier for everyone to change direction. It meant that they could see each other easily too. Which was good, because it was difficult to control a big formation like this!

When they arrived at the scene, before the fight started, the ships would move into a single column, or battle line. Faster ships would be racing about gathering information about the enemy and sending it back to the Admiral in charge. They'd also try to stop the enemy's small ships from doing the same.

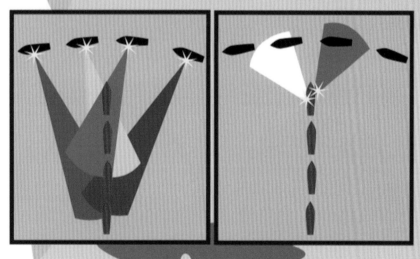

What you really wanted to do in battle was a move called 'crossing the T'. This meant you sailed across the top of the enemy's line at an angle that enabled you to shower as many shells on them as possible while you were still protected from giving them the same chance.

JUTLAND

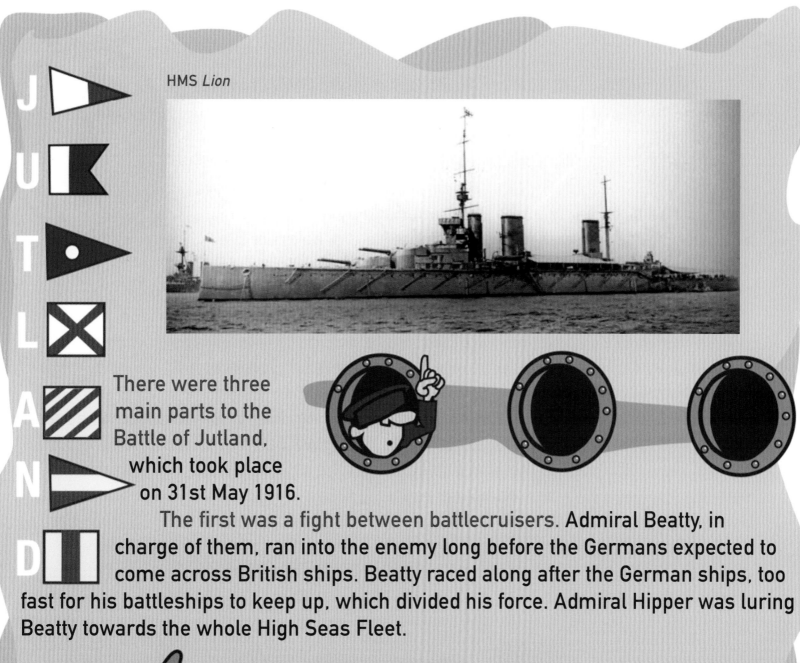

HMS *Lion*

There were three main parts to the Battle of Jutland, which took place on 31st May 1916.

The first was a fight between battlecruisers. Admiral Beatty, in charge of them, ran into the enemy long before the Germans expected to come across British ships. Beatty raced along after the German ships, too fast for his battleships to keep up, which divided his force. Admiral Hipper was luring Beatty towards the whole High Seas Fleet.

The Battle began at 3:48 pm when Hipper opened fire. First they ran to the south, the British chasing the Germans, who were still leading him towards the shocking sight of the High Seas Fleet. It was foggy and overcast, and this made it hard for the ships to hit each other.

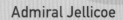
Admiral Jellicoe

At 4:00 pm Beatty's own ship, HMS *Lion* was hit and the shell caused an explosion. Lots of men were killed. The worst thing that can happen to a ship is that its magazine catches light. On *Lion*, Major Francis Harvey of the Royal Marines had been badly burned and wounded by the first explosion. In fact, he was dying, but before he did, he is credited for giving an order to shut and flood the magazine, so that it could not explode. If he had not have done this, the ship would have blown up.

When things like this happened at sea, there was no way to escape. If your ship suffered an explosion like this, there was nowhere for you to run. At 4:02 pm, HMS *Indefatigable* was hit by three shells, which caused her magazine to blow up. 1,019 crew died. In fact, only two men survived the sinking. Within half an hour, it happened again. We think that HMS *Queen Mary* was hit by two German ships at once. Both magazines at the front of the ship exploded and the ship vanished in a massive cloud of smoke. She had 1,275 men on board, and only nine survived. An officer on one of the German ships that hit her, the *Derfflinger*, said: 'A vivid red flame shot up from her… then came an explosion, followed by a much heavier explosion… Immediately afterwards, she blew up with a terrific explosion, the masts collapsing inwards and the smoke hiding everything.'

WHAT IS A MAGAZINE?

These aren't the kind you read!
Magazines are where the explosives are kept, and a big ship will have several. If it came into contact with a spark, or flame, or a shell, the whole ship could blow up in an instant.

Soon after the loss of *Queen Mary*, HMS *Southampton* spotted the German High Seas Fleet. This was a shock to the British, because nobody knew they were even at sea yet, just that they might be plotting something! Southampton dodged German shells to try and take this news to the admirals. As soon as Beatty spotted the edge of Scheer's fleet, he turned, escaping the trap, and now everyone raced to the north. Now the Germans were chasing the British, and Beatty was leading the enemy towards Admiral Jellicoe and the superior Grand Fleet. Beatty had already lost two of his six battlecruisers, and was going to be heavily criticised after the battle for this.

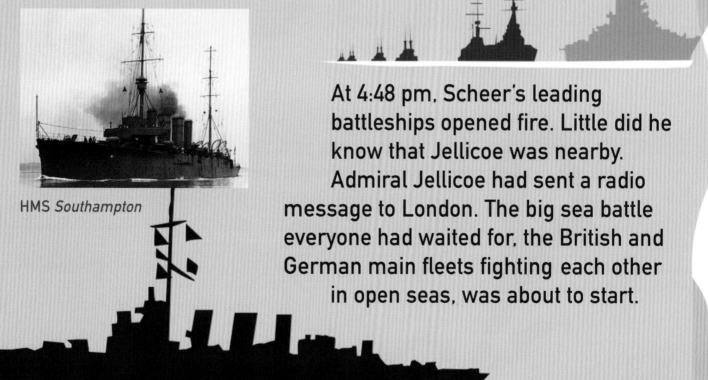

HMS *Southampton*

At 4:48 pm, Scheer's leading battleships opened fire. Little did he know that Jellicoe was nearby. Admiral Jellicoe had sent a radio message to London. The big sea battle everyone had waited for, the British and German main fleets fighting each other in open seas, was about to start.

The second part of the battle was the fleet action. Jellicoe sent a battlecruiser squadron led by Rear-Admiral Hood to help Beatty. At 5:38 pm, one of the ships screening Hood's ships, HMS *Chester*, came under fire. Hood swung round to help, but before he could get there, four German light cruisers filled her with shells.

Jack Cornwell was a 16 year old serving on HMS *Chester*. He was from East London, and his father and brother both served in the army during the war. He was working as a sight-setter, so helping to point one of the guns on deck. All of the men near him were killed or badly wounded by shell splinters. Jack was hurt too, but stayed at his post, standing by his gun for another fifteen minutes. He was found still standing there, with bits of metal stuck in his chest. He died of his injuries two days later.

He was awarded the Victoria Cross, which is the highest award for bravery that someone in the British armed forces can get. Jack became very famous, and lots of money was raised in his name for charity. Not much of it went to his family though, who desperately needed it.

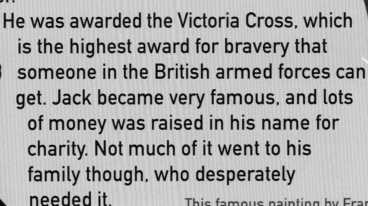

This famous painting by Frank Salisbury shows you how Jack might have looked standing by his gun during the battle.

At about 6:00 pm, Jellicoe's own ship, HMS *Iron Duke*, finally spotted Beatty's damaged *Lion*. The British ships tried to move into their battle line with German shells flying towards them, and there were near collisions and close shaves. This bit of the battle is known as 'Windy Corner'. In the meantime, Scheer was sailing his ships directly towards the Grand Fleet without knowing it. HMS *Defence* was trying to sink the *Wiesbaden*, which was crippled and an easy target, but she sailed right into the path of Scheer and Hipper's combined forces. German battleships flung shells at her and her magazine went up. She disappeared in a massive explosion in front of the rest of the Grand Fleet, taking all 903 of her crewmen with her.

Hipper now took on Hood's ships. His flagship, *Lützow*, was hit many times, including under the waterline by Hood on HMS *Invincible*. But at 6:30 pm suddenly the tables turned. Lützow and Derfflinger found themselves with a clear shot at Hood's own ship. They opened fire and sank *Invincible* in 90 seconds. One shell detonated the magazines in the middle of the ship and she blew up. Of 1,032 men, only six survived. Rear Admiral Horace Hood as not amongst them.

In these photos you see the moment that HMS *Invincible* began to blow up, and afterwards, the wreck sticking out of the water.

In this photo you can see part of the Grand Fleet in Scotland. It must have been scary to find them sailing towards you!

At about 6:30 pm, Jellicoe managed to cross Scheer's T.

Scheer and his leading captains were stunned. Suddenly out of the battlefield smoke came their worst nightmare, the huge, powerful battle line of the Grand Fleet. Scheer later wrote that: 'The entire arc stretching from north to east was a sea of fire. The flash from the muzzles of the guns was seen distinctly through the mist and smoke on the horizon, although the ships themselves were not distinguishable.' He hadn't even known that Jellicoe had put to sea. Realising that the situation was terrible, Scheer ordered his men to turn around and sail the other way. They did this very professionally and escaped. They weaved about, to avoid being chased, but without realising, Scheer sailed his fleet right back towards the British battle line.

By 7:15 pm, Jellicoe had crossed Scheer's T again. This time he was able to cause much more damage, suffering hardly any to his ships in return. Once again, Scheer turned and sailed away from a fight he could not win. This time it was harder, though, and to ensure the escape of the main German fleet, he ordered four battlecruisers into the path of the Grand Fleet. The German sailors called this charge the 'death ride'. Derfflinger alone was hit fourteen times. In return, as Scheer sailed away, his torpedo boats launched more than thirty torpdeos. The British ships managed to avoid them all. This was the end of the significant action between the two fleets. They had directly engaged each other twice, and would not do so again in the First World War.

Below you can see a line of ships firing their guns. Can you imagine how loud it was?!

In this photo you can see some of the German High Seas Fleet on the move.

The last of the main parts of the Battle of Jutland happened after nightfall. Jellicoe did his best to cut the Germans off from returning to their bases, as he hoped to start the battle again the following day. Lots of ships fought through the night, and the situation was very muddled. Torpedoes flew back and forth, ships were sunk and hundreds more men killed. SMS *Nassau* rammed HMS *Spitfire*, ripping a hole in her side, but she managed to get back to port. It was confusing and terrifying. One German ship even managed to ram another, when the dreadnought *Posen* ran into the cruiser *Elbing*. She sank the following day.

The biggest loss of the night happened just after midnight, when HMS *Black Prince* sailed into the path of German battleships. She was a cruiser, and she blew up when shells damaged a magazine. Not one of the 857 men on board survived. The German battlecruisers *Moltke* and *Seydlitz* also sailed into trouble, but the British ships did not open fire on them, because they did not want to give away their positions. Scheer's fleet was sailing away to safety at daybreak on the 1st June.

The battle was at best a draw. The *New York Times* summed it up very well when a journalist wrote that 'The German Navy has assaulted its jailor, but is still in jail'. The German fleet would be trapped in port for the whole war. Bizarrely, the Kaiser began telling everybody in Germany that his ships had secured a big victory over the Royal Navy. His cousin, King George, was very unimpressed, as was the navy, but the Kaiser did things like this from time to time. He had a very unique personality!

Admiral Scheer had failed in his plan to destroy part of the Grand Fleet, but in turn, the Royal Navy failed to engage the High Seas Fleet in a decisive battle. They had the fire power to win, and they had let Scheer get away. By the end of the year, the Germans had decided that they were not going to put their fleet in this dangerous position again, but just having it in port and ready to sail into the North Sea meant that the Royal Navy would always have to be waiting, ready, and that they couldn't sail off somewhere else and cause Germany trouble.

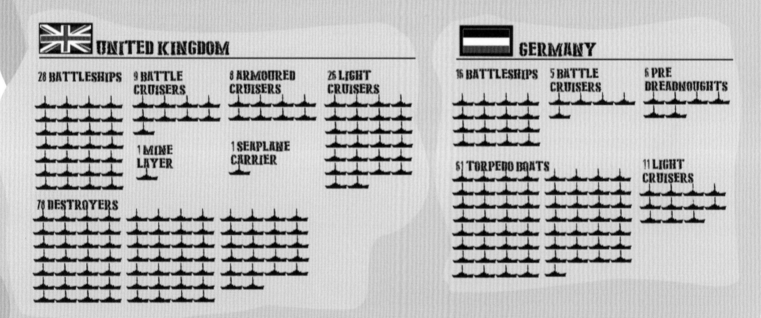

UNITED KINGDOM

28 BATTLESHIPS | 9 BATTLE CRUISERS | 8 ARMOURED CRUISERS | 26 LIGHT CRUISERS

1 MINE LAYER | 1 SEAPLANE CARRIER

78 DESTROYERS

GERMANY

16 BATTLESHIPS | 5 BATTLE CRUISERS | 6 PRE DREADNOUGHTS

61 TORPEDO BOATS | 11 LIGHT CRUISERS

Nearly 10,000 men were killed during the Battle of Jutland, which did not even last 24 hours. This shows you how devastating naval warfare can be. About 250 ships took part. 14 British ships were sunk, and 11 German.

The Battle of Jutland was not the last attempt by Scheer to engage the Royal Navy in 1916, but the others were very small by comparison.

On the 19th August, the German Admiral attempted another raid, sending out zeppelins, submarines and ships. As well as keeping the Royal Navy on its toes, he wanted to improve the morale of his men after Jutland. This time the target was the northeast coast and the town of Sunderland. However, the team in Room 40 obtained intelligence by intercepting German radio messages and breaking the code. A large British force set sail quickly to intercept them. Scheer's plan fell apart, with only minor damage to ships, but the Royal Navy suffered 39 casualties.

Another clash took place in October near Dover with the Battle of Dover Strait. German torpedo boats from the Flanders Flotilla set sail to attack whatever ships they could find and cause damage to the Dover Barrage, which was a set of underwater defences to protect the port from U-boats. In five groups, the torpedo boats attacked, sinking a number of smaller ships. 45 men died, and a few were wounded and taken prisoner. The Germans got away with just minor damage to one ship.

1917

By now everyone was tired of war, and with no real end in sight, people all over Europe were exhausted and very depressed. Men no longer rushed for a chance to fight in their thousands. Even in Britain now, service was compulsory. In some countries people protested about the war carrying on, and Empires began to crumble.

In every country involved in the war, children lied about their age in order to join the army. Boys as young as 12 managed to find their way into uniform because they thought that war would be an adventure. Do you think you would have tried to do this?

Boy Soldiers

Sidney Lewis managed to convince the army he was 18 when he was actually 12! By the age of 13, he had fought on the Somme. He was found out, and sent home, only to lie again at 15 to get back into the army! Luckily, he survived the war.

Paul Mauk was from Germany and wanted to be a doctor when he grew up. He managed to convince the army to take him and was sent to Western Front. In June, 1915, he was shot in the arm in a front line trench. Unfortunately he was carrying lots of ammunition, which caught fire. He died of his wounds that day, aged 14.

Reggie Hobbs was from North London. His mum actually helped him to join the army at the age of 15. She was scared that if she didn't go with him, he would run away and change his name and she would have no idea where he was. He joined the Royal Flying Corps as a wireless operator, and actually had quite a safe job. However, during the Battle of the Somme he volunteered to go further forward to help the artillery. He was hit by a shell and died aged 16.

We think about 20 soldiers under the age of 18 from Australia died in the war. Jim Martin was from New South Wales. His parents' only son, he enlisted as a teenager. Like Reggie Hobbs, he told his parents he would use a fake name and run away if they did not let him. He arrived at Gallipoli in July 1915. He died in October as a result of typhiod, aged 14. We think that he was the youngest Australian soldier to die in the First World War, but it's hard to tell with so many boys lying about their ages!

Children and the War

Aside from boy soldiers, it is impossible for something as big and as long as the First World War not to touch the lives of all children in some way.

Lots of children found a way to work towards the war effort. On the left you can see a boy scout working as a messenger. He would have taken notes backwards and forwards for officials. On the right are Scouts from London who have gone to the country to help with the harvest because the farmworkers have gone off to war.

This Sea Scout is helping protect Britain against spies. The man he is talking to has been taking photographs on the beach and the scout is checking to make sure he has proper permission.

There were no air raid sirens during the First World War. Sometimes policemen rode about warning people on bicycles. It is this scout's job to sound an all clear when it is safe to come out again.

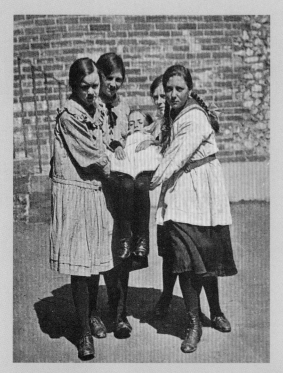

Air raids became more and more likely as the war went on. Here you can see schoolgirls practising what to do if one of their friends is hurt. You can also see women at a nursery practising getting all of the babies down into a shelter.

Children always, always suffer in war. Sometimes they became refugees when their families had to leave their homes. A lot of them came home afterwards to find their house gone and that they had nowhere left to live. Economies are always ruined in war too. This means the way money moves, and how people buy and sell things. Prices get higher, and it can be hard to feed a whole family. Millions of children went hungry during the war,

On the Western Front, the winter of 1916-17 was the coldest in living memory.

The German line was very messy after the battles at Verdun and on the Somme. Since the summer of 1916 they had been constructing a new defensive position, called the Siegfriedstellung, The Allies would call it the Hindenburg Line. Thousands of men helped dig the trenches, make strongpoints for machine guns and lay out thousands and thousands of miles of brand new barbed wire. There was so much that it sparkled and could be seen for miles!

Starting in February 1917, the Germans began to fall back to their new line. They called this Operation Alberich. The Allies called it the Retreat to the Hindenburg Line. German soldiers caused lots of damage as they left, because they did not want to leave anything useful for the Allies. They also laid booby traps too, to try and cause casualties. These could be anything from a trip wire to a packet of cigarettes that was rigged to explode if a soldier tried to pick it up.

It was a retreat; but the Germans were doing it not because they were running away and giving up. They had shortened the line they had to defend by thirty miles and made their job on the Western Front much, much easier.

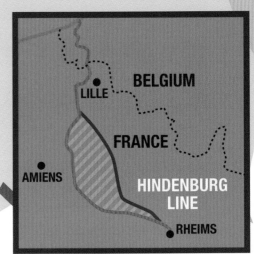

BELGIUM
LILLE
FRANCE
AMIENS
HINDENBURG LINE
RHEIMS

General Nivelle had taken part in the limited success at the end of the Battle of Verdun in 1916, and made a good name for himself. Now, he told the French Government exactly what they wanted to hear. He told them that he could beat the Germans, kick them out of France and win the war very quickly. And they believed him.

He began making plans for spring 1917. He planned to win the war in a big, quick battle and said that he could do it in just a couple of days. It was really the Second Battle of the Aisne, but lots of people just call it the Nivelle Offensive.

General Robert Nivelle

This photo shows you a very cold-looking German trench on the Somme at the beginning of 1917

VIMY RIDGE

The first part of Nivelle's masterplan to win the war was the British Arras offensive and the attack on Vimy Ridge on Easter Monday, the 9th April. This would be called the Battle of Arras. The artillery had been shelling the whole 24-mile line around Arras since the 4th April. They had used an enormous two and a half million shells! This was over a million more than at the beginning of the Somme offensive, which shows you just how big these battles were getting! These bombardments were terrible for the Germans on the ridge. Even if they were not being killed by the shells, the noise shook them to the bone for days at a time. Their nerves were shot to pieces. They could not move in and out of the lines, or get hot food. Some of them could not get any kind of food or water brought to them. Their trenches were completely destroyed and by the time the battle started, men were just sitting in scattered holes in the ground. For the last ten hours, the British also started firing shells with poisoned gas.

These photos show you two very different endings to the Battle of Arras. In one, wounded men wait on their stretchers for treatment. In the other, men who have come back from the battle celebrate after capturing Monchy le Preux.

232

BELGIUM

• MONS

• VIMY RIDGE

ARRAS
• CAMBRAI

FRANCE

• PARIS

In this photo you can see men on their way into battle. What else can you see?

Zero-hour, the time that the infantry were to attack, was at 5:30 am. Snow fell heavily as the British troops went forward, but luckily for them, the sleet was being blown into the faces of the Germans. The enemy was taken by surprise, and the British took men prisoner who had their boots off, or were just waking up.

The Germans had not defended this area strongly. The reason that so often the Germans, when attacked, could kick the Allies out of their trenches again, was because they were defending in depth. Really, they were happy to let their enemies into the trenches, because they had reserves waiting to come up and get rid of them

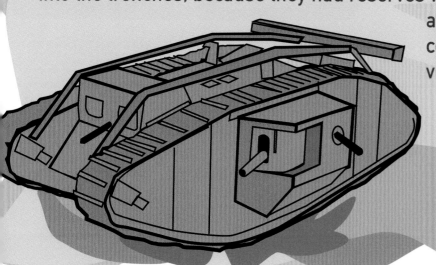

again. They let the British, or French come towards them and make themselves vulnerable, then they attacked. During the opening phase of the Battle of Arras, German reserves were too far away, so they could not carry out their usual plan. The British pressed on, and did very well.

It was Canadians, led by the British General Byng, who were entrusted with capturing the all-important Vimy Ridge, They carried with them lots of machine guns, and lots of Lewis guns, which were a special kind of light machine gun. They had been well trained, and their attack was well planned. Men were given very specific goals, which meant that it was easy for them to understand what to do even if their officers were killed. Remember that communications were difficult in battle on the Western Front, so this was very important. They conquered the ridge and now they had the view, watching German soldiers retreating away on the other side of the ridge.

This battle was the first time that troops from all over Canada had fought together under one flag, so it is an incredibly important part of their history. The famous flag you see today though, with the maple leaf, would still not be used for many years.

General Byng was a British general who commanded the Canadians at Vimy. When he first took charge of them, he joked that he did not even know a Canadian, but he came to love his men very much.

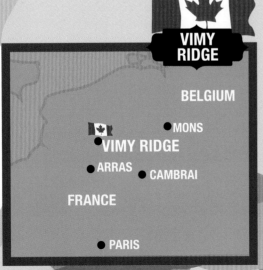

VIMY RIDGE

BELGIUM

MONS

VIMY RIDGE

ARRAS
CAMBRAI

FRANCE

PARIS

The battlefield was such a mess, that there now needed to be a break so that the British and Canadian forces could prepare to go forward again. Roads needed to be built, guns needed to be moved and new pits needed to be dug to put them in. Food for men and horses needed to be brought up and the wounded taken care of. It would have been easy to get over-excited, but the Allies could not afford to throw all of their men in the battle and risk having nothing left if it went wrong.

The Second Battle of the Scarpe began on the 23rd April after more freezing cold weather delayed the attack. Once more they made gains, though not everything went to plan. The British and Canadians then advanced even further whilst trying to tie up German troops for the French, who had started their part of the Allied offensive. Finally, the Third Battle of the Scarpe took place at the beginning of May to try and capture a major German defence in the area. This last attack was a failure, with heavy casualties, but the British learned a lot about how to use tanks, artillery and infantry together, and these lessons would be useful later in the year.

This photograph shows soldiers having a rest by the side road during the Arras Offensive.

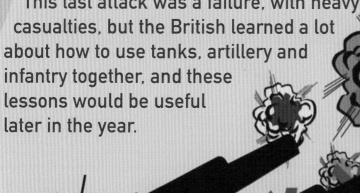

What happened when a

There were lots of men ready to help a soldier when he was wounded either in the trenches or on the battlefield. Lots of them belonged to the Royal Army Medical Corps, or RAMC. Here is a rough idea of how a man might go from the battlefield to hospital if all went to plan on the Western Front:

First of all, stretcher bearers would go looking for the wounded. Some of them might be able to walk, and they would make their way to a Dressing Station. Sometimes, though, all medical units were very busy and it was difficult to keep up. Men could wait a long time to be found. Days, even. The Dressing Station would patch a man up as best they could. If he was able, he'd go back to his unit, or he'd be sent back further for more treatment.

soldier was wounded?

Stretcher bearers or ambulances would taken men to a bigger, better place called a Casualty Clearing Station. These could be very big, and sometimes looked like a whole village made of tents. Here operations could be done, and men could be made comfortable for a long trip to hospital. A lot of men died at these stations, because sometimes they could not be helped.

If a man was safe enough to be moved, casualty clearing stations were usually near railway lines. Men would be loaded onto hospital trains and sent as far away from the enemy as possible. Britain had lots of big base hospitals by the sea where men could stay as they recovered. In many cases the men were sent back to Britain from here if their recovery was taking a long time. If not, they would return as soon as they were better.

237

Medicine & the War

SHELL DRESSINGS

We've looked at how war makes weapons advance very quickly, but this is also true of medicine. All sorts of medicine was developed during the First World War, from how to make artifical limbs, to plastic surgery. It also advanced simple things we take for granted now like blood transfusions, and doctors and nurses got better at keeping wounds clean. They also had to deal with completely new problems, like what to do with men who had been gassed, trench foot, men who were suffering from strange illnesses like trench fever, and of course, shell shock and mental health problems. Do you think you can say that medical development can be called a good outcome of the First World War?

One thing that some countries got very good at was making artificial limbs. Instead of just making lots of identical ones and posting them to men who had lost an arm or a leg to use, they made them to measure. This Senagalese soldier in France is learning to write again after losing both of his arms.

Plastic surgery also developed quickly. Harold Mann, from Sheffield was shot in the face in 1917. Here he is in the middle of lots of operations to repair his face. He lived a long life when he went home.

This photo shows an x-ray machine that is able to travel about the front to help treat wounded soldiers.

Here are some medical aspects of the war you might not have thought of! There was a lot more to it than just treating men who had been shot or injured by shells.

It is so important to keep soldiers healthy. Winning wars is all about being efficient, and if all of them are sick, you cannot be efficient. You are wasting time and money. These Indian soldiers are all having a general exam in Salonika to make sure that they are fit and well.

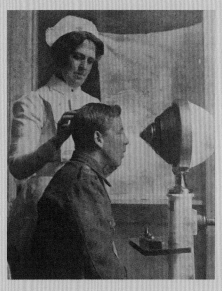

This man is sitting in front of a giant magnet! How many soldiers do you think got bits of shell and other metal in their eyes? You can't shoot straight if you can't see, and so this magnet will draw the metal out.

How did you find all your wounded soldiers? Some armies used dogs to help, which is a simple idea when you think about it!

This is a vaccination kit used by the French Army. It is to stop men catching typhoid. Disease was always a problem in war.

BLOOD TRANSFUSION SET

At the same time as the main British offensive, there were also attacks at Bullecourt, which was to the southeast of the main battlefield. This village was an important part of the Hindenburg Line, and the job of attacking it was given to Australian soldiers, who had been fighting on the Western Front for nearly a year by this point. The first attack was a failure. A second attempt went ahead on the 3rd May, again carried out by Australian soldiers. This time the fighting lasted for two weeks, and British troops were sent in too to try and break through the powerful Hindenburg Line. Bullecourt was finally captured by British soldiers, but the fighting was very costly. The offensive was called off on the 17th May.

The gains at the beginning of the Arras offensive, including Vimy Ridge, were very impressive by the standards of the Western Front. But after that the progress was slow and fell short of what was intended. Really, you can argue that the attacks only went on as long as they did for the benefit of the French, who, you are about to learn, were in trouble further south. The British Army suffered about 150,000 casualties, and this included 11,000 Canadians at Vimy Ridge. We think that the numbers were similar for the Germans.

In this photo you can see Australian soldiers cleaning their rifles in a trench at Bullecourt.

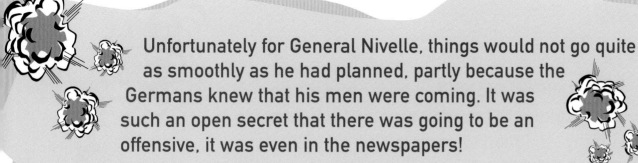

Unfortunately for General Nivelle, things would not go quite as smoothly as he had planned, partly because the Germans knew that his men were coming. It was such an open secret that there was going to be an offensive, it was even in the newspapers!

The French planned to make their breakthrough on fifty miles of the Chemin des Dames, a famous road which runs high along the top of a ridge near the River Aisne. Nivelle's big offensive began in foggy weather on the 16th April. From the beginning, French troops faced lots of damaging fire from machine guns. In some places his troops were successful. In one spot the French troops managed to get two and a half miles into German territory. In other areas though, things were terrible.

For several days the battle continued, and it did achieve success. French troops advanced several miles in some places, and 29,000 Germans were taken prisoner.

For the Western Front, the gains were huge, and they included very strong positions along the Chemin des Dames. About 160,000 German casualties had been suffered.

For France, the Battle of the Hills, which can also be called the Third Battle of Champagne, also took place as part of the attempt to finish the war in Spring 1917.

The French, including Moroccan soldiers and men of the Foreign Legion, attacked before it became light on the 17th April in the middle of rain, wind and snowstorms. The dark helped them get forward. You won't be surprised to learn that as always, the problem was not getting into the enemy trenches, but holding onto them when the enemy counter-attacked. Fighting was bloody, but the French got to the high ground. The Germans could no longer watch them from there, and the fact that they tried 16 times in ten days to take the high ground back should tell you how badly the Germans needed it!

This photograph shows a French soldier helping his wounded comrade.

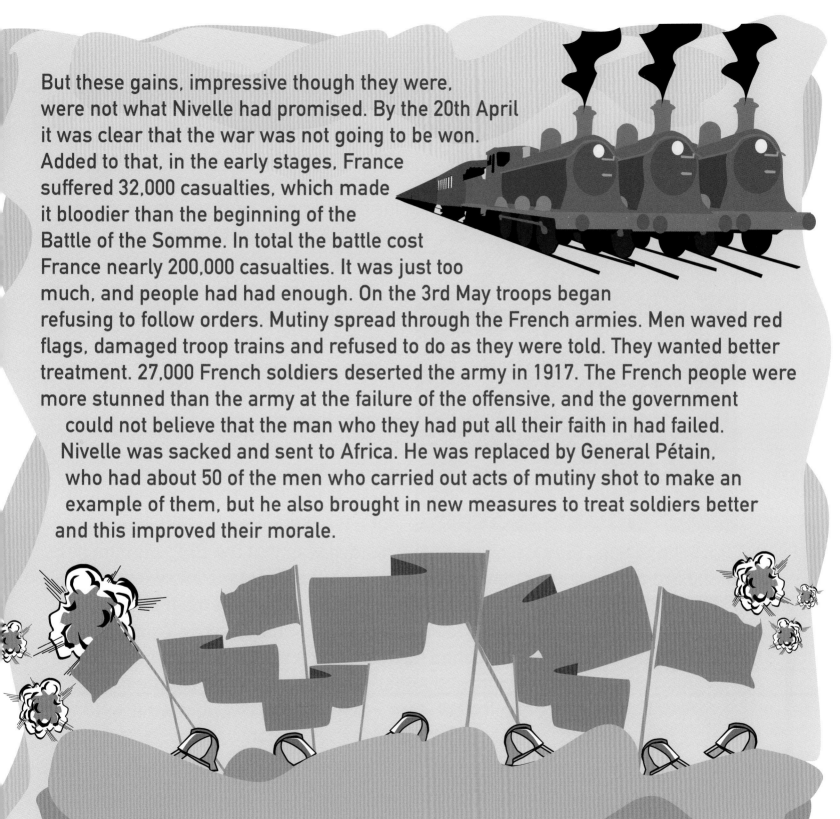

But these gains, impressive though they were, were not what Nivelle had promised. By the 20th April it was clear that the war was not going to be won. Added to that, in the early stages, France suffered 32,000 casualties, which made it bloodier than the beginning of the Battle of the Somme. In total the battle cost France nearly 200,000 casualties. It was just too much, and people had had enough. On the 3rd May troops began refusing to follow orders. Mutiny spread through the French armies. Men waved red flags, damaged troop trains and refused to do as they were told. They wanted better treatment. 27,000 French soldiers deserted the army in 1917. The French people were more stunned than the army at the failure of the offensive, and the government could not believe that the man who they had put all their faith in had failed. Nivelle was sacked and sent to Africa. He was replaced by General Pétain, who had about 50 of the men who carried out acts of mutiny shot to make an example of them, but he also brought in new measures to treat soldiers better and this improved their morale.

It was lucky for France that Sir Douglas Haig and the British Army had been planning their own offensive for the summer of 1917. Whilst the French Army dealt with mutinies and tried to recover from the disaster caused by General Nivelle and his plans, they would need Britain to distract the German armies. The summer offensive in Belgium was the attack that General Haig had wanted to make all along.

It's very famous, and it's proper name is the Third Battle of Ypres, but a lot of the time it's just called 'Passchendaele'. (Say Pash-en-dale). The idea was that the BEF, with the help of the French playing a small role, would push the Germans away from Calais, Boulogne and Dunkirk towards their own borders. Most importantly, the German Army would be pushed further away from Britain and from the English Channel, which was used to supply the BEF on the Western Front. The Allies would wear out the enemy and capture the Belgian coast, which would mean that Germany would no longer have their U-Boat bases.

YPRES   BELGIUM

MONS

VIMY RIDGE

ARRAS   CAMBRAI

FRANCE

PARIS

One thing we haven't really looked at so far is tunnelling. This had been going on for most of the war. Tunnellers were often soldiers who came from mining backgrounds and were used to working underground. They earned more money than a normal soldier because their work was so dangerous. These men would dig long galleries out into No Man's Land, and plant mines. These could be blown up in battle and help the beginning of an attack by causing lots of damage and confusion.

The most famous result of tunnelling was the opening day of the Battle of Messines. This battle was an introduction to the rest of the summer. If Haig wanted the BEF to succeed in his big summer offensive, then first of all he needed to make sure that his soldiers were in the best position. Flanders is very flat, but there was one bit of high

ground around the village of Messines. It had been captured by the Germans in the First Battle of Ypres in 1914. He ordered General Plumer and his men to take this back at the beginning of June.

Before the battle, tunnellers from Britain, Australia and Canada spent months getting ready. The battle was due to start on the 7th June and as it did, 21 mines would explode all at once to help try and defeat the enemy. The mines all exploded in a twenty-second period at 3:10 am.

Nineteen of the mines exploded, and we think they killed thousands of German soldiers. The explosion caused is one of the biggest tnon-nuclear explosions ever created by man. It could be heard in England. The result was terrible. One journalist who saw it happen wrote: 'Suddenly…there rose out of the dark ridge of Messines… enormous volumes of scarlet flame throwing up high towers of earth and smoke all lighted by the flame, spilling over into fountains of fierce colour, so that many of our soldiers waiting for the assault were thrown to the ground. The German troops were stunned, dazed and horror-stricken if they were not killed outright. Many of them lay dead in the great craters opened by the mines."

In this photo you can see tunnellers hard at work. It was dangerous and hard work.

This photo shows just how big some of the mines on the Western Front were, This photo was taken in 1916.

The Battle of Messines is remembered as one of the most successful operations carried out by the British Army in the First World War, and it was not just because of the mines. Artillery was helped by lots of high-tech innovations, like surveying the ground, analysing the weather and the drawing of very accurate maps. They also used sound-ranging and flash-spotting. This means advanced ways of listening to guns and watching their firing to learn more about where the enemy's guns were. All of this meant that the BEF knew where 90% of the enemy's artillery was before the battle.

These men are looking at a very large model of the Messines battlefield. Models like this were made to look exactly like the ground they were going to attack, so that the men could learn all about what they would face in battle. In the second picture you can see men building a road at Messines. Work like this was essential when carrying out an attack.

The attack was carried out by troops from Britain, Australia and New Zealand. The BEF was learning to use tactics called 'bite and hold'. This meant that the troops would not try to achieve everything at once. They would bite a little bit of German territory off then make sure that they did not get kicked out of it again. They would hold it. Then they would repeat this again and again. It was a safer way to attack and would hopefully mean less lives were at risk each time.

However, the battle still caused lots of casualties. We think that in just a few days, both the British and the German armies lost more than 20,000 men each who were killed, wounded or taken prisoner.

The battle was a success for the British Army, but it was not a big offensive, more like the introduction to one. Everything really depended on the Third Battle of Ypres, for which the Allies now had to prepare.

This German soldier has been taken prisoner. What do you think he is thinking and feeling when he looks at the camera?

In this photo men pose for the camera after the fighting at Messines.

This photo shows the centre of Ypres in 1917. The men passing the ruins of the cloth hall are from New Zealand.

The Third Battle of Ypres began on the 31st July, 1917. The first part of it was called the Battle of Pilckem Ridge, and not only involved British troops, but French too. At the northern end of the Ypres Salient, things went well, partly because the Germans had already given up some ground on the Yser Canal.

But further south, on a piece of ground called the Gheluvelt (Gel-oo-velt) Plateau, it was a very different story. For the next few days, troops would try and make their positions better, but it began to rain and this made life very difficult. But what could they do? This was now the Allies' big chance to try and win the war in 1917. They had to try to do something.

For the next few weeks, the Allies, led by General Gough, tried to improve their situation at key points on the battlefield, even though the rain turned everything to sticky mud. Because the ground was so cut up, all natural drainage had been ruined. Shell holes filled up with water, and sometimes if men fell in, weighed down by heavy equipment, they drowned.

On the Gheluvelt Plateau, soldiers were sent forward in lots of attacks that failed, and lots of them were killed. The month of August saw lots of badly managed fighting, and finally Haig decided that Gough was not the man to win the war in this offensive. Instead, he gave the job of managing the rest of the fighting to General Plumer, who had been in charge at Messines.

This photo shows men trying to take a wounded man away from the battlefield during the Third Battle of Ypres. Can you see how muddy it is?

As September approached, the rain stopped, which gave the ground a chance to start to dry out. While this was happening, Plumer began making plans. He was determined not to try and do everything at once. Instead of giving his men too much to try and achieve, he was going to use bite and hold tactics. They were going to make smaller advances and make sure that they could not be thrown back again. Think of it like bunny hops!

He was also not going to throw his men into silly attacks and have lots of them killed or wounded. Instead, he would only attack when he had had time to get ready, when his men could be properly prepared and supported by other arms like the artillery. Because of this, the offensive did not start again until the 20th September, with the Battle of the Menin Road.

Once again the point was to try and get across the Gheluvelt Plateau. Men would attack, stop, consolidate their positions and then new troops would pass through them and carry on the attack. These tactics worked, and bit by bit the plateau began to fall into Allied hands.

General Plumer had his army stop. There would be a break while they prepared again. New troops would be brought in, the guns would be moved, and then the offensive would start again on the 26th September with the Battle of Polygon Wood. Like the woods on the Somme, there weren't really any trees left. Shells had destroyed the area and it had been captured back and forth several times. Once again the plan was only a limited attack and it went well.

General Plumer had been more successful than General Gough, but once again, an offensive that had been planned to win the whole war had been reduced to small fights for little gains on the battlefield. The last of Plumer's real bunny hops came very quickly on the 4th October with the Battle of Broodseinde, which was another lurch across the Gheluvelt Plateau.

This photograph shows wounded men waiting to be treated during the Battle of the Menin Road.

These men are at Broodseinde a few days after the battle, standing next to a covered trench.

By now the weather was deteriorating again. This made moving guns, equipment and men very difficult. But there was no thought of stopping. It was now that the third phase of the Third Battle of Ypres began, and it's the famous part. It's the advance towards the village of Passchendaele in horrible conditions. The battlefield became like a swamp, and now it was getting colder and colder. The Battle of Poelcappelle achieved very little, except more loss of life, but the Allies still wanted to capture Passchendaele.

The first attempt, on the 12th October, was carried out despite the weather and the ground conditions. Morale was getting worse among the Allied troops. The Germans took back almost all of the ground captured with counter-attacks. The First Battle of Passchendaele cost the Allies 13,000 men. Of these, nearly 3,000 were from New Zealand. It is one of the worst days of fighting in New Zealand's history.

By October the battlefield was in a disgusting state. There was no way for any of the water to drain away, and the ground had been destroyed.

After this, General Haig and his army commanders, like General Plumer, decided that until the weather got better, and equipment could be properly brought up, they would stop sending men into attacks. After that, they would carry on the offensive until they reached the best line that they could to rest in for winter. Once more, they were giving up on the idea of winning the war, and starting to think about the next year.

The Second Battle of Passchendaele began on the 26th October. By now, the Canadians had arrived on the battlefield to replace the exhausted men from Australia and New Zealand that had been fighting alongside British troops. The plan was a number of small advances, which would gain the British Army safer positions and a better place to rest for the winter. It took many days of bitter fighting by both British and Canadian forces, but finally, on 6th November the village of Passchendaele finally fell.

These Canadian soldiers are trying to lay a pathway across the battlefield at Passchendaele.

In these aerial photo of Passchendaele you can see that there is nothing left of the village. You can just about see where the roads were, and everything else is shell holes and ruins.

It is very, very difficult to try and count how many men were casualties during the summer offensive of 1917. People have been arguing about the numbers for a hundred years, but we think that about half a million men on all sides were killed, wounded or taken prisoner during the Third Battle of Ypres.

PASSCHENDAELE
• YPRES   BELGIUM
                    • MONS
• VIMY RIDGE
• ARRAS   • CAMBRAI
FRANCE

• PARIS

The end of the offensive at Ypres was not the end of the fighting on the British front in 1917. Cambrai was an important town because of the railway line. It was very important for supplying the German Army up and down the line. Capturing the town would ruin this and put the whole German line at risk.

The Battle of Cambrai is famous because the attack was carried out using lots of tanks, but that was not the only use of new technology. There had also been big advances in artillery and using aeroplanes to support troops on the ground.

YPRES
BELGIUM
MONS
VIMY RIDGE
ARRAS
CAMBRAI
FRANCE
PARIS

At about 06:30am on the 20th November, more than 1,000 guns began firing at the German lines. Infantry went forward with the help of more than 400 tanks. They had come a long way since their introduction on the Somme in 1916.

Things started very well. The British troops broke through the Hindenburg Line and advanced nearly five miles in some places. They went further in six hours than they had in three months at Ypres! But the Germans responded with one of their biggest counter-attacks of the war. By the end of the battle at the beginning of December, more than 10,000 British soldiers had died, and almost 9,000 Germans.

This photo shows German soldiers trying to salvage a British tank after the Battle of Cambrai. They were a long was behind with this technology, and catching up was made easier if they could fix and use tanks built by someone else.

In this photo Canadian cavalry is on the move at Cambrai.

In this photo long lines of men are making their way across the battlefield on their way to fight.

The War in the Air

Would you want to try flying one of these fragile looking machines?

The first aeroplane to fly only took off in 1903, and so they were still quite a new invention in 1914. At the beginning of the war, nobody knew that they would play such a huge role. There weren't many military pilots and armies had not fully developed ideas about what to use aeroplanes for in war. Flying was really just an expensive hobby for people with a sense of adventure. When pilots first got to the Western Front, they didn't always know what to make of each other. They tried some very basic ways of attacking the enemy, like leaning over the side and throwing a hand-held bomb or a big metal dart at the enemy. Sometimes, they would even fly past each other and cheerfully wave! Things would change before long. War makes technology move very fast, because both sides would always be looking to gain the upper hand. This was very true of flying and aeroplanes. Military flying would hardly be recognisable by 1918!

Nations had already formed air services before the beginning of the war. The French were first, with the Aéronautique Militaire and the Aéronautique Navale in 1910. Germany formed Die Fliegertruppen des deutschen Kaiserreiches (The Imperial German Flying Corps) in the same year. They had a naval equivalent too. The Royal Flying Corps and the Royal Naval Air Service were formed in Britain and the Imperial Russian Flying Corps in Russia. During the war, the Italians had the Corpo Aeronautico Militare and Austria-Hungary had the K.u.K. Luftfahrtruppen and the K.u.K. Seefliegerkorps.

Lots of different ways were developed to use aeroplanes during the First World War. Firstly, they could help armies get ready for battle.

Reconnaissance (re-con-a-sans) is a French word and it means 'recognition'. In military speak, it means going out to try and spy on your enemy to see what he is up to. Aeroplanes were very useful for this right from the beginning of the war, because they could get to places that soldiers on the ground could not.

Obviously you can't always remember everything that you have seen, and so soon airmen began to carry out aerial photography. They would fly over the lines to the enemy's side and take thousands of photographs. These would be printed and made into huge picture mosaics that were used to plan battles. Making the mosaics over and over again showed you what had changed too, so you could learn what your enemy was up to!

259

Aeroplanes could also be very useful after battles had begun. First of all they flew contact patrols. These were a new way of following what was happening when troops were fighting on the ground. This was always a problem in the First World War because soldiers did not carry radios. Troops on the ground would wear special markers, or lay out signals. The information would be collected by the men in the air, and then, when they returned home, they passed it on to the people commanding the battles so that they could decide what to do next.

Artillery spotting was an important job too. Big guns were the kings of the battlefield. It was very important the men who fired them received as much information as possible about where their shells were landing, and where the enemy was, so that they could adjust their aim and get the best results. Pilots and observers would go up and spot everything that was happening and help them with this.

This is a photgraph of the front taken from an aeroplane. What can you see?

This photo shows German scout planes lined up at an aerodrome on the Western Front

In this photo you can see that light machine guns could be attached to an aeroplane. This was a new way of arming them in the First World War.

Not all work in the air was aimed at gathering information. Late in the war a new job developed for airmen. This was called ground strafing. Aeroplanes were by now all equipped with guns in order to defend themselves in the air and attack other machines. By 1918, they had been ordered to turn these guns onto targets on the ground, such as groups of soldiers, and shoot as they flew low over the top of them.

Of course, it was in the best interests to stop your enemy from trying to carry out all of this work. As the war went on, whilst slower machines carried out these important jobs, smaller, faster aeroplanes would be sent up to defend them and try to take control of the sky. These were called scouts. More and more were sent up until great crowds of them scrapped with each other in the air. These were the world's first dog fights, and the men that took part in them were the world's first fighter pilots.

Famous Types of Aeroplanes

Not all experiments worked! This odd looking Austro-Hungarian plane from 1916 did not last very long at all.

France was a world leader in making aeroplanes before the war. This is a Nieuport 17, one of the most famous flown by French airmen. It is called a biplane because it has two wings.

It was very important during the Battle of Verdun, and helped to give the Allies the edge in the air after a horrible year famous for German Fooker machines in 1915. They were so devastating that this was called 'the Fokker Scourge'.

But lots of nations flew French machines, because they were so good. This is a Morane-Saulnier in Russian colours. In August 1914, Lieutenant Pyotr Nesterov famously rammed an Austrian aeroplane in mid-air, sacrificing himself, whilst flying in one of these machines.

This Albatros D.II from 1916 is painted in the colours of Manfred von Richthofen. German pilots were allowed to be adventurous in decorating their machines. This earned him the nickname 'the Red Baron'.

Italy had different versions of this Ansaldo SVA. It was used for jobs like reconnaissance, but in 1918 some of them went on a special mission to Vienna. Eleven machines dropped thousands of propaganda leaflets on the city, telling people in the Austrian capital that they were about to be defeated and that Italy would be on the winning side at the end of the war.

The SE5a was one of the best British aeroplanes of the First World War. It was a scout machine, and in 1917 and 1918 it was flown by famous pilots like Albert Ball and James McCudden.

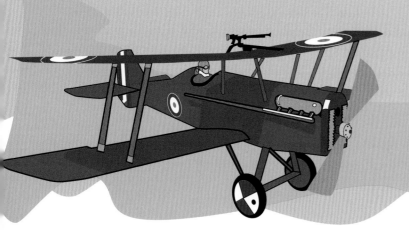

263

Aces of the First World War

A pilot scored a victory if he shot another aeroplane down or forced it to land. If he did this five times he could call himself an ace. There lots of famous aces in the war, and some of them became huge celebrities.

Some of the younger aces like Britain's Albert Ball and Frenchmen Georges Guynemer were very brave but reckless. They flew into battle without thinking, and used risky tactics. Both were very talented, but they were shot down and killed in 1917.

Other pilots were older and more sensible. Britain had James McCudden and Germany had Oswald Boelcke. They thought a lot more carefully about how they flew, but both were killed in flying accidents.

A lot of aces are still regarded as national heroes. Francesco Baracca was idolised as a result of his flying. Italians loved Francesco so much that the emblem he used, a prancing horse, is still put on every Ferrari today! The Red Baron, whose real name was Manfred von Richthofen, was also very famous. Both men were killed towards the end of the war in 1918. Flying was a very dangerous job in the First World War.

It was all about getting higher than your opponent and diving down on him. And you wanted to be behind, so that he couldn't see you coming! Because of all the diving, as fights were carried out, aeroplanes got closer and closer to the ground. They chased each others' tails until someone got shot down, was forced to land, or until it all got a bit too scary and one pilot gave up and broke away from the fight.

How to win an aerial fight

One of the first things we think about now, when we look at aeroplanes in war, are bombing raids. This is when an aeroplane bombs a target on the ground. This was developed on a large scale for the first time in the First World War, and the targets were not only military. Paris was the first major city to be bombed. Dover was the first British city ever to be bombed by an aeroplane in December 1914.

This photo shows a nighttime bombing raid on Paris. It's not often you get to see a photograph like this, because cameras at the time were not as good as they are now!

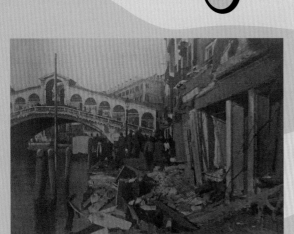

In this picture you can see damage done near the famous Rialto Bridge in Venice by Austrian airmen and their bombs.

The worst bombing raid carried out by aeroplanes in the First World War on Britain took place on the 13th June 1917. It was carried out by a big new type of aeroplane called a Gotha. Lots of them took off at once and dropped bombs on the city. The East End was hit badly, with more than 100 people killed. Eighteen children died when a bomb fell through three classrooms at Upper North Street School in Poplar.

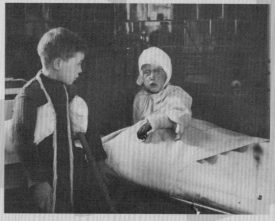

In the photos on the left you can see children putting down flowers for the children killed in the air raid and of the damage done to the school. Above is an image of two children being treated for injuries sustained in the air raid on the 13th June.

We've already looked a little bit at problems in Russia. The way that things were done was very old fashioned, and lots of Russians were unhappy with how little a say they had in how the country was run. There had

In this photo you can see a barricade set up by revolutionaries in Moscow in 1905.

already been a revolution in 1905. Men in the army refused to follow orders, people refused to go to work, or went on strike. The Tsar was forced to create the Duma, or Parliament and give elected officials the chance to take more of a part in running the country. However, change was slow and not carried out very well. Things weren't really settled by 1914, but the situation was forced into the background because the country was fighting a war.

CONFUSED?

You will be! When the city was founded in 1703 it was called St. Petersburg. During the war, the Russians decided that this sounded too German so they renamed it Petrograd. After the war, the name changed to Leningrad. And now, it's St. Petersburg again!

Remember how the Tsar had taken over command of his armies in 1915? Well, not even the Brusilov Offensive improved morale. Yes, the battle was a big success, but casualties were high. Russians were struggling to get by, because there was not enough food and prices had got so high. One estimate claims that women in Petrograd were standing in line waiting to buy food for forty hours. People looked at the Tsar as the man who should have fixed these problems.

WHAT IS GENOCIDE?

Genocide is a deliberate attempt to destroy an entire people. Usually, the people are chosen based on either their ethnicity, such as the Kyrgyz people during Urkun, their nationality, race, or their religion. The Holocaust in the Second World War was an act of genocide. Genocide is one of the most evil things that human beings can do to each other.

But before anything happened in Europe, another uprising had taken place in another part of Russia. The Central Asian Revolt in 1916, which is called 'Urkun' happened when men from Russian Turkestan protested about being conscripted into the army. Like in the western part of the country, people were angry about how things were done and about a lack of basic rights under the Tsar's rule.

Hundreds of thousands of people of Kyrgyz and Kazakh backgrounds left for China, and those that were left behind suffered when the army tried to supress the protests. There were also Tajikr, Turkmen and Uzbek victims. For a long time, the Soviet Union would not let anyone learn about what happened in 1916, but it was important because nearly half of the Kyrgyz people might have died. It is very difficult to try and count how many died, but hundreds of thousands may have been murdered. Those that tried to flee to China had to pass through the Tien-Shan Mountains. It was a very difficult journey and many more thousands died trying to make it. Now, more than 100 years later, some people argue that we should call Urkun a genocide, but the Russian government did not agree.

CENTRAL ASIAN REVOLT 1916

MONGOLIA

KAZAKHSTAN

CASPIAN SEA

UZBEKISTAN

KYRGYZSTAN

CHINA

TURKMENISTAN

TAJIKISTAN

PAKISTAN

AFGANISTAN

269

Putilov's was a huge factory in Petrograd. On the 7th March (it was the 22nd February in Russia, because they used a different calendar then) closed because of a strike. In the days that followed, society began to break down. Thousands protested about food shortages and political issues. Eventually, work in the city had ground to a complete halt. The Tsar hoped the army would fix the problem, but they were unhappy too. On the 11th March he ordered his soldiers to stop the riots by force, and soldiers began to refuse to follow their orders. Officers who tried to make them were shot, and law and order collapsed. The Tsar sent the Duma home, which was a terrible decision, because now they got angry too. Protestors organised the Petrograd Soviet to speak for workers and soldiers, who were fed up with being told what to do. They wanted more democracy, better rights and an end to discrimination against ethnicities and religions, like Russia's Jews.

This photo shows you the kind of scenes that took place in Petrograd during the February Revolution.

WHAT IS A SOVIET?

A Soviet was a committee elected by the people. It could be chosen to operate at local or national level. So the Soviet Union was a union of different soviets that all came together to make a country.

The first picture shows the Tsar with his wife, the Empress Alexandra, their four daughters and their son.

The second picture shows Nicholas II at the window of his personal train.

Tsar Nicholas had been at the headquarters of the Russian Army. He decided he needed to go back to Petrograd to try and sort things out for himself, but he never got there. His train was stopped by revolutionaries, which is what you call those supporting a revolution. His advisors convinced him that the game was up, and that he was going to have to abdicate. This is the word we use when a monarch gives up their throne. He abdicated for himself and for his son too. This meant that his brother Michael was offered the crown, but he turned it down, saying he would only take it if the people voted for him to be Tsar.

Tsar Nicholas became plain Nicholas Romanov. His family had ruled Russia for more than 300 years, so of course he felt like a massive failure. The Provisional Government was now taking charge of the country, and they placed him under house arrest. Along with his wife, the Empress Alexandra, his four daughters, Olga, Tatiana, Marie and Anastasia, and his sick son, Alexei, he would have to remain under house arrest at his palace just outside the capital.

FABERGÉ EGG
STEEL MILITARY 1916

So the monarchy was gone, but what happened next? When things like this happen we say that they create a power vacuum, because it sucks a big hole in how things work. And there is never just one person or group that wants to step into that hole and take that power.

In Russia, the situation led to dual power. On the one hand there was the Provisional Government, which was eventually led by Alexander Kerensky. Then there was the All-Russian Central Executive Committee of Soviets. But you have to remember that Russia is a very, very big country and all of this was just happening in Petrograd. Events began spiralling out of control everywhere, and nobody had proper control of the country.

Kerensky had to deal with other politicians who didn't agree with him, and the fact that Russia was still fighting a war, which many people did not want. Added to that, getting rid of the Tsar did not suddenly mean that everyone had money and food to eat. Would you have wanted his job?

This photo shows Kerensky inspecting Russian troops in 1917. He did not try to take Russia out of the war, which was good news for Britain and the rest of the Allies!

RUSSIA

RUSSIA

EUROPE

INDIA

AFRICA

AUSTRALIA

Vladimir Ilyich Lenin was a revolutionary from a city on the River Volga in Russia. In 1887, his brother was executed for being a revolutionary. Vladimir followed his lead, and was expelled from University in Kazan for protesting against the Tsar. Until 1917, he was living in Switzerland, but was still a fierce revolutionary who wanted drastic political change not just in Russia. but everywhere.

The man who was going to cause the biggest problems for Kerensky and the Provisional Government was called Lenin. He had been living in Switzerland, because he was already a revolutionary and Russia was not safe for him. The Russian Revolution was great news for Germany, because if their enemy was too busy trying to stop their own country collapsing, they would not have time to fight a war. German officials helped Lenin pass through their territory to get back to Petrograd. They hoped that if he took power with his Bolshevik Party, that Russia would quit the war. This would put Germany in a much better position to try and win it. He famously arrived by train at Finland Station in Petrograd in April 1917. He wanted all the power for his cause, and to shout down people with less extreme views. Throughout the spring, more and more people grew frustrated that the Provisional Government couldn't fix the country, and began to support the Bolsheviks.

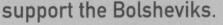

So what did all of this mean on the Eastern Front? Well, Kerensky had promised the Allies that Russia would stay in the war. In July 1917, General Brusilov led the army once again in an attack in Galicia, but so much had changed since 1916. 'Soldier committees' decided whether they wanted to follow orders or not. Mutiny and riots occurred all along the front. Some officers were even murdered by their men. If men who didn't want to fight anymore decided to just go home, who was going to stop them?

The Kerensky Offensive began on the 1st July 1917, and at the beginning, the Russian armies did advance. But soon discipline collapsed and by the 16th July their attack had fallen apart. Then the troops of the Central Powers advanced 150 miles the other way! It was to be the last Russian offensive of the war.

These pictures show Russian troops being moved, and Germans inspecting prisoners they have captured during the offensive. On the right you can see General Brusilov.

WHAT IS SOCIALISM??

Socialism is a type of political philosophy. There are lots of different kinds, but generally socialists believe that society will be better if power is given to the people, not men like the Tsar in Russia.

In this photo you can see Lenin talking to a crowd in Moscow.

The consequences of disaster in Galicia caused chaos in Petrograd. We call this the October Revolution. In Soviet Russia it was called the Great October Socialist Revolution.

Trotsky

On the 10th October 1917, the Petrograd Soviet, led by Leon Trotsky, another famous revolutionary, voted to support a military uprising to overthrow the Provisional Government. Bolshevik sailors arrived in the city, and thousands of soldiers joined the uprising. The Bolsheviks seized government buildings, then the Winter Palace; the Tsar's home in the city. Russia was now plunged into a civil war between the Bolsheviks and their enemies.

The Suez Canal was crucial because it is how all the troops arrived in Europe from the rest of the Empire.

If the Turks can come from the east and take it, they'd have to sail the whole way around Africa instead, which would make the journey much, much longer. The Turks first tried to attack the Canal in 1915, but failed.

During 1916, there were clashes east of the canal, but again, they did not manage to take control of it.

SUEZ CANAL

The Middle East as it looks today

MEDITERRANEAN SEA
PORT SAID
ISRAEL
PALESTINE
JORDAN
SUEZ CANAL
CAIRO
SINAI PENISULA
SAUDI ARABIA
SHARM EL-SHEIKH
EGYPT
RIVER NILE
RED SEA
SUDAN

MIDDLE EAST

This photograph shows you what the Suez Canal looked like at the time of the First World War.

The two sides fought the Battle of Romani. Troops from the Central Powers launched an attack on men from around the British Empire. The Australian Light Horse were fighting before dawn on the 4th August 1916, and were slowly forced back, but they were joined by more of their countrymen and by the New Zealand Mounted Rifles Brigade. Together they forced the Ottoman and German attackers into deep sand, where the enemy also found themselves against British soldiers. The attack, which also included Austro-Hungarian troops, collapsed thanks to their bad position and the heat. They were chased by mounted troops, who found this a much more traditional battlefield suited to horse action, and eventually retreated to El-Arish. This was the last attack by large numbers of Ottoman soldiers on the Suez Canal.

These Indian soldiers are posing with their machine gun along the Suez Canal.

In this photo you can see Turkish mounted troops in camp near Beersheba.

In the weeks after the Battle of Romani the Egyptian Expeditionary Force, which was the name given to the British and Empire troops who had driven the enemy away from the Canal, consolidated their position in the desert. This means they made it stronger. Not only that, but they were thinking about chasing them further while building a water supply and a railway line to help them keep going. Just before Christmas 1916, they felt ready to advance again. The enemy had abandoned El-Arish, but left an Ottoman force guarding the way across the desert at Magdhaba. In Egypt men from Britain, Australia and New Zealand all attacked the strong Ottoman position. They were mounted infantry, which meant that they rode in as close as they could, then got off their horses to fight on foot. With the support of artillery and machine guns, the EEF forced the Ottomans to surrender. A final battle at Rafa in January 1917 secured the Sinai peninsula for the Allies. Instead of panicking about the Suez Canal, they were now on an offensive campaign into Ottoman territory with Palestine in front of them.

In this picture you can see men of the ANZAC Mounted Division on the move in Palestine.

By the end of February 1917 the British Government had decided that the advance into Palestine should continue that spring. By this time the Ottoman defenders in southern Palestine had withdrawn to form a long line between the city of Gaza on the Mediterranean coast and Beersheba. 22,000 men set out to surround Gaza and the first attempt to take the city took place on the 26th March.

The attack was made by a combination of infantry and mounted units, and looked like it was going to be successful very quickly. But by nightfall they had not managed to crush the Ottoman defences and so advancing further was out of the question. The troops were pulled out of Gaza to safety. More men arrived, and in the meantime, the idea of doing well in Palestine was starting to look very important. The Nivelle Offensive was not going to win the war on the Western Front after all, and U-boats were causing havoc at sea. Added to this, the idea of capturing Jerusalem was made to look a lot easier than it really was, because of the way the first battle at Gaza was reported to London.

Everything in Palestine depended on the construction of railways and water supplies to support troops across the desert.

The Second Battle of Gaza began on the 17th April. In the three weeks since the last fight, the Ottomans had poured more defenders into the city, and in fact all along the line to Beersheba, which they had been strengthening. They were not going to be surprised again. This meant that the second battle for Gaza was very different. Infantry poured across open ground supported by tanks [Mk1]. The attack failed and the EEF suffered a large number of casualties. The men in charge of the offensive, Generals Murray and Dobell, were sent home and removed from command.

During the summer both sides reorganised. Edmund Allenby came in to command the EEF, and General Falkenhayn arrived to command the Thunderbolt Army Group. Interestingly, both men had failed to find glory on the Western Front. The British were serious about progressing, and by the end of October the EEF was made up of 50,000 soldiers and many thousands more Egyptians.

ALLENBY

General Allenby started the war in charge of cavalry troops. He had a son killed in the war, and is most famous for his work in Palestine.

In these pictures you can see Mustafa Cemal and the German officer, von Kressenstein, who was sent to help the Ottoman Empire.

In the photo on the right you can see troops with their motorcycles. There was a lot more movement in Palestine than in France and Belgium!

This photograph shows Ottoman troops keeping watch in Palestine.

On the 31st October, Allenby's forces attacked Beersheba at the other end of the Ottoman line. It was well defended, but foot soldiers attacked from the west, whilst mounted troops also attacked from the west. It was a hard fought battle, but in the end a gap opened up, men of the 12th Light Horse galloped through and grabbed Beersheba. At this point Allenby was told to cause the Turks as much trouble as possible, so that Ottoman forces would have to be sent to Palestine. It was hoped that this would make life easier for the campaign in Mesopotamia.

The Ottoman forces did their best to hold up the EEF, including at the Third Battle of Gaza, but throughout the opening days of November they could do little more than occupy the attackers so that the rest of their men could get away. The pursuit included one of the last cavalry charges in history at Huj.

From here Allenby's force carried on advancing, with their sights set on Jerusalem. After the Battle of Mughar Ridge on the 13th November, Falkenhayn ordered a general withdrawal and the Ottoman forces fell further back into the Judean hills towards Jersualem. The EEF had now moved about 50 miles beyond the defensive line that had stretched

The above photo shows Australian soldiers scouting in Palestine. Below, you can see Allenby entering Jerusalem after it fell. He walked for a reason. It is a very religious city and riding in on a horse would not have been very respectful.

JERUSALEM

between Gaza and Beersheba. They had captured thousands of prisoners and guns, but Jerusalem, a huge prize, was in sight. Not for the value it had for trying to win the war, but for what marching into it would do for Allied morale after a miserable year. By the middle of November the march was on. Both Jaffa and Jerusalem fell to the Allies. On the 11th December, Allenby, a Christian conqueror, entered the city on foot instead of on horseback as a mark of respect for the holy city.

At the same time as the Palestine campaign, the Arab revolt was also starting in what is now Saudi Arabia. It was a joint uprising against the Ottoman Empire by different Arab groups, led by Hussein bin Ali, the Sherif of Mecca. His ambition was to create one big Arab state stretching from Aleppo in Syria, all the way to Aden, which is now in Yemen. There is a famous saying: 'The enemy of my enemy is my friend'. Hussein had the support of the British for exactly this reason. They promised to help with the fighting, and recognise the Arab state if Hussein managed to make it happen. By the end of 1916 the Arab forces had conquered Jeddah, Ragbeh and Yenbo, capturing many thousands of Ottoman prisoners, although it was Hussein's sons Abdullah and Feisal who were doing the fighting.

This photo shows Hussein's third son, Prince Feisal. He was to become the most famous of them because of the film, *Lawrence of Arabia*.

Hussein's eldest son, Ali, was really not cut out to be a military leader. The picture on the left shows his second son, Abdullah. Like his famous brother, Feisal. Abdullah was important during the First World War because he took part in the Arab Revolt. He hasn't had nearly as much attention as his younger brother, though.

One very famous character emerged from the Arab Revolt, a young man named Thomas Edward Lawrence. He was nicknamed 'Lawrence of Arabia' and was one of a number of British officers sent to the Hejaz region to help Hussein's forces. His biggest contribution to the revolt was convincing Hussein's two sons to work towards British plans. In 1917, he also helped to occupy the Ottoman troops in the area by helping to attack the Hejaz railway, who desperately needed it to fight the campaign. Lawrence even laid bombs under rails himself to try and blow up trains!

One legendary figure in the Arab Revolt was Auda Abu-Tayeh. He was a leader of the Huwaytat tribe, who were Bedouin people. Lawrence called him 'the greatest fighting man in northern Arabia'. He claimed to be married 28 times and that he'd killed 75 men with his bare hands! He was, however, a very friendly man and always smiling.

Thomas Lawrence was nicknamed Ned. He came from a large family of five boys and was educated at Oxford University. Before the war, he had spent lots and lots of time travelling in the Middle East and working as an archaeologist. He spoke the language, and knew how to behave in a way that would not offend local people.

In this photo you can see Lawrence dressed in traditional Arab clothing on a camel. Eventually he wore this almost all the time when he was in Arabia.

The photo above shows you a scene from the battle for Aqaba.

Above is another scene from the Arab Revolt. Not all of the men were mounted on camels though. There were infantry troops, too. Some of them had even started the war fighting for the Ottoman Empire. Then they were caught, and changed sides!

Lawrence was present in the spring when the Arabs captured Aqaba on the Red Sea. Lawrence then travelled to Suez himself to arrange supplies. At the end of the year, the Arab forces assisted Allenby's advance into Palestine. Lawrence was there too as they carried out raids on Ottoman transport and the railway in order to make their lives more difficult. In the end, the Arab troops got as far as Damascus. At the end of the war Britain and France betrayed the Arabs and instead of overseeing a big Arab state, like Hussein wanted, they split the region up into smaller parts based on their own best interests.

In every theatre of war, there were groups and small units that you could be forgiven for forgetting all about. It would be impossible to include them all in one book. In Arabia, the Royal Navy's Red Sea Patrol was very small, just a handful of not very impressive ships led by an officer named William Boyle from 1916-1918.

The work they did was very important. Here is what T.E. Lawrence had to say about them:

'The Red Sea patrol-ships were the fairy-godmothers of the [Arab] Revolt. They carried our food, our arms, our ammunition, our stores, our animals. They built our piers, armed our defences, served as our coast artillery, lent us seaplanes, provided all our wireless communications, landed landing parties, mended and made everything. I couldn't spend the time writing down a tenth of their services.'

RED SEA PATROL

HMS *Fox* a cruiser, was William Boyle's ship in the Red Sea.

Italy

In Italy at the beginning of 1917, attention was still focused on the River Isonzo. So far the Italians and the Austro-Hungarians had fought nine battles in the space of a year and a half, and overall, they had not been successful. General Cadorna was still in charge, and he was worried that German soldiers would come to Italy to help Austria-Hungary. He was so worried, that in the end the British and French promised that if there was an emergency on the Italian Front, then they would rush soldiers there to help their ally. In exchange, the French encouraged Cadorna to attack yet again.

The Tenth Battle of the Isonzo began on the 12th May. The Italians greatly outnumbered their enemy, and made it to within 15 miles of Trieste, but then a big Austro-Hungarian counter-attack pushed them almost the whole way back to where they had started. By the time Cadorna called off the fighting on the 8th June, his Italian troops had not achieved much at all. Nonetheless, Italy had suffered another 157,000 casualties.

10

ISONZO

ITALIAN FRONT

ALPS

ITALY

This photograph shows a big gun in action during the battle.

This was still not enough to convince the Italian general to stop trying. Instead, he planned his biggest attempt yet. The Eleventh Battle of the Isonzo started on the 9th August. The Italian attempt involved an attack on different sides of Gorizia. North of the city, the Italian troops broke through, and although they did not manage a big victory, the Austro-Hungarian Army in front of them was exhausted. It was now that they asked for German soldiers to come to the Italian Front and help them. They believed that if the Italians attacked again, they would be done for. They did not know it, but the Italians were exhausted too.

They could not have attacked again, even though they were close to victory.

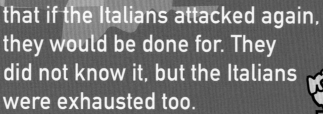

11

ISONZO

German troops came from the Eastern Front, where the Kerensky Offensive had failed. They began working hard with the Austro-Hungarian Army, not only to collect everything they needed to carry out a big attack, but also to help them develop battle tactics. On the other side of No Man's Land, much like in France, Italian soldiers had had enough Men were refusing to follow orders, and were living in horrible conditions. Morale was terrible and they felt like all they ever did was attack and watch their friends die for nothing.

On the 24th October the Battle of Caporetto began. This is the most famous name for it, but you can also call it the Twelfth Battle of the Isonzo or the Battle of Kobarid, which is what Caporetto is called now. On a misty winter morning, using lots of gas shells and more than 2,000 guns, the Central Powers burst into the Italian line. Cadorna refused to let his men retreat to an easier place to fight from, ordering them to stand firm in the face of the attack instead.

German stormtrooper tactics continued to press the offensive on. Finally, on the 30th October Cadorna allowed them to fall back to the other side of the Tagliamento River. Bosnian troops fighting for Austria-Hungary crossed the river a few days later, but by now the Central Powers were getting tired too. It was a complete disaster for Italy, and they carried on running. In the end, the Italian Army retreated to the Piave River, nearly 100 miles away from where they started! The army suffered more than 300,000 casualties and the city of Venice was under threat. They had lost thousands of machine guns and artillery pieces. Things were so bad that the Government was overturned in Rome! In Italy, people still say 'it's all a bit Caporetto' if they mean something has gone really badly wrong! Cadorna's time had finally run out. He was replaced by General Armando Diaz. Italy stopped making wasteful attempts like the first eleven battles of the Isonzo and were more cautious from now on.

These photos show you scenes from Caporetto. On the right, you can see just a few of the many, many Italians taken prisoner during the fighting. Underneath that are some troops who have managed to get away, retreating from the battle-field. The last photo shows you German troops resting during the battle.

ISONZO

12

Here you can see the conditions at the end of the year at Monte Grappa. It was cold!

This photograph shows you a very detailed model of the battlefield at Monte Grappa.

The Central Powers made one more attack in 1917, but this time they were beaten. Austro-Hungarian and German troops attacked at the First Battle of Monte Grappa, which is a mountain nearly 6,000 feet tall that stands in the middle of the front.

Here, General Armando Diaz ordered his men to stop retreating and fight. They were outnumbered three to one, but managed to stop the advance of the Central Powers. In this region, they could not get across the Piave River, which was a good natural barrier, and were stopped about 70 miles from Venice. Diaz gave his officers much more freedom to do their jobs than Cadorna, and being flexible meant that they could stop the advance of their enemy. Now, of course, the Italians turned to their Allies for help. This was the emergency that they had talked about. Despite a long, hard year on the Western Front, both France and Britain now sent soldiers and airmen to Italy.

The Caucasus

The Caucasus is the name given to a thick strip of land in between the Black Sea and the Caspian Sea. Now, the area includes the independent countries of Azerbaijan, Georgia and Armenia, but in 1914, these were part of Russia. This meant that the Russian border met that of the Ottoman Empire in the Caucasus. Parts of the front were in remote, mountain country with bad roads, which could get very, very cold.

Russia crossed the border first in 1914 to carry out the Bergmann Offensive. This was their first attempt to capture ground from Turkey. We don't get to read a lot about the Caucasus in English, but this was not a small fight. Russia alone lost 40,000 men in this offensive! The Ottomans got the better of them here, and in late December, the Ottoman 3rd Army went on the Offensive. They were ill prepared for fighting in the winter, and while they did take some ground, they soon found themselves partly encircled outside the city of Sarikamish. The Russians counter-attacked and captured many Ottoman troops, the rest of 3rd Army retreated and tens of thousands froze to death in the snow-covered mountains. The Ottoman offensive had been smashed to pieces, but the Russians needed time to recover too though, and when they asked for their allies to distract the Ottoman armies, this eventually led to the idea for the Gallipoli campaign.

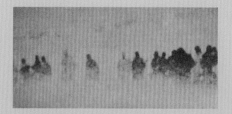

In these photos you can see Turkish officers in the Caucasus and men trying to advance in a blizzard!

In 1915 Ottoman troops on this front were heavily outnumbered and had nowhere near enough guns. Turkey was much, much more occupied by the attempt to defend Gallipoli from Allied invasion.

They were hoping that the Russans would not attack, but in January 1916 General Yudenich started by surprising an Ottoman division that expected to be resting until the weather got better. The Ottoman troops were forced to retreat.

By the end of the summer, the Ottoman force had been defeated at Bitlis, which was disastrous because it was the last line of defence stopping the Russians from trying to enter both central Anatolia and Mesopotamia. In August, Mustafa Kemal arrived to reorganise the Ottoman defence of the front, and to try and turn the situation around. They would lose 30,000 men before the end of the year, and were not able to defeat the Russian forces. Much like in Europe, the winter of 1916-17 was bitterly cold and so for a while not much happened. It was just impossible to fight in some conditions.

Then the Russian Revolution happened. The same problems that caused Russian soldiers on the Eastern Front to just give up and walk away, or disobey orders, affected the men in the Caucasus and soon the Russian Caucasus Army was useless. When an army falls apart like this, it is not only fighting that becomes impossible. All of the work to supply food and medical care for soldiers also disappears. There were outbreaks of scurvy and typhus and other diseases as a result.

All of this was good news for Turkey. Until now they had been constantly pressed by the Russians and had tried desperately to hold back invading armies. But don't forget, they were fighting Allenby in Palestine, and more British troops in Mesopotamia. They were so busy that they were unable to take advantage of the total chaos caused by the revolution. On the 5th December 1917, Russia and the Ottoman Empire signed the Armistice of Erzincan.

This photo shows you how it was easier to get about on skis sometimes on this front!

In this photo you can see Russian troops near Erzurum. It could get very cold in the Caucasus.

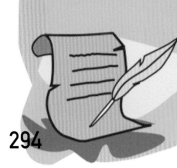

In this photo you can see Turkish cavalry on the move in terrain that looks very different to the Western Front!

But as the Russians went home, they passed men moving in the opposite direction. Some men still wanted to fight too. Armenia had now declared itself a new state, and the Armenians who had fought against the Ottoman armies in the Russian Army so far still wanted to defend their region. They would be joined by Cossacks, Georgians and Pontic Greeks who were all willing to carry on the fight against the Ottoman Empire in the Caucasus. They would also be joined by the new Central Caspian Dictatorship. There were even British troops in the area! Their unit was nicknamed Dunsterforce, after the man that commanded them. This was because of the Anglo-Persian Oil Company which could end up being threatened by the Ottoman armies. Don't forget, Britain needed that oil to keep the ships of the Royal Navy moving! In June, Germany troops arrived too. They were very interested in the oilfields at Baku, which put them in conflict with the Ottoman Empire. Eventually, the Turks were pressured into giving in, because they needed German support in the war. It is very difficult to work out how many casualties were suffered in the Caucasus. For Russia, it might have been nearly 100,000 men. The Ottomans suffered at least a quarter of a million.

Armenians had volunteered and fought bravely as part of the Russian armies in the area. They also formed the Fedayi, which were armed groups of civilians who were willing to defend their homes and their families. Unfortunately, this was necessary in the years before the First World War because there was a lot of bad blood in the region between Turks, Kurds and Armenians and some ugly fighting. When the Ottoman forces were defeated badly at the Battle of Sarikamish in January 1915, they blamed the humiliation on Armenians. They said that they had been beaten because Armenians had acted against them. Armenian soldiers serving in the Ottoman Army were put into units where they had no guns, like labour battalions. Some were later killed.

In April 1915, the Ottoman authorities began rounding up Armenian political activists, intellectuals and leaders in Constantinople and beyond. This was based on the theory that if you remove the smart people and the leaders of a people, the rest of them will not be able to organise themselves against you. Lots of the people arrested were killed.

This was followed by the Tehcir Law, which said that Turkey wanted to force all Armenians out of the Ottoman Empire. The plan was to force them all to move to the Syrian desert. They would have to walk there, forced along by armed men. Most were women and children. They were denied food and water, left behind if they could not walk, or killed. These were called death marches. This was the fate of hundreds of thousands across Turkey, but those in areas affected by the war were treated even worse. Many civilians, including women and children were just executed instead.

It is impossible to say exactly how many Armenians died, because there were no Ottoman officials writing down what was happening. Lots of clever historians have spent a lot of time doing their best, because we want to be able to remember what happened and those that lost their lives. The best we can do is say that about a million people died and that by the time it was over, 90% of the Armenians living in the Ottoman Empire were gone. They also had their money, their property and their belongings taken away from them. These events are called the Armenian Genocide, and some people even call it the first Holocaust. Turkey does not agree. The country says no crime was carried out against the Armenian people. Actually, there is even a museum and a memorial that claims that the Armenians carried out genocide against the Turks, and not the other way around. What do you think of that?

We need to learn about events like this, even if they make us sad. By learning about when things went terribly wrong, we can try to make sure that they never happen again. You can say a prayer for the victims of the genocide if you like, before you go to bed tonight. Or, why not go online and listen to a traditional piece of Armenian music or read an Armenian story? People commit genocide to destroy a people and make the world forget them. The Armenian people have their own country now, and the more we take the time to learn something about Armenian culture, the more we celebrate the fact that it all survived.

Salonika

The Allies had failed to defeat the Bulgarian armies on the Salonika front in 1916, and so they would try again. In spring 1917, the French would attack German and Bulgarian positions in the Second Battle of Monastir. In France, they call this the Bataille de Pelister, after a nearby mountain. In Bulgaria it is called the Battle of Chervena Stena, which means the Battle of the Red Wall. This is the name of a full mountain range nearby.

The Allies had captured Monastir, but they could not use it properly because it was still within range of all of the Bulgarian guns in the Pelister mountains, on a nearby hill called Hill 1248.

On the 14th March, French troops attacked. They managed to capture the whole of Hill 1248, but the Central Powers counter-attacked and took some of it back. It made life a little bit easier in Monastir, but half of the town was still within range of the enemy guns and would be for the rest of the war. To achieve this, 14,000 French casualties were suffered, which was a very expensive way to fight a war. Civilians in Monastir suffered badly too during the war. More than 500 of them were killed and lots more injured. More than 20,000 shells fell on the town and destroyed a lot of it. The Bulgarians were the real winners in this battle.

This photo shows Serbian soldiers on the march in Macedonia.

There would be more fighting for the Allies. At the Second Battle of Doiran General Milne would command British troops as they fought against the Bulgarian forces again. The Bulgarians had been improving their positions, and making their defences stronger with proper trenches and barbed wire. The battle began on the 22nd April and lasted for nearly three weeks.

Thousands of shells were fired; more than 100,000 by the British! The infantry attack started well, and they got into the Bulgarian defences, but counter-attacks pushed them all the way out again. In the days that followed, the British soldiers were under constant fire, and on the 27th April they were back where they had started. Vladimir Vazov was in charge of the Bulgarian forces and he would become a national hero. The British tried again on the 8th May. They went forward again with five waves of soldiers attacking the lines that were being quickly repaired by the enemy. There were four attacks before the end of the following day, and the British were defeated badly. The Bulgarians had lost 2,000 men, General Milne had lost 12,000. The British soldiers that had survived apparently called the area the Valley of Death.

Map labels: PRILEP, REPUBLIC OF MACEDONIA, DEMAR HISAR, RESEN, HILL 1248, KOZJAK, MONASTIR, MOUNT PELISTER, LAKE PRESPA, KRANI, GREECE, FLORINA, SMALL PRESPA

The last major battle of 1917 in Salonika was another offensive fought at Crna Bend, which Bulgaria and Germany considered one of the most important points on the Salonika front. Here, in May, French, Italian and Russian troops clashed with Bulgarian and German soldiers. The enemy knew it was coming and were told to protect them at all costs, until the end if necessary.

The infantry finally attacked on the 9th May, at 6:30 am. The battlefield was dry and so the shelling made it very smoky and dusty. The Italians attacked with men from Sicily and the northwest of the country. They were attacking strong positions on Hill 1020 and Hill 1050. Battlefield hills are named like this for how high they are in feet. Some of the the Italians got into Bulgarian and German trenches, but were pushed out either by counter-attacks or shelling. By the end of the day, the Italians had lost nearly 3,000 of their men and had called off their attack. The attacking French troops were colonial forces. Here the artillery bombardment had achieved more, and they managed to get into the enemy trenches. They were driven out again though, partly because the Italian troops next to them had failed. Within an hour and a half, the French were beaten. It was the same old story. They could get into the enemy trenches, but couldn't hold onto them and were pushed back out again.

These photos show British soldiers in Macedonia, and you can also see a view of Lake Doiran.

In this picture you can see troops on the Salonika front wearing a more advanced type of gas mask. How did they see where they were going!

This photo shows Italian troops arriving in Macedonia.

Russians also took part in the battle. They only arrived shortly before the battle, and they too attacked at 6:30am, and enjoyed a rare success. They managed to get into German trenches at Dabica and seized an entire hill within an hour and a half. It was the biggest achievement of the battle, but the Russians could not carry it on because the French attack next to them had failed. You don't want to carry on attacking without friendly troops next to you, no matter how easy it is, in case you get cut off! German and Bulgarians recaptured the position and the Allies were well and truly beaten. About a thousand Russians became casualties. General Sarrail did try again, on the 11th and the 17th May, but both attacks failed. The entire offensive in Salonika was abandoned on the 21st May. After this, there was a long period of quiet at Salonika, and it was seen as a very boring place to go.

But would you rather be here or on the Western Front?

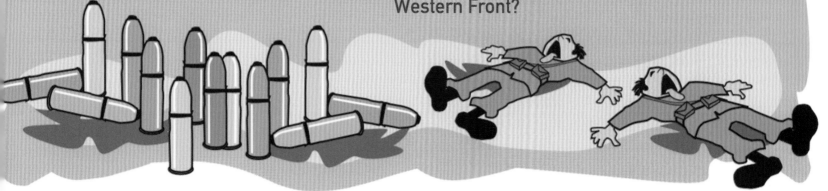

When we looked at Greece in 1916, a tricky situation had emerged. A huge argument had taken place between the government, who wanted to join the Allies, and the pro-German King, who wanted to stay neutral. Some men were furious and refused to obey orders, and started the Movement of National Defence at Salonika.

This meant that Greece had a second government led by Venizelos, who had been the Prime Minister. It quickly declared war on the Central Powers. Things were very confusing and the Greek people were divided into two groups, those that supported the royalist government and King Constantine, and those that supported Venizelos and his Committee. Most Greek military men stayed loyal to King Constantine and his government, but by wanting to avoid starting a fight with the likes of France and Britain, on 31st August most of them had surrendered.

In this photo you can see a ship bringing Greek soldiers to Salonika to join the Allied war effort.

King Constantine had powerful relatives, including the Tsar in Russia, who was his cousin, and it was hard for the Venezelists to remove him, but after the revolution in Russia he could no longer count on this support. He was also a cousin of George V, who thought that Constantine was wrong and was not about to support him, In June, Constantine gave up his throne, just like the Tsar, passing it on to his second son, Alexander. Venizelos and his supporters had wanted a Republic, like France, not a monarchy. But this was better than nothing, as Alexander was nothing like his father.

Venizelos was able to take control of Greece and the country properly declared war on the Central Powers on the 30th June 1917. They would contribute both soldiers and the Royal Hellenic Navy to the Allied war effort.

Constantine went to live in exile in Switzerland after his abdication. He actually returned to the throne in the early 1920s, after his son King Alexander was bitten by a pet monkey and died of sepsis. It was an unpopular decision, and once again King Constantine abdicated and ended up in exile. He died in Italy in 1923.

This photograph shows King Alexander, Constantine's second son. When he died, he was only 27 and it was a big shock.

Romania may have been beaten badly in 1916, but the country did not leave the war. They still had enemy soldiers on Romanian soil to worry about, but first of all they needed to rebuild their army after the disasters of the previous year. But it was also really important that the country looked after things like food production and the refugees who had moved across the country to escape the war.

When Romania went back into battle, they made sure that they were much more organised. This time they would not risk whole armies on rushed offensives. Now, they would only fight if the country could gain something important. By July 1917, they were ready. A huge force came together, starting with nearly a million men, to fight three battles that would be crucial for Romania's future.

In this photo you can see troops of the Central Powers looking at church bells in Romania. This is because they will want to melt them down and use the metal to make equipment for the war.

In this photo you can see Romanian soldiers looking after their rifles.

The first was the **Battle of Mărăști** in July 1917. Here, Romanian and Russian soldiers launched an offensive and forced the Germans and Austro-Hungarians to retreat. In fact they did so well, that they might have completely overrun the enemy, but the Russian High Command did not want to take risks because of the failure of the Kerensky Offensive on the Eastern Front. However, this had been a huge achievement for the rebuilt Romanian Army. They had advanced nearly 20 miles in some places!

This photo shows Romanian guns in action during the Battle of Mărăști.

The Central Powers had also been planning to attack. They planned two offensives into Moldavia: one by the German 9th Army against the city of Adjud, and one by an Austro-Hungarian force towards Oituz. The first attack, known as the **Battle of Mărășești**, began on 6th August. It was the most important battle in Romania during the First World War. Romanian soldiers, with Russian help, managed to hold back the enemy for almost a week. The attack against Oituz, known as the **Third Battle of Oituz**, began on the 8th August, but was also stopped by the Romanian defenders. By the 3rd September, it was all over, when the Central Powers stopped all further attacks. Romania had prevented their enemies from entering Moldavia, and had not been forced out of the war. It was a stunning achievement for a country that had almost been destroyed in 1916.

In this photo you can see men rushing into battle in Romania in 1917.

TREATY OF BUCHAREST

These photos show you how a peace treaty is made. In the first one, you can see a meeting taking place. Each side needs to agree what the rules will be.

For Romania, the war took a sudden turn when the October Revolution changed everything in Russia and their closest ally dropped out of the war. This left Romania surrounded by the Central Powers. They had no choice but to agree to peace, and agreed a truce on the 9th December 1917.

The Treaty of Bucharest in May 1918 finished the war for Romania, but after Bulgaria was defeated during the Vardar Offensive they entered it again, rejoining the Allies on the 10th November. Although the First World War finished a day later, fighting would continue between Romania and Hungary. When Germany lost the war, the truce was scrapped and Romania got back everything they had had to give up.

When everyone is happy, the two sides sign a treaty, or agreement to try and make sure that fighting will not start again,

ROMANIAN

306

The photo shows one of General Maude's bases full of supplies.

Mesopotamia

The British Army in Mesopotamia was not in a good way after the siege at Kut. Things had to change. A new man was put in charge, General Frederick Stanley Maude. His nickname was 'Joe'. He was perfect for this job, because he loved organising and planning, and making sure that the important things like medical care and supplies were taken care of before soldiers were sent into battle.

The War Committee in London wanted more progress in Mesopotamia. They thought if Britain did nothing in the Middle East, then it would encourage problems for the empire in India, Persia and Afghanistan. More soldiers were sent to General Maude, and at the same time the Ottoman force was getting weaker. He took over in April 1916, after being one of the last officers to leave Gallipoli. He spent months organising supply lines, and training the men. British engineers also built a railway for him to use. Proper medical arrangements were made, so that men would get help if they were wounded in battle next time. One thing he also understood was how important the River Tigris was. The port at Basra was improved, and he made sure that he had lots of armed boats and ships that could carry things up and down.

General Maude began a new advance along the Tigris in December 1916. He had 50,000 men, and most of them were from India, but he had also brought with him the men he had commanded at Gallipoli. Maude was a very careful general. He never went too fast, and he always tried to make sure that his men were ready and in the best position to attack before they went forward. His advance was a complete success.

The British took Kut back in February 1917. The Ottoman troops were determined not to be trapped in the town like General Townshend had been, and removed their men. Instead, the Ottoman commander, Khalil Pasha, chose to defend Baghdad where the Diyala and the Tigris met, about 35 miles south of the city. At the beginning of March, General Maude sent his men forwards again. Maude managed to outwit Khalil Pasha, and on the 10th March the Ottoman ordered their men to evacuate Baghdad. General Maude captured the city without another fight on the 11th March 1917.

These photos show you some of the challenges of moving about in Mesopotamia – always making sure that you have enough water and moving supplies. Disease was another, and the heat.

This photo shows the British entry to Baghdad.

In this picture you can see Ottoman soldiers being taken away from Baghdad.

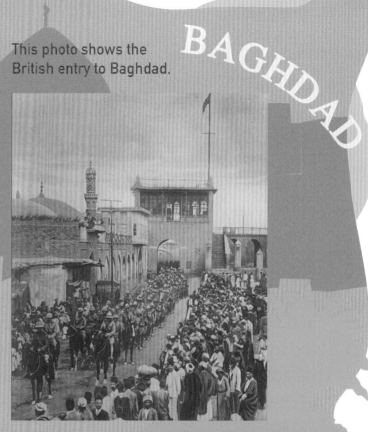

And in this one, Indian troops are marching into the city.

At home, General Maude and his troops were heroes. He had made up for the humiliation in Kut, and taken an important city from Turkey. Lots of the people in Baghdad had no love for the Ottoman Empire, and he issued a proclamation that said: 'Our armies do not come into your cities and lands as conquerors or enemies, but as liberators'. He was telling them that the arrival of British and Indian soldiers meant that they were now free from Turkish rule. Maude now took charge of the city.

9,000 Ottoman soldiers were captured along with Baghdad. The rest went further up the Tigris with Khalil Pasha and he established a new headquarters in Mosul. He still had about 30,000 men, but things did not look good. A battle might have beaten some of Maude's men, but now that the British Army were organised and Baghdad was being sorted out, it meant that strategically there was not a lot to gain. This means that there was not a good way to plan a better overall situation for Turkey in the area. Maude knew when to stop, and he had paused at Baghdad to arrange himself and his men again.

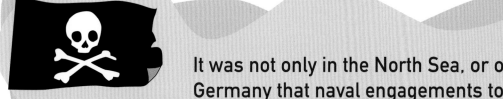

It was not only in the North Sea, or only between Britain and Germany that naval engagements took place in the First World War. Remember the naval fighting at Gallipoli? Then, the biggest fight on the surface of the Adriatic happened in May 1917 when the Austro-Hungarian navy raided the Straits of Otranto. They were hoping to break back into the Mediterranean, because the Allies had blocked their access.

At the beginning of the war, Britain had agreed with France that they would take care of the North Sea and both countries' coastlines in that area, whilst the French would take charge in the Mediterranean. After the Italian declaration of war in 1915, activity increased. The Austro-Hungarian navy bombarded the port of Ancona, which led to four Allied raids on the Austrian coast carried out by British, French and Italian troops. As an ally of Britain, Japan sent a dozen ships to the Mediterranean too. They proved to be very good at making a nuisance of themselves with enemy submarines.

One place that British submarines were used was in the Baltic. Max Horton was the most famous commander there, and the man who started the tradition of sailing home flying the Jolly Roger after a successful trip. The Black Sea was also the site of naval action in the First World War, and a combined German and Ottoman fleet was dominant there. But it took them most of the war to be able to break out into the Aegean, and when they did their ships were damaged.

On the left you can see drifters at the Battle of Otranto. On the right is British submariner Max Horton.

For the whole of the First World War, the Allies carried out a blockade of the Central Powers. This means that they used their superior naval power to stop things getting to the enemy. This did not just mean bullets and guns, but also things like food. This was especially bad for Germany, because they relied a lot on importing food from other places to make sure that people had enough food to eat.

The idea was to make enemy countries as weak as possible, so that they could not carry on fighting. This makes it an economic weapon, because it was planned to destroy the economy of German so much that they gave up. If Germany decided to come out and fight the blockade, then that was fine too, because Britain still had the better fleet. The effects of the blockade were made even worse because Germany did not have proper plans to feed the people through a war. The Blockade did not have a positive impact with neutral countries, because in places like America, they were angry that their trade was being affected badly by the Allies.

In these photos you can see a war-time cartoon that shows the blockade shaking all the leaves from a tree that is in Germany. In the middle, Germans are waiting to be given soup. At the bottom, people stand in long queues for bread.

Germany looked for a way to turn things in their favour. They had abandoned the idea of unrestricted U-Boat attacks after 1915, because they made Germany look so bad after tragedies like the sinking of the *Lusitania*. Now, they decided to resume unrestricted U-Boat warfare. Germany did not have enough ships to create a blockade, but they could try and impact Britain receiving food and war materials by sinking as many ships carrying these things as possible. They believed that if they could sink enough ships, they could make Britain surrender in six months and win the war. The Kaiser signed this off on the 31st January 1917, after being told that Germany could be defeated without it. In March nearly 150 ships were sunk on their way to Britain. That's 25% of the total ships trying to make the journey. Again, it made Germany look bad, and Brazil joined the war on the side of the Allies when their ships became victims on the way to Europe too.

This angry poster to raise money for the war was made after a hospital ship called the *Llandovery Castle* was sunk in 1918. More than 230 men and women died when she sank, or were killed whilst they were in the lifeboats waiting for help. It was considered a war crime.

The Allies tried lots of different things to avoid German submarines during the war. They tried running away – sailing a zig zag course was a good way of doing this. It made it harder to target a ship with a torpedo if it kept changing direction!

They also invented things to try and destroy submarines. A depth charge was sunk to try and sink submarines under the surface. The First World War also saw the beginnings of sonar.

And then there were Q-ships. You had to be brave, or mad, or maybe both to serve on one of them! A Q-ship was usually a dirty old vessel, that looked very unimpressive and very vulnerable. It probably looked like a little fishing boat, or something similar. Because it looked weak, the U-Boat would try and attack it. But now it was the U-Boat that was vulnerable, and suddenly, the Q-Ship would throw off its disguise and attack. Really, they were naval ships armed with guns and trained crews ready to try and sink the submarine!

This is a Q-Ship. Can you tell that she is dangerous? Would you be scared if you met her at sea?

But the most important invention in the First World War for avoiding U-Boats was the convoy system. This would be hugely important in the next war too.

The Allies had been using convoys since the very beginning of the war. The idea was that if ships sailed in a big group, with naval vessels for protection, then they were less likely to become victims of U-Boats. There were some downsides. They made transporting things slower because of the organising involved, and a convoy could only sail as fast as its slowest ship. It was also hard work for ports when lots of ships arrived at once, but it was the best option.

In April 1917, German U-boats sank nearly a million tons of shipping. There was only enough grain in Britain to feed the country for six weeks and the Royal Navy approved convoys for all shipping crossing the Atlantic and these began in the middle of the year. When America joined the war, their ships took part too.

The Atlantic convoy system was so successful for incoming ships that U-Boats began to concentrate on outgoing vessels instead. So convoys began to operate both ways. Then the U-Boats began to concentrate on the Mediterranean. Escorts were provided by British, French, American, Japanese, Italian and Brazilian ships. Aeroplanes, airships and balloons were also used when convoys got close to the coast. They were very effective, because they could see the outline of submarines when they were under the surface. Only five ships were lost in convoys when the escort included an air force.

There was some incredibly good news for the Allies in the spring of 1917, because America finally declared war on their side. The United States had been angered by the death of Americans as a result of U-Boat action, such as the sinking of the *Lusitania*. But there were still lots of Americans who preferred Germany or Austria-Hungary to the Allies. Some hated the idea of the blockade keeping food from the Central Powers and thought that it was illegal. And there were lots who didn't see why America should get involved in a war happening thousands of miles away. America was also making a lot of money from the war, without having to meet the massive cost of being involved in it. In 1916, there was a presidential election, and Woodrow Wilson won after he travelled the country promising to keep America out of the war.

But then Germany resumed a policy of unrestricted U-Boat warfare, which threatened American shipping. Then something disastrous happened for Germany as far as their relationship with America was concerned. The document responsible was called the Zimmerman Telegram, and it was intercepted by British naval intelligence and Room 40. Of course, Britain wanted America to be angry with Germany, so it was published. The telegram was sent from Germany to Mexico, promising that if Mexico joined the war on their side, if they won together, Mexico would get to take back Arizona, New Mexico and Texas. America was now furious. President Wilson went to Congress and asked them to vote for war. They did, and on the 6th April 1917.

America declared war on Germany. They did not declare war on Austria-Hungary until December, and never did so against the other Central Powers like Bulgaria and Turkey. For this reason, they would not fight on certain fronts.

It would take until 1918 for lots of American soldiers to start arriving on the Western Front, but their joining the Allies was a disaster for the Central Powers. America was massive, and rich. She could provide millions of soldiers, and more equipment and supplies than Germany could ever hope to manufacture. The Central Powers were already tired after three years of war, and they were already running out of men to put in the army. Think of America as the biggest kid in the playground. This was an enemy you did not want to make.

The Allies were thrilled, especially the French, who threw huge celebrations when the first American soldiers began to arrive in the summer of 1917. But the Allies had learned a lot since 1914, and it would take time for American forces to learn these lessons. There were lots of men who could be made soldiers, yes, but it would take time to train them and send them to Europe.

South America

Brazil was the only country in Latin America that was directly involved in the war. War was declared in 1917 because of the sinking of Brazilian merchant ships by German U-Boats. Brazil's main contribution to the war was at sea.

Admiral Frontin

Brazil's navy carried out anti-submarine work. The fleet was called the Naval Division for War Operations, or the Divisão Naval em Operações de Guerra. Under the command of the British Admiralty they went to look after a triangle of the Atlantic between Dakar, the island of São Vicente, Cape Verde and Gibraltar. The officer in charge was Admiral Pedro Max Fernando Frontin.

A small group of Brazilian soldiers visited the Western Front in 1918, but the main work carried out by the country here was by medical staff, who spent lots of time looking after French victims of the Spanish flu.

BRAZIL

This photo shows the members of the Brazilian medical mission that went to France.

SPAIN
GIBRALTAR
AFRICA
CAPE VERDE
SÃO VINCENT
DAKAR
ATLANTIC OCEAN

1918

With thousands of Americans on their way, Germany had no choice but to try and win the war. Countries were finally putting all of the lessons they had learned together, but still nobody knew who would win, and how much the world would change.

Women at War

Women worked hard in the First World War, and you'll be surprised to learn just how many different things they did! First of all, they did jobs that you might think of very quickly. Thousands of women from all over the world trained to be nurses so that they could help the wounded. Nurses even came from Japan to work on the Western Front! As air raids became more lethal, women were more and more at risk while they were doing their work. Some of them were killed by the enemy, just like men.

Above you can see a German nurse. She is treating a German sailor and a French colonial soldier. If you were caught by the enemy, and wounded, it was their responsibility to take care of you. You would do it, because you wanted them to do it for your men.

In this picture you can see two South African girls working at recruitment. Do you think you could convince a young man to join the army and go to war?

This photo shows two American nurses.

But women did not just perform traditional roles in the First World War. So many men went to fight, that they were needed to fill jobs not only for the war effort, but to help keep the country running. This meant that in some countries, they were enjoying freedom and independence they could only have dreamt of before 1914! It could be an exciting time to be a young woman, despite all of the hardships of war. Women did every job you can think of. They delivered coal, they became bus and train conductors, swept chimneys, brewed beer, joined the police and went into industry. Basically, any job that you can think of, a woman probably gave it a go during the First World War. King George V said that he loved to see this, and that it proved that if Britain won the war, it would be just as much because of the hard work of the country's women as the men in the trenches.

This young Frenchwoman is repairing carriages on the Paris Metro.

Queen Mary spent lots of time meeting women during the war. In this photo she is talking to women in East London.

These Italian girls have found jobs in their local area unloading munitions for the army

There were also lots of new jobs for women to do during the First World War. The main one was working in munitions. Remember how badly everybody needed shells in 1915? To make them you needed lots of workers and hundreds of thousands of these jobs were filled by women. This could be very dangerous work, and some munitions workers were killed in accidents and explosions.

This photo shows munition workers at Ibrox Stadium in Glasgow. They were attending a medal ceremony.

Working in munitions could be exhausting and dangerous work. This woman is making shell cases.

This picture shows American girls painting tanks with camouflage in 1918. By the end of the war, women helped to build tanks, aeroplanes, guns; everything you can think of!

By the end of the war women's work had got even more organised! In Britain they joined special female units of the Army, the Royal Navy and the new Royal Air Force. They had gone out to the front and were doing important war work that directly helped the men doing the fighting. Women had made themselves completely indispensible in the war effort.

Another job that lots of women did was mechanics and driving! This freed up more men for fighting. In 1918, a girl chauffeur was even allowed to drive the King!

These women are baking bread for soldiers. Another important job!

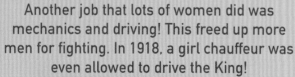

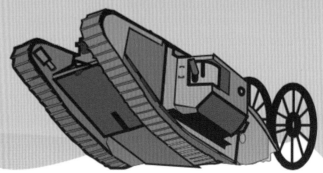

A handful of women did actually fight in the First World War. One of these was **Maria Bochkareva**. She was a Russian peasant women who had lived a miserable life before 1914. She left her husband to try and help the Russian war effort, and ended up in charge of the 'Women's Battalion of Death'. These women bravely fought with Russian men. In fact, if you believe Maria, when the men refused to fight after the Revolution, it was her girls who made them carry on! She was executed in 1920, fighting against the Bolsheviks.

This photo shows women who served with Maria.

Ecaterina Teodoroiu started her war work as a nurse. However, after her beloved brother, Nicolae, was killed, she decided that she wanted to become a soldier. This was odd, but she had the support of the Romanian Royal Family and so she was allowed to join an infantry regiment. She was good at it! She managed to stop her company being captured by the enemy, after she lied to the enemy to make them think they were about to surrender. She was captured at the end of 1916, but managed to escape. She was later wounded in both legs by a shell, but survived. She won gallantry medals and eventually became Romania's first female army officer. On the 3rd September 1917 she was leading her men in a counter-attack when she was killed by German machine-gun fire. She is still regarded as a heroine of Romania and it is said that her last words were: 'Forward, men, don't give up, I am still with you!'

Religion

On the left, you can see an Orthodox priest praying with Russian troops before battle. Below, on the left you can see a Catholic Austro-Hungarian soldier at confession and on the right, an Imam prays with Bosnian muslims in the same army.

Lots of people relied on their religion during the war. Religious organisations all over the world also helped to feed soldiers, help the wounded and otherwise look after them. We call people that go to war but not to fight non-combatants. As you can see from the picture on the right, not holding a gun did not mean that you were safe in the First World War. The grave on the right belongs to the Reverend Hubert Allan, who was Canadian. He died on the Western Front in 1915.

The Western Front

With the Americans on their way, German military leaders knew that they had to try and win the war as quickly as possible. Once that pipeline of men and supplies was properly open for the Allies, they would never be able to win. They put everything they had into a group of battles we call the Spring Offensives in the first half of 1918. In Germany it was called Kaiserschlacht, which means the Kaiser's Battle. The Germans decided that they would throw all of their effort at the British, believing that if Britain was knocked out of the war, the French would collapse. They dreamt up lots of operations and gave them code names. The British knew that an attack would be coming, but because the Germans were preparing for other attacks too, they were not sure where the blow would come.

This picture shows a giant German railway gun.

By 1918, the way that men fought on the Western Front had changed a lot. Neither side stuffed front line trenches full of soldiers anymore. Remember how we looked at the idea of letting your enemy attack, take some of your territory, and get far from safety before you attacked them and kicked them out again? This theory got more advanced by the last year of the war and defences were split into three zones.

The Forward Zone – A few men in outposts perhaps with machine guns as far forwards as you could get. If you were attacked, you never planned to try and hold onto these positions.This would not be where the fighting happened.

This would be further back in the Battle Zone. This would be much better defended, with concrete bunkers and strong points and lots of men ready to fight and hold on to their positions. By now, the attackers would have got further from their artillery, and their reserves, and their supplies, so you were fighting them in your strongest positions, just as they were getting weaker.

And finally, in theory behind that, you would have the Rear Zone. For Britain, this zone did not really exist as a proper military structure, partly because there had been no time or men available to build it.

FORWARD ZONE

FRONT LINE

BATTLE ZONE

REAR ZONE

At 4:40 am on the 21st March, thousands of German guns suddenly burst into life as Operation Michael began. German gunners would fire 3.2 MILLION shells on just the first day, lots of them filled with gas! The Germans had further developed their storm trooper tactics. These men were trained even harder in how to attack quickly, moving past any strong point that might hold them up, leaving that for the men behind to deal with. Their job was to get as far as possible. In German, we call these units Sturmabteilung. These men quickly overran the British forward zone and moved to the positions behind. The attack was so powerful, that there was little that the British soldiers in front of them could do.

For several days, the German offensive surged on, taking back all of the territory on the Somme won so slowly by the British and the French in 1916. The French sent help, but things got so bad, that the Allies decided to put everyone under one command to try and stop the German advance. Ferdinand Foch was now in charge of the Western Front. Though General Haig remained commander of the BEF, he agreed that this was best.

Finally, the German advance ran out of steam. The German soldiers were as tired as the Allies by now. They had won lots of ground, but it was largely empty, and not a lot of use for winning a war. Operation Michael was finally called off on the 5th April. Germany suffered nearly 240,000 casualties in two weeks. They would find it very, very difficult to replace these men. Britain, France and American lost 255,000 soldiers. Eventually all of these could be replaced thanks to their new ally. If you look at war just in numbers, then it is a much better result for the Allies. But this battle killed or hurt half a million men. It's very hard to feel that this is a good result for anybody, and that is OK too. War is not an easy thing to get your head around.

This is a very famous photo of a German tank moving through the streets of Roye in Spring 1918.

But Germany had more than one plan. Even before the enemy gave up on Operation Michael, they were already beginning to carry out Operation Georgette. The main point of this attack was to capture Hazebrouck. This town had a crucial railway that the BEF needed to supply the British armies. We call this area the Lys, after the river that flows through the area.

HAZEBROUCK
9th APRIL
10th APRIL
NEUVE CHAPELLE

HAZEBROUCK

Things got very, very busy on the Western Front in 1918! During the German offensives there was a lot of confusion, as you can see in this photo.

Also important was the town of Bailleul, which had hospitals and other army units in it to help men when they came out of the trenches.

329

Operation Georgette, which can also be called the Battle of the Lys, began on the 9th April. It was a foggy morning, and the Allies were completely surprised. Once again, the British Army was staring at possible defeat. The Allies were forced to give up the ground that they had won during the Battle of Passchendaele. On the 11th April, General Haig issued a very famous order to his troops, encouraging them to hold on. He said:

'There is no other course open to us but to fight it out. Every position must be held to the last man: there must be no retirement. With our backs to the wall and believing in the justice of our cause each one of us must fight on to the end. The safety of our homes and the freedom of mankind alike depend upon the conduct of each one of us at this critical moment.'

His men did hang on. The operation finished on the 29th April. Once again, although Germany had achieved a lot, it was not enough, and they had still not defeated the Allies on the Western Front. In this part of the Spring Offensives the Allies suffered about 120,000 casualties. For Germany, the figure was about 100,000.

In this photo you can see what the town of Bailleul looked like just before it was taken by German soldiers.

For hundreds of years, Portugal had considered itself a friend and ally of England. Technically, the country had been neutral since the beginning of the war, but

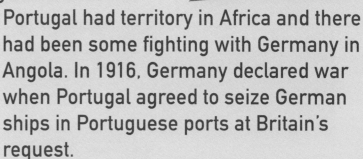

Portugal had territory in Africa and there had been some fighting with Germany in Angola. In 1916, Germany declared war when Portugal agreed to seize German ships in Portuguese ports at Britain's request.

The top picture shows you lots of Portuguese men on their way to the Western Front. Below, you can see a man writing a letter for his friend. Lots of the soldiers that Portugal sent to war were poorer and uneducated men who did not know how to get out of military service.

During the First World War, Portugal was a new republic, and the way that the army operated was very old fashioned. By 1917 Portuguese soldiers were on the Western Front, but they did not have enough equipment, no new men arrived when troops were killed or wounded, they did not have enough officers and the British Army decided it would be better to remove them from the line.

LYS

Unfortunately, this did not happen fast enough. The exhausted Portuguese were still in the line when the Battle of the Lys began, and it was a disaster. At the time, lots of people accused them of just running away like cowards. Now we know this is not a fair account of what happened.

The picture above shows many, many Portuguese soldiers taken prisoner in 1918. The photo on the right shows Soldier Milhais. He is wearing a bravery medal given to him after the Battle of the Lys.

Some Portuguese soldiers were very brave. Anibal Milhais was a farmer from the north of Portugal near Braganza. For four days and three nights during the battle he stayed with his light machine gun, stopping only to find ammunition and to reload. He had no food or water other than what he could take from the packs and bottles of his dead comrades. When he could find no more ammunition, he picked up his Lewis gun and left. He soon found a Scottish officer, wounded in both legs, in the middle of a swamp. With the Scotsman on one shoulder and his Lewis gun on the other, he crossed the German lines and No Man's Land, and got into a British-held trench, refusing to hand over his wounded Scot to anyone but a medical officer. He then accepted a mug of tea.

CHINESE

At the beginning of the First World War China was a country still dominated by other nations. We have already looked at how the port of Tsingtao was affected by the war in 1914, but the war impacted Chinese people in many ways. In 1915, Japan also issued a list of demands that put large parts of China under foreign control. The anniversary of this was later remembered as the 'National Day of Humiliation'. China now refers to this whole period as 100 years of humiliation.

China was mostly motivated by unrestricted submarine warfare to join the Allies, especially when more than 500 Chinese victims were lost in the sinking of the *Athos I*. Going to war was not necessarily a popular decision, but society in China would change a lot because of the war. Sending workers to Europe was a huge change for China, because the Qing dynasty, who ruled the country, had tried to dissuade people from going abroad. Emigration was not allowed until the 1800s!

In this picture, you can see Chinese labourers in a camp on the Western Front.

Talks began in 1916 about employing Chinese workers to help with the massive amount of labour that needed doing on the Western Front. China hoped that if men went to Europe, they would return smarter and with a knowledge of the world that would benefit Chinese society. Recruitment centres were set up in many places across China. Nearly 150,000 men were recruited. Although they were not fighting troops, many Chinese labourers found themselves in danger. We think about 3,000 of them were killed in the war.

Do you remember that we talked about uncomfortable attitudes to men who were not white? Men like those in the Chinese Labour Corps did very, very important support work behind the lines. However, they were often not treated the same as white men, or given the same recognition for their contribution to the war effort.

This photo shows hundreds of men serving with the Chinese Labour Corps in France and Belgium.

This picture shows a Chinese labourer. In his spare time he has been making a toy model of a traditional Chinese boat.

The war was so big, and so many labourers were needed that Britain asked South Africa for help too. Once again we see uncomfortable attitudes to race, because they were specifically looking for black men to do manual labour. The South African Native Labour Corps was formed. Some white South Africans were worried about what they might learn while they were away, and that they might return realising that they were unfairly treated at home. How might this change South African society? Despite this, more than 21,000 black labourers sailed for the Western Front to work in Europe.

Britain also recruited men in the West Indies, or the Caribbean. More than 15,000 men from Jamaica, British Honduras, Barbados, Trinidad and Tobago, the Bahamas, British Honduras (Belize), Grenada, British Guiana (Guyana), the Leeward Islands, Saint Lucia and Saint Vincent. Once again, these men were primarily used as labour, because it was thought that only white men made good soldiers. The same idea prevailed with a large Egyptian Labour Corps. Where do you think silly ideas like this came from?

On the right, you can see men of the Egyptian Labour Corps on the Western Front. Below are recruits from Trinidad joining the army and a picture of the King meeting men of the South African Labour Corps.

WEST INDIANS

335

Siam (Thailand) was another country that entered the closing stages of the war on the side of the Allies. By 1917, the King of Siam, Rama VI, thought that declaring war on Germany and Austria-Hungary (again, the sinking of merchant ships by U-Boats was a problem) would make his country look strong and important. He even redesigned the national flag using the dominant colours of the Allies; red, white and blue. Siamese troops began arriving on the Western Front in 1918, 19 men died, as a result of sickness or accidents.

In these pictures you can see men from what is now Vietnam on the way to war, and some of them at prayer on the Western Front.

Elsewhere in southeast Asia, France had colonies. They were known as French Indochina, and included countries we know today as Vietnam, Laos and Cambodia. The French forced lots of men to serve. Unlike Britain's attitude to lots of non-white colonial subjects, they did allow these men to serve in fighting units, but thousands more served as labourers. We think about 100,000 men from Vietnam alone served on the Western Front. They would return home with lots of ideas and a wider perception of the world and fight for independence from French rule. About 12,000 men from French Indochina died during the First World War.

INDO-CHINESE

Germany now turned the Spring Offensives on the French. They still believed that the British were the key, and that destroying them would win the war, but the French had been sending men north to help. They thought that if they attacked the French further south, then they would have to concentrate on that. Then the Germans would be able to attack the British again in the north a few weeks later. This attack included Operation Blücher-Yorck, named after two Prussian generals in the Napoleonic wars. You can also call it the Third Battle of the Aisne. It began on the 27th May. Again the Germans managed to achieve total surprise. They got across the River Aisne, and made it nearly fifteen miles! But Foch and Haig had figured out the German plan. They suspected that all along Ludendorff was planning to attack the British line again, and so Foch refused to move men south in large numbers. Haig even began to think about evacuating everyone back to Britain.

This photo shows both British and French soldiers. They worked very hard together to stop Germany from winning the war in spring 1918.

RIVER AISNE

General Ludendorff decided that he would try and extend the gains his men had made during their attack on the French. Operation Gneisenau and Operation Hammerschlag were launched in the middle of June and were supposed to improve his armies' positions. General Ludendorff refused to believe that the Spring Offensives had failed. But by now, the German Army had suffered so much that they would not be able to carry out big new attacks in Belgium, Britain and France who had all survived their offensives, and Americans continued to arrive in Europe.

Ludendorff tried once more with a battle called Marneschutz-Reims. We also call this the Second Battle of the Marne. It began on the 15th July when German soldiers attacked French and Americans and tried to split the Allied force in two. But this time the French were expecting the attack. It was not planned with anything like the depth of thought that went into the first offensives. Ludendorff had forgotten all about the idea of destroying the British. The attack was a complete disaster.

The French people loved seeing American soldiers. You can see that with their unique hats they were very distinctive. Their nickname was 'Doughboys', but we don't know why!

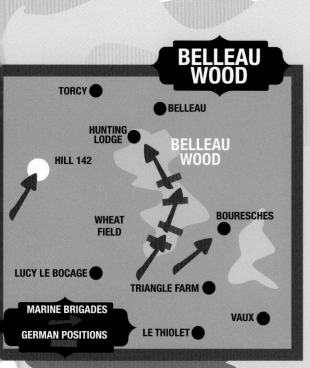

BELLEAU WOOD

TORCY

BELLEAU

HUNTING LODGE

HILL 142

BELLEAU WOOD

WHEAT FIELD

BOURESCHES

LUCY LE BOCAGE

TRIANGLE FARM

MARINE BRIGADES

GERMAN POSITIONS

LE THIOLET

VAUX

This period saw some of the first battles involving large numbers of soldiers from the United States. Belleau Wood is near the River Marne and has become very famous in American history because of the United States Marine Corps. The French wanted to retire away from the woods and dig trenches further back. The Americans had other ideas. In total the Americans would attack Belleau Wood six times before finally capturing it. On the 26th June, the last Germans were cleared out. United States forces suffered 10,000 casualties in one of the bloodiest battles they fought in the war.

At the end of the Third Battle of the Aisne, the closest part of the Allied line was only 35 miles from Paris. France, Britain and the United States suffered 137,000 more casualties, the Germans suffered slightly less. Most importantly, Germany had failed to win the war before the arrival of the Americans. The country was exhausted. Surely, now there could only be one result?

This is a famous piece of art that imagines what the fighting looked like in Belleau Wood.

WOODS NOW U.S. MARINE CORPS ENTIRELY

Eastern Front

Treaty of Brest-Litovsk

In Russia, the Bolsheviks, led by Vladimir Lenin, took power on the 7th November 1917. They wanted the war to end, because they said it was all about imperial powers. At the same time though, they launched an attack on Ukraine and other enemies. Now that the Tsar was gone, many parts of the Empire wanted to claim their independence. The new Russia agreed peace with Germany in March 1918, with German troops less than a hundred miles from Petrograd. The Treaty of Brest-Litovsk was a disaster for the Allies. All of the fighting on the Eastern Front stopped, which meant that the Central Powers could now move troops to the Western Front and carry out the Spring Offensives. This was a terrifying thought for the Allies.

Russia suffered a huge amount of casualties in the First World War. Good records were just not kept, but we think it might be that more than two million people died as a result of the fighting, from disease and as prisoners. This does not include hundreds of thousands of civilians. When the Treaty of Brest-Litovsk was signed, more than two million Russian men were still prisoners in German and Austrian captivity.

This photo shows you a protest happening in Kiev, which is the capital of Ukraine. Lots of people were not happy that Lenin and his party had taken over.

340

The picture above shows you the Tsar as a prisoner in Tobolsk. When he was here he was allowed outside, to exercise, and he and his family were allowed some space.

Life got much harder when the Imperial Family was moved to the Ipatiev House in Ekaterinburg. It was much smaller, and the rules were much more strict.

In the summer of 1917, the former Tsar and his family were moved from their palace outside Petrograd to Tobolsk in Siberia. The Provisional Government did not really know what to do with them. They lived together in a house there, and still had quite a bit of freedom. By the following year, though, the Bolshevik Revolution had taken place and their position was far more dangerous. By the end of May 1918, the whole family had been moved again, this time to the Ural Mountains, to live in a house belonging to an engineer called Ipatiev in Ekaterinburg. The civil war was raging, and enemies of the Bolsheviks were approaching the city. The Bolsheviks panicked. In Moscow, they still wanted to bring the Tsar to trial in front of the world. But things were disorganised, and the leadership in the Urals had other ideas. On the 17th July 1918 17the family was woken up and taken to the basement of the house where they were executed with some of their faithful servants who had refused to leave them. Bodies were discovered in nearby woods in 1979, and in 1998 new DNA technology, with help from samples from relatives (one of these was Prince Philip), confirmed that these were the remains of the royal family. A funeral was held on the 80th anniversary of their deaths and Tsar Nicholas, Tsaritsa Alexandra and their children now lay at St Peter and Paul Cathedral, St. Petersburg.

Arthur Balfour

After the capture of Jerusalem, just like in Baghdad, there was administration to take care of. The city needed to be run properly after the departure of Turkish officials. Food and supplies needed to be brought in, and money. Things like postal services needed to be sorted out. It was also at this time that the famous Balfour Declaration was made. This was a famous document that said the British Government supported the idea of there being a whole country provided for Jews to call their own. As time went on, this idea would have a huge impact on the future of the Middle East.

For now though, General Allenby had a plan. In 1918, he wanted to take Jericho and part of the Dead Sea. He also wanted to cross the Jordan River towards Amman. Finally, he wanted to destroy more of the Hejaz Railway so that Ottoman troops would be stranded much further south in Medina. This would not only help his troops, but it would help the Arab Revolt too. He didn't really need to do any of this. The Arabs still wanted their own country, but Britain had achieved everything necessary in Palestine and in Mesopotamia, too. Nonetheless, not everyone in the government agreed. They wanted to make sure that Turkey was knocked out of the war and its Ottoman Empire destroyed. They said that this could only mean good news for the Allied war effort.

HEJAZ RAILWAY

Palestine

General Allenby's force took Jericho in February. The first attack on Amman, which the Ottomans named the First Battle of the Jordan, started on the 21st March, the same day as Operation Michael on the Western Front. British, Australian and New Zealand troops occupied Es Salt. They also attacked part of the Hejaz Railway east of Jericho. Amman was defended not only by Ottoman soldiers but Germans too, and although the British tried to capture the city, they were forced to fall back throughout. It was the first time they had failed in Palestine since the Second Battle of Gaza in April 1917.

The Central Powers did try an offensive themselves with the Affair of Abu Tellul. They attacked Australian Light Horse units on the edge of the Judean Hills, but were defeated by a large group of British and Indian soldiers, as well as soldiers from the Caribbean, before they got started in some places. It was the last time that they attacked in this theatre of war, and at the begnning of October, the Ottoman defenders in the area surrendered.

The first picture shows you Ottoman defences at Abu Tellul. The second one shows you what men of the Australian Light Horse looked like.

343

It's important to remember that the Arab Revolt was carried out by infantry as well as the men on camels.

Since the capture of Aqaba in the middle of 1917, lots more Arabs and lots more British officers had joined the Arab Revolt. T.E. Lawrence might be the most famous, but there were lots more. The British representatives were there to help provide rifles, explosives, machine guns and all types of weapons, including some artillery. Egyptians and Indians also served, usually because they had particular training and were operating specialist equipment like machine-guns, or armoured cars. Sometimes, even the Imperial Camel Corps or the Royal Flying Corps helped too. France also provided officers, but they operated mainly further south. The ranks of the Arab armies were made bigger by Arabs who had been in the Ottoman Army earlier in the war. They had been taken prisoner by the Allies, and then switched sides to fight for their own people.

This photo shows you what part of the Hejaz Railway looks like in Jordan today.

This picture shows you T.E. Lawrence just after an attack on the railway. How do you think he is feeling?

It might not sound like a big deal, carrying out small attacks on the Hejaz Railway, but it was important. The Ottoman Army desperately needed it to move men and supplies, so one bit of damage to the line by just a handful of Arabs, or Hashemites, as they were also called, could tie up thousands of men. They either destroyed bits of rail, or locomotives, or bridges. It was a complete nuisance for the Ottoman Empire, and turned out to be very helpful indeed for General Allenby in Palestine. In one attack by the members of the revolt, 1,000 Ottoman casualties were caused at Tafileh, whilst they suffered only 40 themselves. In 1918, in Operation Hedgehog alone, 25 bridges were destroyed. Once again the Imperial Camel Corps was involved, and one important attack was on the station at Mudawwara Station. In August men of the ICC stormed it with help from pilots above, taking more than 100 prisoners and once again disrupting the line to Medina.

The Battle of Megiddo is called Megiddo Muharebesi in Turkey. It took place in September 1918 after the threat of the German Spring Offensives had died out on the Western Front. It was the last big offensive of the campaign in Palestine. A lot of the places that General Allenby and his men were reaching now, you might recognise from the Bible. Megiddo is an ancient fortress, and it has been important to soldiers for a long time; as far back as the ancient Egyptians! In 1918, the position helped the Ottoman armies to defend all of their positions in Judea.

In charge of the Ottoman forces now was General Otto Liman von Sanders. Remember him? He was the German general who had helped the Ottomans defend Gallipoli. Turkey had reason to feel good about things by September 1918. Their situation looked better than the rest of the Central Powers, and they trusted that General von Sanders would be a hero again and stop the British invading Palestine.

General Otto Liman von Sanders

In this photo you can see Indian troops entering the city of Haifa.

This picture shows you refugees running away from Es Salt. How would you feel if war came to your town?

General Allenby spent the summer reorganising his men, receiving new troops, lots of them Indians and planning his offensive. His men worked very, very hard to keep their plans a secret. They moved at night so they couldn't be seen, and carried out fake marches. They created dust clouds so that it looked like men were moving, and had fake camps built; and when the men really did move towards battle, they hid in orange groves and plantations.

British and Australian airmen policed the skies so that German and Ottoman pilots would not see what was really going on. On the 16th September Arabs, Egyptians, Gurkas, British, Australian and French troops, partly led by T.E. Lawrence, began attacking the vital part of the railway at Daraa. Here there was a junction that helped supply Ottoman troops in Amman and in Palestine. This disturbed the Ottomans and acted as a distraction. Soon 3,000 more tribesmen, among them the famous warrior Auda Abu Tayi of the Howeitat tribe, turned up too. This was not supposed to be such a big uprising, but local communities also began to revolt against the Turks.

The top picture shows you just some of the many, many camels needed to carry bread for soldiers on the march in Palestine. The second photo shows tanks. By 1918, they had reached the desert too, not just the Western Front.

347

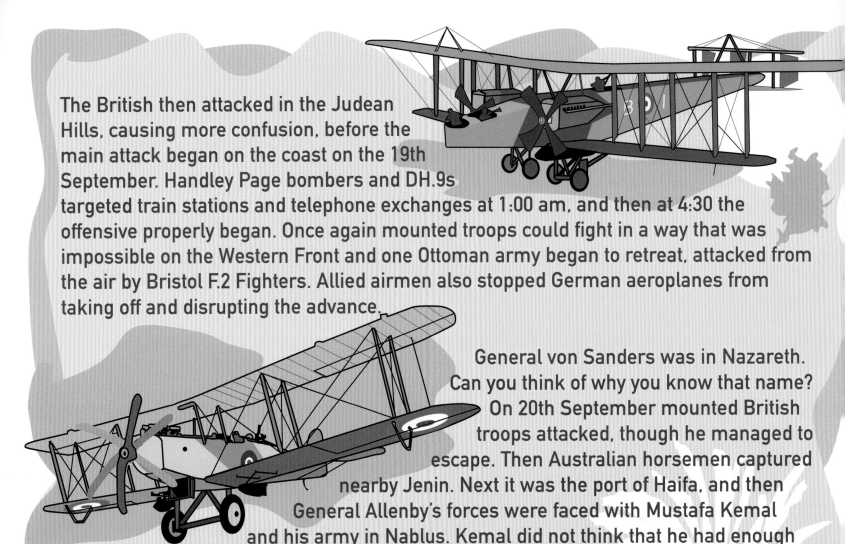

The British then attacked in the Judean Hills, causing more confusion, before the main attack began on the coast on the 19th September. Handley Page bombers and DH.9s targeted train stations and telephone exchanges at 1:00 am, and then at 4:30 the offensive properly began. Once again mounted troops could fight in a way that was impossible on the Western Front and one Ottoman army began to retreat, attacked from the air by Bristol F.2 Fighters. Allied airmen also stopped German aeroplanes from taking off and disrupting the advance.

General von Sanders was in Nazareth. Can you think of why you know that name? On 20th September mounted British troops attacked, though he managed to escape. Then Australian horsemen captured nearby Jenin. Next it was the port of Haifa, and then General Allenby's forces were faced with Mustafa Kemal and his army in Nablus. Kemal did not think that he had enough men to fight, and so they began to leave on the 20th September. Like the other Ottoman troops, they were bombed and attacked from the air as they retreated, and in one hour, the army was destroyed.

The Battle of Megiddo is important because it is so different to others in the First World War. General Allenby had not done that well on the Western Front, but here, he used tactics that belonged more in the Second World War than the first.

Hussein bin Ali,

This photo was taken at the peace conference in France after the war. Prince Feisal is right at the front, and behind him, on your right is Lawrence in his British uniform.

Amman was captured. Arabs, with T.E. Lawrence, took Daraa. Forces of the Arab Revolt moved on Damascus, too, as the fighting reached Syria. The first Arab horsemen reached the city on the 30th September and inside, their flag was raised. The following day Auda Abu Tayi, T.E. Lawrence and Arab troops entered Damascus. The war in Palestine ended on the 30th October 1918 when Turkey signed an armistice with the Allies.

The fate of the Arabs after the war left them very bitter. T.E. Lawrence was ashamed. Although Britain had said that it would support Arab independence if they helped defeat the Central Powers, after the war Britain and France divided up the area in a way that benefited them instead. The Balfour Declaration, which talked about giving land to the Jews for their own country also went against what the Arabs wanted. Eventually, this would happen when Israel was formed after the Second World War. Sharif Hussein did make his own country, but it was not recognised by everyone. It was taken in 1925 by Ibn Saud, and it is now part of Saudi Arabia.

Mesopotamia

After the capture of Baghdad, Khalil Pasha established a new headquarters in Mosul. He still had about 30,000 men, but things did not look good. A battle might have beaten some of Maude's men, but now that the British Army were organised, and Baghdad was being sorted out, it meant that there was not a lot to gain. The Ottomans would be wasting their effort because the results would not be worth it.

This photo shows British and Indian soldiers with a machine gun in Mesopotamia.

General Maude stopped at Baghdad to arrange himself and his men again. He was very good at making sure he was prepared. But he would not live to see the next part of the campaign. He died in the city from cholera in November 1917. We think he might have drunk some milk that gave him the disease, but there is another suggestion that he might have been poisoned.

The photo at the top is of General Maude's grave in Baghdad, where he is still buried. Below, you can see the man that took over, General Marshall, telling everyone that the war is over. He is reading what we call a proclamation, which is an official announcement.

His men began their offensive again in February 1918. They captured Hīt, Kifri, then Najaf, but like the Turks, strategy had moved away from this area for Britain. The troops in Mesopotamia were taken away and sent to Palestine for the Battle of Megiddo. Others went to Persia. There was no enthusiasm left for the fighting on the Tigris. In October, General Marshall, Maude's successor, knew the war was about to end, but he was told to fight again, and that 'every effort was to be made to score as heavily as possible on the Tigris before the whistle blew'. Ottoman forces under Ismail Hakki Bey were heavily defeated.

MESOPOTAMIA

PALESTINE

POISON

The Armistice of Mudros was signed on the 30th October 1918 by Britain and Turkey. Both sides agreed to stop where they were, but General Alexander Cobbe carried on advancing and captured the city of Mosul despite the anger of the Turks. Mosul had lots of oil (though the British would pretend they didn't know this), and whether or not Britain should be able to claim it after they marched into the city on the 14th November became a very important question. On this day, the war in Mesopotamia ended. British and Indian troops had suffered 85,000 casualties on the battlefield, and the Ottoman Empire more than 300,000. These numbers do not include hundreds of thousands more men who became sick or died of disease in Mesopotamia.

Britain brought people from India who had experience in how to run a country. It was disappointing for the Arabs in the area, who had been glad to see the Turks go, that they did not gain more independence after the war. Secret societies like the Jamiyat al Nahda al Islamiya (The League of the Islamic Awakening) Al Jamiya al Wataniya al Islamiya (The Muslim National League) and the Haras al Istiqlal (the Guardians of Independence) were formed to stand up to British rule. An Arab monarchy was formed in 1921, with British protection. Iraq gained its independence in 1932.

MOSUL

OIL

Italy

In this picture British soldiers have stopped to look after their lorries.

In Italy fighting continued in 1918 on the new Piave front, where the Italian Army's retreat ended at the end of 1917, after Caporetto.

After Russia left the war, Austria-Hungary was able to concentrate more on the Italian Front, and Germany had men they could move away from the Eastern Front too.

RIVER PIAVE

RIVER ISONZO

PIAVE FRONT VENICE

The Austrian Emperor Franz Josef had died in 1916, and his replacement, the Emperor Karl, was pressured by the Germans to carry out a new offensive against the Italian, and now British and French troops in front of them. After all, they were not far from Venice now. The Germans really hoped that this offensive would force the Allies to American troops from the Western Front, and make their life easier there.

This photo shows the new Austrian Emperor, Franz Josef.

The Italians knew exactly when the attack, which is called the Second Battle of the Piave, The Battle of the Solstice (in Italy) or the June Offensive (in Austria-Hungary) was coming. It was to begin on the 15th June at 3:00 am. Half an hour before this, the Italian artillery opened fire all along the enemy trenches. Men were waiting to attack.

The Austro-Hungarians got across the Piave on a large front, before they were finally brought to a stop. They tried again over the next few days, but they found it very hard to get supplies across the river, and more men. The River is deep and moves very fast, and lots of Austro-Hungarians drowned trying to get across. On the 19th June, General Diaz ordered his men to counter-attack.

In the meantime, more Austro-Hungarians, under General Conrad, who had been demoted, were attacking high on the Asiago (A-see-ah-go) Plateau, trying to capture Vicenza. His men did get forward, but the Italians held firm. The Austro-Hungarian Army was spread too thin. In the end, Emperor Karl took control himself. He ordered a retreat, and by the 23rd June his army was back where they started, having suffered more than 110,000 casualties. It was the last big offensive in history carried out by Austria-Hungary. Morale in the army and in the country was terrible. The political situation got very tense, and the survival of the Hapsburg monarchy was now in serious doubt. After this battle, the German General Ludendorff is supposed to have said that for the first time, he believed that the Central Powers might lose the war. If this is true, he was right. It was definitely the beginning of the end of Austria-Hungary.

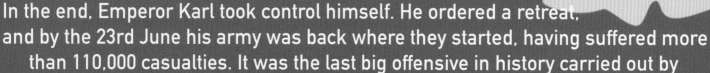

2

PIAVE

In this picture you can see Italian soldiers in action on the Piave.

The final blow came four months later at the **Battle of Vittorio Veneto**, which took place to the north of Venice.

General Diaz had been sensible after the Piave battle, and waited for his Italian troops to be ready before they tried to carry out a big offensive. British troops under General Lord Cavan played an important part too. The Allies launched their attack on the first anniversary of the Battle of Caporetto, but things were very different this time. By the 27th October, Italians and British troops were across the Piave. Austro-Hungarian soldiers refused to follow orders to counter-attack in places. The army was beginning to fall apart. The following day, Czech soldiers declared independence for Bohemia. Other groups followed their lead. On the 31st October the Hungarian parliament announced their separation from Austria.

This photo shows the damage done to the town of Nervesa on the Piave River.

In this photograph you can see Italian soldiers celebrating after victory at Veneto.

Meanwhile the Allies pressed on over the battlefield. An advanced guard of cavalry and cyclists entered Vittorio (the rest of the name was added after the war) on the 30th October and seized the town the next day. An American regiment had even arrived now too, and Allied soldiers were pouring across the Piave and moving on towards the Tagliamento River. The Austrian city of Trieste was captured on the 3rd November.

In this battle, the Arditi, a special kind of Italian soldier, were very brave, To help the army across the river, armed with knives and two handheld bombs, they were trained to stay in the fast, freezing waters of the Piave for hours on end. More than half of them became casualties. At Vittorio Veneto, 30,000 Austro-Hungarians were killed.

The Allies captured 5,000 pieces of artilley and more than 350,000 prisoners. They included Austro-Hungarians, Ukranians, Romanians, Poles, Slavs, Slovaks, Czechs and Germans. Casualties for the Allies were much lower. Italy suffered 38,000, most of them at Monte Grappa, Britain just over 2,000 and the French nearly 1,000.

The war on the Italian Front was over. The Austro-Hungarians signed the Armistice of Villa Giusti and the fighting stopped on the 4th November 1918.

This was disastrous for Germany too, who saw their biggest ally disappear from the war. It meant that even more so than before, the writing was on the wall for Germany.

All of these Austro-Hungarian prisoners were taken during the Battle of Vittorio Veneto. It was a disaster for Austria-Hungary.

In the aftermath of the war, the Austro-Hungarian Empire crumbled, with more countries declaring independence like Hungary. The monarchy was deposed, and Emperor Karl went to live in Switzerland and later the island of Madeira. He tried very hard to get his throne back, but died in 1922 at the age of just 34.

ARMISTICE OF VILLA GIUSTI

This photo shows damage done to a shop in Vienna. Order quickly began breaking down in Austria-Hungary at the end of 1918.

The Caucasus

In this photo you can see Armenians being trained in how to use rifles.

Why was everyone so interested in this region? The answer is oil. In this photo you can see oil fields at Baku in what is now Azerbaijan.

After the October Revolution in 1917, all of the territories in southern Russia were left to protect themselves, with a small number of local Armenians who had held onto weapons left behind by others and some refugees from Anatolia in Turkey. The Ottoman forces attacked in February 1918, and by the 22nd had captured the port of Trabzon. More troops came in by boat, and by the end of March the Ottomans were crossing the border into what had been the Russian Empire. Despite the end of the First World War, the region would see conflict into the 1920s. Finally, the territories of Azerbaijan, Armenia and Georgia became part of the Soviet Union. When this broke up in the 1990s, they finally became independent countries.

Salonika

There had been a long gap on the Salonika front in between battles. The Battle of Skra di Legen began on the 29th May 1918. It was a Bulgarian strongpoint, and it is important because it was the first time that a large number of Greek troops took part, fighting for the Army of National Defence. Allied forces captured Skra on the 30th May, and managed to hold off all of the enemy's counter-attacks. Finally, they had broken through the defences of the Central Powers in Macedonia. The Bulgarian Prime Minister quit his job on the 21st June. To make things worse for the country, it was clear that the Allies were planning a new offensive in Salonika, and Germany did not look too enthusiastic about helping. Bulgarian troops began making emergency preparations, but in some areas soldiers refused to help. They were tired, and hungry, and some of them deserted their units.

At times, troops found themselves with a lot of spare time. In the picture below, French soldiers have made their own circus!

In this photo, you can see Bulgarian prisoners taken during the fighting at Skra.

The Vardar Offensive had two parts to it. One of them was the Third Battle of Doiran which saw Greek and British troops attacking the Bulgarians on the lake again. Don't forget, British and French troops had failed here in 1916, and then the British failed twice more in 1917. Bulgarian engineers had built very strong defences and were determined to hold on. The ground was also very difficult and rocky to cross if you were trying to attack. For these reasons, and because the attack was not very well carried out, this attack was a failure too. The British and the Greeks suffered about 7,000 casualties in two days, and the Bulgarians about 2,700.

In this photo a British mule team is practising evacuating wounded soldiers.

The photo above shows soldiers talking with a local priest in Macedonia.

The photo below shows Russian troops on the move on the Salonika front.

The other part of the Vardar Offensive was a French and Serbian attack at Dobro Pole. This means 'Good Field' and is a mountain in Serbia that had been used very well as a defensive position by the Bulgarians. At the same time as the fighting at Doiran, this Allied force attacked on the 15th September. The artillery bombardment had already had a terrible effect on Bulgarian morale, and men had deserted. Despite this, the soldiers left behind put up a strong fight, but the line eventually collapsed and the Allies broke through towards Vardar.

In this photo you can see German soldiers swimming in the River Crna.

These French soldiers are on the march at Salonika. The Allied force there remained very multi-national.

361

Back at Doiran the Allies went forward again and found that the Bulgarians had run away. Now, they were far more interested in defending their homeland. Army deserters forced the Bulgarian High Command to flee Kyustendil, before they looted the city. They then gathered at Radomir, which was only 30 miles from the capital, Sofia. On the 27th September, leaders of the Bulgarian Agrarian National Union took control of these troops and declared that Bulgaria was now Republic.

Tsar Ferdinand of Bulgaria. He lost his throne, but not his money, and lived a comfortable life in Germany after the war. When he was 86 he married again, and his wife was so much younger than him, that she only passed away in 2015! He died in 1948.

The Tsar, Ferdinand I, abdicated and went into exile, just like the Russian Tsar, the Greek King and the Austrian Emperor. In Germany, the Kaiser was furious. Whilst all of this was happening, Bulgarians arrived at Salonika to ask for the war to stop. The Armistice of Salonika was signed on the 29th September, and then Bulgaria was no longer at war with the Allies. Together, troops from Serbia, along with French soldiers, took back their country.

ARMISTICE OF SALONIKA

The War at Sea

This is HMS *Vindictive*. It's a good name when you think about what the Royal Navy decided to use her for!

On St. George's Day 1918, the Royal Navy made a bold attempt to block the Belgian port of Bruges (Broogshe) The German Navy were using it as a base for their U-Boats. The plan was to take old ships and sink them at Zeebrugge (Zee-brooger) and Ostend, so that they blocked the narrowest part of the canal and the path out to sea for enemy submarines. This was a very dangerous mission and so the navy asked for volunteers to take part in what they called 'special service'. They did not know exactly what they would be doing. The first attempt failed, but the second one went ahead on the 23rd April, at the same time as another, smaller raid on another nearby port, Ostend. The plan was for HMS *Vindictive* to land 200 sailors and a battalion of Royal Marines at the entrance to the Bruges–Ostend Canal, where they would destroy German gun positions. But during the attack the wind changed direction and suddenly the smoke cleared and the Germans could see them. There were heavy casualties, and *Vindictive* was spotted by German gunners and forced to land in the wrong place.

There were submarines filled with explosives, but the main part of the plan was to sink three old ships: HMS *Thetis*, *Intrepid* and *Iphigenia* (Ifi-gee-nia) so that they would block the way to Bruges. Because the attack by the men on *Vindictive* failed, it meant that the Germans were still able to shoot at these ships and although they were sunk as planned, it was in the wrong place. They only managed to partially block access to the harbour. 1,700 men took part in the operation, with about 220 killed, and more than 300 wounded. The Germans suffered 24 casualties.

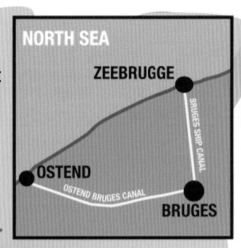

Along the coast at Ostend, two more cruisers were going to be sunk at the mouth of the canal. The attack failed because the German marines defending Ostend were well prepared and managed to force the British ships off their course. They gave up on the operation, but tried again three weeks later. This time the Royal Navy managed to sink a ship in the canal but it did not block the way to Bruges completely.

Die versenkten engl. Dampfer
in Zeebrügge

This photo shows you how the ships ended up at Zeebrugge. As you can see, they did not completely block the harbour for German submarines, and so the raid was a failure.

364

Towards the end of the war, the United States Navy and the Royal Navy worked together on a new way to try and limit the way U-Boats could move about. They laid a huge minefield from the Orkney Islands to Norway. At the time, it was the biggest minefield ever created.

The Mark 6 mine was round, and nearly three feet wide. Inside was stuffed 300 lbs of TNT. It was lowered on a steel cable with an anchor on the bottom so that it would hang in the water. A copper wire floated above it, and when a steel ship touched it, the circuit was completed and the mine detonated. The mines could float for more than two years waiting to go off! In all, the Allies laid more than 70,000 mines in this 230-mile long belt. We know that the mines definitely destroyed four U-Boats, and perhaps four more. We know that another eight German submarines were damaged by the mines, and lastly, there are five more U-Boats that disappeared without a trace, which we think may have run into the minefield. Lots of civilian vessels were also needed for such a big project as mine-laying.

In these photos you can see mine-layers in action.

SHETLAND ISLANDS

ORKNEY ISLANDS

NORWAY

NORTH SEA

SCOTLAND

DENMARK

NORTHERN MINE BARRAGE

On the 1st April 1918, the Royal Naval Air Service and the Royal Flying Corps joined together to become the brand new Royal Air Force. The RAF carried out many important actions before the end of the war, including the Tondern Raid, which is also known as Operation F.7. This was the first ever attack carried out by aircraft launched from an aircraft carrier at sea.

Their mission was to attack the German naval airship base at Tønder. On the 19th July 1918, in weather that was getting worse very quickly, seven special Sopwith Camels took off from HMS *Furious* just after 3:00 am. They reached Tønder about an hour later, and took the airship base by surprise. The base had three huge sheds. One of them, codenamed Toska, had both L.54 and L.60 inside. Three bombs landed on the shed and a fire destroyed both of the Zeppelins. The RAF suffered one casualty, and shortly afterwards, the Germans stopped using the base for anything but emergency landings.

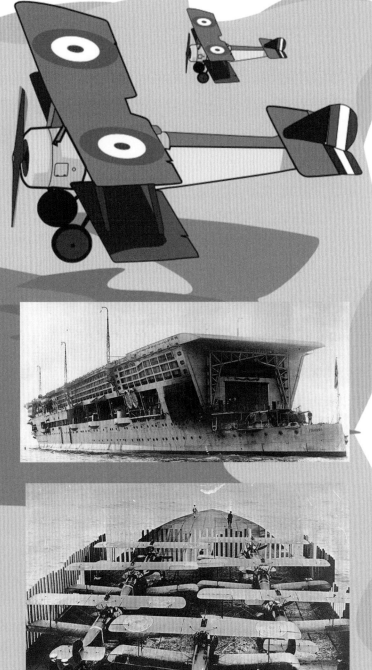

These photos show HMS *Furious* and the deck of the ship on her way to Tønder crowded with Sopwith Camels.

As the situation on land got worse and worse for Germany at the end of October, 1918, it was decided that the Imperial German Navy would issue the Naval Order of the 24th October 1918 to try to tempt the British Grand Fleet out to sea so that they could destroy it. However, Germany's sailors had had enough of the war. When orders were issued on the 29th October to get ready to go to sea, a string of mutinies broke out, with thousands of German naval men refusing to listen to their instructions. The war was almost over, and the operation was cancelled, but the mutinies were the beginning of a revolution that would destroy the German monarchy and leave Kaiser Wilhelm II without a throne. He abdicated two weeks later, Germany became a republic and he went to live in exile in the Netherlands.

In this photo you can see disorganisation at Kiel during the mutinies. Sailors just did not want to follow orders anymore. This was the beginning of revolution in Germany.

These sailors have taken their picture with a sign that boasts they are there at the beginning of Germany's journey towards becoming a republic.

On the Western Front, after the failure of the German spring offensives, the Allies decided that the time was right for them to carry out their own massive attack. The Americans were arriving in large numbers and were keen to fight. British numbers had been finally made up too, with men moved to the Western Front from Palestine. The French, who had been reluctant to get involved in more offensives before the American Expeditionary Force arrived, now viewed the situation very differently. General Foch and General Haig agreed that the first strike should be on the Somme. The situation here was not good, the ground was suitable for tanks, and they believed that the German defences were weak in this area. They didn't know it, but the beginning of these offensives marked the beginning of what we now call The Hundred Days. These were the famous last 100 days of the war.

Thousands of Americans had arrived on the Western Front by the middle of 1918. On the right, you can see some shaking hands with French soldiers, who were very pleased to see them.

Generals Foch and Haig

The Battle of Amiens began on 8th August 1918. A combination of British, Canadian and Australian troops advanced about seven miles in one day. This was unheard of on the Western Front. One of the things that made it so successful was the use of nearly 600 tanks. The attack was such a surprise that the Germans could not even fire back at first. They just weren't ready. General Ludendorff called it the 'black day' of the German Army, not just because it was defeated so badly, but because it destroyed morale. Some German soldiers ran away. They didn't want to fight and thought that the orders for the them to keep going were just making the war last longer.

Just like in all the other battles, soon the attackers began running out of steam. Within four days, only a few tanks were still able to take part in the fighting. The important thing about this battle was that for once, the Allies did not keep going. They stopped, and instead of waiting for the Germans to push them back again, they moved the focus of the fighting somewhere else, to hit the enemy hard again before they could organise themselves. They began doing this again and again.

This soldier is looking at the ruins of Amiens. Many of the places liberated from German occupation were in ruins.

100 DAYS

In this photo, Australian soldiers have just entered Bapaume to find bits of it completely destroyed.

The British Army began the Second Battle of the Somme on the 21st August. All along the German line, the troops began falling back. Albert was captured on 22nd. Then Australian troops crossed the River Somme again and broke the enemy at Mont Saint-Quentin and at Péronne.

The Allies were not only beating back the enemy on the Somme. Bapaume fell on the 29th August, too. To the south, the French had also been attacking. By the beginning of September, the Allies had pushed the Germans almost all the way back to the Hindenburg Line again. They were right back where they had started their spring offensives.

This French family have just returned to Amiens. Lots of families came home to find their houses and their belongings gone.

Now, it was time to try and break the very strong Hindenburg Line, and make the German Army collapse on the Western Front. This was their strongest position, and so troops from all over the world would be used; including the French, British and American armies.

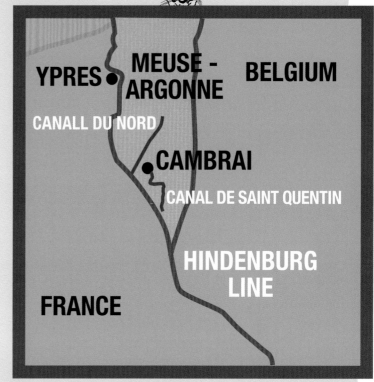

YPRES • MEUSE - ARGONNE   BELGIUM

CANALL DU NORD

CAMBRAI

CANAL DE SAINT QUENTIN

HINDENBURG LINE

FRANCE

Trench warfare as the men knew it was finished on the Western Front. There were lots of new challenges in chasing the enemy. The top photo shows a gun team rushing to get into position. In the second, French soldiers have found a ruined church to defend themselves from, and they are trying to hold up the enemy.

The Hindenburg Line was broken for the first time on the 12th September, when troops from Britain and New Zealand attacked. It was starting to feel like the German Army did not want to fight anymore, and this encouraged the Allies to plan a full-scale attack on the line.

175 miles away, French (including colonial soldiers) and American troops also advanced towards the salient at St. Mihiel, to try and get to the city of Metz. This was the first time that an attack was mostly carried out by American soldiers, and the planning was very detailed. In the end, the plan changed, and the American Expeditionary Force did not take Metz, but the fighting made Britain and France respect their new ally more.

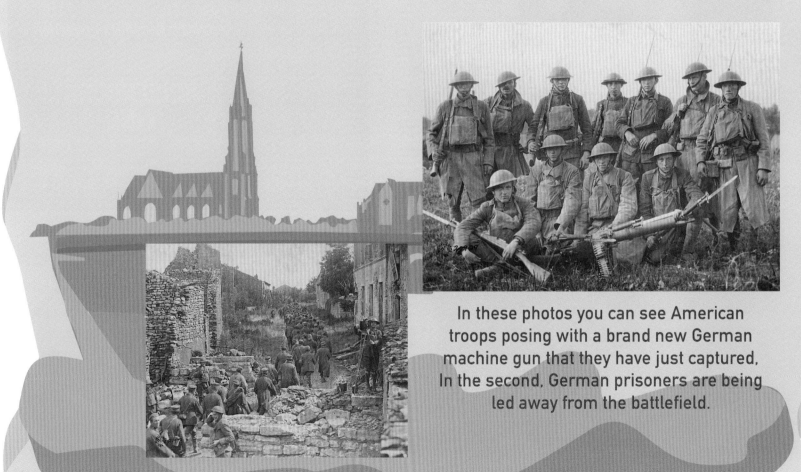

In these photos you can see American troops posing with a brand new German machine gun that they have just captured. In the second, German prisoners are being led away from the battlefield.

As you can see, tanks had come a long way by 1918! Both France and Germany had them. One of the most famous was a mini tank called the Renault FT. You can see it was only a little bit taller than a man, but you can still get two men inside!

Tanks were valuable machinery. You can see from the photo on the left that this one was British, but became German, when they captured it, because it has their markings on, before eventually being wrecked on the battlefield.

The French and the Americans began the Meuse-Argonne Offensive on the 26th September 1918. The point of the battle was to advance towards the town of Sedan. If the Allies could take the town, and it's important railway connections, then it would be very difficult for the Germans to carry on supplying their armies and moving their soldiers about on the Western Front.

For this reason, they were determined to try and defend their positions.

Before the battle began, the Allies fired so much ammunition that it was calculated to cost a million dollars per minute! American troops went forward at 05:30 am. They were brave, but very inexperienced, and they still had a lot to learn about fighting this new type of war. Results were mixed on the 26th September, and in the days that followed more and more German soldiers arrived. French troops got further than the Americans, but on easier ground.

100 DAYS

In these photos you can see American soldiers fighting during the Meuse-Argonne battles, and a German dugout in the Argonne forest.

100 DAYS

BELGIUM

YPRES•

CANAL DU NORD

•NAMUR

MONS

CAMBRAI ╲ CANAL DE SAINT QUENTIN

HINDENBURG LINE

There were still some difficult German defences in the way of the advancing Allies. They included the half-built Canal du Nord. Bits of it were still dry, but it was more than 100 feet wide, and in places the banks were 15ft high! The day after the attack began at Meuse-Argonne, the British Army stormed the Canal du Nord. Canadian soldiers were the first to break the enemy. The way to Cambrai was now open to the British Army.

CAMBRAI

All of the armies on the Western Front had got good at sitting still. Now they seemed to be rushing all over the place!

Meanwhile, in Belgium, French, British and Belgian troops also began to advance in Flanders on the 28th September to try and reach Liège. In command was the Belgian King, who would be the only monarch to actually lead a battle during the war.

The Allies quickly broke into the German lines, and began to take back the ground lost in the Spring Offensives. Despite bad weather, which meant that rations for troops had to be dropped by British and Belgian aeroplanes from above, the combined force continued advancing until the 2nd October, when German reserves arrived. Britain suffered about 5,000 casualties, and the Belgians 12,000, but they had advanced up to twenty miles in some places, and captured thousands of German prisoners, artillery and machine guns.

The top photo shows celebrations when Belgian soldiers re-entered Liège, which had been one of the first cities occupied in 1914. Below, you can see smiling British soldiers in another liberated Belgian town called Tournai.

100 DAYS

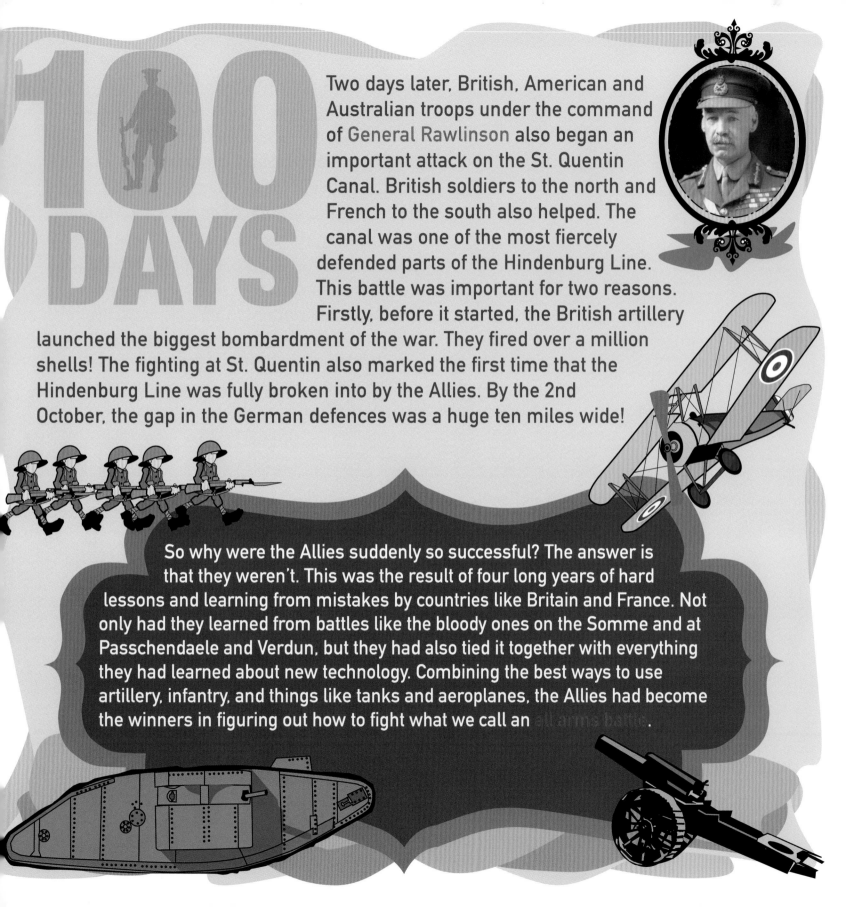

100 DAYS

Two days later, British, American and Australian troops under the command of General Rawlinson also began an important attack on the St. Quentin Canal. British soldiers to the north and French to the south also helped. The canal was one of the most fiercely defended parts of the Hindenburg Line. This battle was important for two reasons. Firstly, before it started, the British artillery launched the biggest bombardment of the war. They fired over a million shells! The fighting at St. Quentin also marked the first time that the Hindenburg Line was fully broken into by the Allies. By the 2nd October, the gap in the German defences was a huge ten miles wide!

So why were the Allies suddenly so successful? The answer is that they weren't. This was the result of four long years of hard lessons and learning from mistakes by countries like Britain and France. Not only had they learned from battles like the bloody ones on the Somme and at Passchendaele and Verdun, but they had also tied it together with everything they had learned about new technology. Combining the best ways to use artillery, infantry, and things like tanks and aeroplanes, the Allies had become the winners in figuring out how to fight what we call an all arms battle.

100 DAYS

Meanwhile, during the Meuse-Argonne fighting, the battle entered a new phase at the beginning of October. American soldiers threw themselves at the Germans, suffering thousands of casualties. However, they managed to break through the toughest defences at the Battle of Montfaucon and clear the enemy from the Argonne Forest. The Meuse-Argonne offensive was the biggest battle in the history of the USA. It lasted for nearly fifty days, and involved more than a million American soldiers. More than 26,000 of them were killed.

MONTFAUCON

The photo above shows American soldiers outside Montfaucon. The two concrete pillars behind them have been put there by the German Army to try and stop tanks getting through.

This famous photo shows an American soldier being helped after he has been wounded at Montfaucon.

The French, too, had advanced about twenty miles and reached the Aisne River again. This was not the end of the offensive, though, the fighting would carry on until the very last day of the war. By the time the guns stopped, the French would have captured back Sedan, and the railway lines that were so important for the German Army were lost to them.

To the north, three British armies were about to do battle for the city of Cambrai, which had been in German hands since the beginning of the war. However, by October 1918, the city was not defended well. Once again the British combination of infantry, tanks and aircraft completely overran the enemy. On the 8th October, Canadian troops entered the city. By the time they had 'mopped up' and made sure that it was clear of the enemy, they had suffered less than 20 casualties. It was about now that the German commanders finally accepted that the war was lost. The Allies were flooding towards them, tens of thousands of Americans continued to arrive in Europe, and the Central Powers were exhausted.

These photos show Canadian soldiers entering Cambrai during the 100 Days. You can also see the kind of thing they, and returning civilians, found – lots of destruction, as well as ruined churches and homes.

For the last five weeks of the war, the Allies continued to pursue the enemy back towards Germany, and the Germans did not make their advance easy. After the fall of Cambrai, the British and French Armies were finding that they were almost right back where the war had started in 1914. In mid-October British troops crossed the River Selle and captured Le Cateau. Further north, in Belgium, a mixture of Belgian, French and British troops liberated King Albert's homeland. Cities like Ostend, Bruges and Zeebrugge. Across the border in France, Lille, Douai and Valenciennes were retaken. Many, many prisoners were taken. They did not want to fight anymore. The Germans were in full flight, though their commanders were still in control of their retreat. By the time the war ended, the line of the Western Front had advanced nearly fifty miles from where it had sat for more than three years.

This photo shows a French girl holding hands with Canadian soldiers who have entered Valenciennes.

In this photo, a Canadian motor machine-gun unit are waiting to find out where they need to go next.

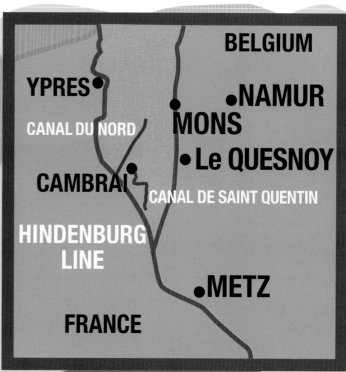

100 DAYS

The Allies continued to press on. The Battle of the Sambre was launched on the 4th November using British and French troops. New Zealanders also climbed the walls of Le Quesnoy and captured it from the enemy. The idea of the battle was to go towards Namur, and it was hoped that when this attack was combined with the French/American offensive in the Argonne, that the Germans would be stopped from making a defensive line to try and fight back. On the night of the 10th November something very symbolic happened. Canadian troops reached Mons, where the very first battle on the Western Front had happened, and began entering the town the next day.

Henry Gunther

Meanwhile in a railway carriage in the Forest of Compiègne, the Allies signed an armistice with Germany, the last enemy left, which meant that the fighting would stop. Everyone agreed that on that day: the 11th November 1918, they would put down their weapons. It was, at this point, a temporary measure, but Germany agreed that their troops would move towards home, that they would hand over their aeroplanes, their ships and their submarines and lots of the equipment they had made to fight, and that they would release the prisoners they had captured in four years of fighting. Unfortunately, knowing what was happening, some men were still sent into battle on that last morning of the war. Nearly 3,000 men were killed on the 11th November. France was so embarassed that this had happened, that on the headstones of those killed on the last day, they marked their date of death as 10th November instead. As far as we know, the very last soldier to be killed in action on the 11th November was an American named Henry Gunther. He died one minute before armistice began.

This photo was taken outside the train, and shows the men who agreed the terms of the Armistice. General Foch is at the front.

Armistice

TOTAL NUMBER CIVILIANS, SOLDIERS DEAD & MISSING

RUSSIA – 2.5 MILLION

FRANCE – 2 MILLION

GB & IRELAND – 1.3 MILLION

ITALY – 1.1 MILLION

SERBIA – 0.5 MILLION

ROMANIA – 0.5 MILLION

USA – 0.2 MILLION

BELGIUM – 0.1 MILLION

INDIA – 74 THOUSAND

CANADA – 61 THOUSAND

AUSTRALIA – 61 THOUSAND

GREECE – 25 THOUSAND

NEW ZEALAND – 18 THOUSAND

MONTENEGRO – 13 THOUSAND

PORTUGAL – 7 THOUSAND

JAPAN – 1 THOUSAND

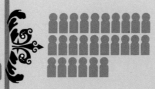

GERMANY – 3 MILLION

TURKEY – 2.3 MILLION

A/H – 2 MILLION

BULGARIA – 0.5 MILLION

These Bolsheviks have been taken prisoner by American troops. Lots of countries sent men to take part in the Russian Civil War because they did not want to see Lenin in power.

Although the war officially ended in November 1918, it is important to remember that the world remained very unstable. In every corner of the world there were civil wars, rebellions and revolutions. People were scared, and it felt like nobody was safe, and that the world was on fire.

The middle picture shows Greek soldiers in the war with Turkey in 1920. At the bottom you can see American soldiers in the Caribbean during the Banana Wars.

This photo shows men of the French Foreign Legion in Morocco during the Zaian War.

The Spanish Flu

This photo shows patients being treated in Washington

Just as the war was beginning to come to an end, the world had to deal with another crisis. The 'Spanish Flu' was a pandemic. We don't name diseases after places anymore, but at the time, people picked this name because it is where they thought it started. We know now that this was a strain of bird flu.

It was a strange disease, because it killed lots of people aged 20-40 who you would imagine would have been strong and healthy. It also killed lots of small children. At the time, there were no vaccines and no antibiotics if people developed complications. Instead, people had to rely on staying away from each other, lockdowns and lots of disinfectant. Does this sound familiar?

These Canadian schoolchildren are wearing masks to protect them from the flu.

Despite all of the precautions, we think that 500 MILLION people caught this flu virus. That's one in every three people on the planet. We think that 50 million people died as a result of the pandemic.

We don't really know where it started, there are lots of suggestions It might have been America, or France, or even China. There were four waves, beginning in Spring 1918 and continuing until 1920.

Some historians think that the flu helped the Allies to win the war, because of how it was affecting Germany and Austria-Hungary. There was a huge financial effect on many countries and some people even claim that there were long-term effects, such as people whose mothers had the flu when they were pregnant having babies who were not as smart!

These pictures show a lady typist in New York wearing her mask at work and a special hospital in Kansas for flu victims.

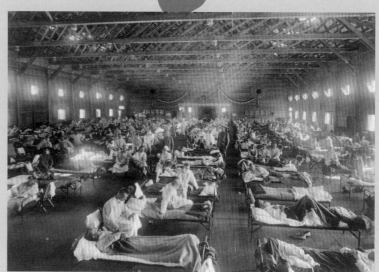

TREATY OF VERSAILLES

The Armistice on the Western Front just meant that both sides agreed to put down their guns. The path to peace was a long one, and there were lots of meetings at the Palace of Versailles which is on the outskirts of Paris.

The result was a huge document which was very strict with how it treated Germany. A lot of people see this document as one of the causes of the Second World War because it made Germans very angry and bitter. One of these angry men was called Adolf Hitler.

But Germany was in a terrible state having lost the war, and could not refuse to sign. The Treaty of Versailles was signed in summer 1919, and on the 29th June the First World War was officially at an end with all sides agreeing not to fight again.

Versailles was the most famous treaty, but to try and ensure that war would not break out again in other parts of the world, the Allies also signed the Treaties of Saint-Germain-en-Laye with Austria and Trianon with Hungary, the Treaty of Neuilly-sur-Seine with Bulgaria, and the Treaties of Sevres and Lausanne with the Ottoman Empire.

This photograph shows the delegates from the peace conference in the famous Hall of Mirrors at the Palace of Versailles.

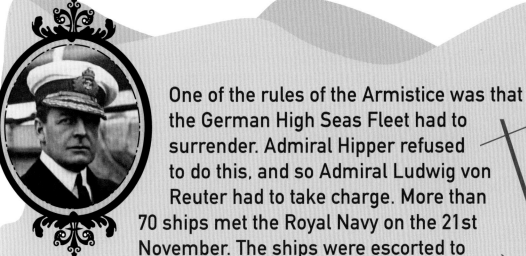

One of the rules of the Armistice was that the German High Seas Fleet had to surrender. Admiral Hipper refused to do this, and so Admiral Ludwig von Reuter had to take charge. More than 70 ships met the Royal Navy on the 21st November. The ships were escorted to Scotland and their German flags taken down.

Admiral von Reuter

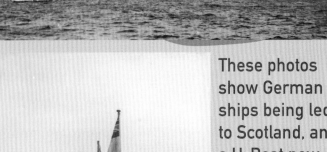

These photos show German ships being led to Scotland, and a U-Boat now flying a British flag.

One of the biggest punishments for Germany in the Treaty of Versailles is that she was no longer allowed to have a big navy at all. By now, the German ships were being held at the Royal Navy base at Scapa Flow in the Orkney Islands. Admiral von Reuter was worried that if war broke out again, Germany's ships would be used against her. To stop this, he scuttled the fleet. This means he sank his ships on purpose! More than fifty ships were lost, and if you go diving at Orkney, you can still see the wrecks of some on the bottom of the sea! People also still bring up steel parts and use them!

For some men, the war was never over. Millions of men had lasting physical and/or mental health problems as a result of being wounded or falling sick whilst serving.

What to do with them was a huge, huge problem in the years after 1918. All over the world, men remained in hospitals and homes for the wounded as late as the 1960s and 1970s.

Lots of companies in Britain pledged to find jobs for disabled veterans so they could earn a living, and there were lots of programmes for retraining men to work around their injuries. Some countries, however, were in the midst of revolution and big changes and not all of them could look after their disabled men.

In this picture you can see lots of wounded soldiers. They are at a special war hospital.

This photo shows a German soldier begging for money on the street in 1923. He is wearing a medal for bravery, and has lost his leg.

389

One way in which the First World War still has an impact on us today is how we remember the conflict. We call this Remembrance. How people remembered their loved ones changed a lot after the war because so many people had died. Nothing like this had ever happened before.

For Britain, it was too expensive to try and bring all of the men who had died home, and so instead they stayed where they fell. In those countries, land was given to Britain for cemeteries, and what we now call the Commonwealth War Graves Commission was formed to look after their graves. Everyone was given the same headstone, no matter how high his rank was.

But there were lots of men who had gone missing, and we don't know where they were buried. Huge memorials were built so that their names could be put on and their families would have somewhere to go to remember them.

In this picture you can see the uniform headstones provided by the Commonwealth War Graves Commission. It was important that nobody who died was treated any better than anyone else killed in the war, but this was not an idea that was popular with everybody at the time.

Countries also wanted to build national monuments to the dead. In Britain we have the cenotaph. Lots of countries also have an 'unknown soldier', to honour the many that disappeared on the battlefields. The idea was that one of them was brought home and buried somewhere special. In Britain they chose Westminster Abbey. This one unknown man was buried as a symbol of all of those who would not have a grave, again, so that their families would have somewhere to go to remember them.

One of the other things that was put into place in 1920 was the two-minute silence. The idea came from a South African man who wrote to Buckingham Palace and we still follow this today in Britain. at 11:00 am on the 11th of November, the moment that the guns fell silent in 1918, the whole country falls silent for two minutes, to remember those killed in war. Why is it important that we still do this?

Shortly after the war, General Haig helped make the poppy the symbol of remembrance. Other countries did the same, like America and Canada. Other countries picked different flowers. In France they use the cornflower, and in Belgium it is a daisy. This is why we wear poppies every November to show that we haven't forgotten all of the people who have been killed in wars in the last 100 years.

This ossuary at Monte Grappa in Italy holds the remains of more than 20,000 Italian and Austro-Hungarian soldiers who died nearby.

A lot of space was needed on the Western Front for graves. At Langemarck, as many as 12 soldiers are buried together.

Not all graves are crosses. This Senagalese soldier buried in France is a Muslim, so his grave has a star and crescent instead,

Jewish graves look different too. This American one is shaped like the Star of David.

Lots of graves have soldiers buried in them, but we don't know who they are. You can see examples of how America and France mark these graves in these pictures.

Lots of memorials have been built since the war to remember those who have no known grave, On the left, the Thiepval Memorial remembers more than 70,000 who died on the Somme. On the right are South African names on the memorial in Delville Wood, which is also on the Somme.

On the left is part of the huge Turkish memorial at Gallipoli. Each red marker remembers lots of Ottoman soldiers who died in the war. Lots of graves were lost, and on the right you can see that parts of Austro-Hungarian headstones have been rescued and turned into a memorial.

Towns all over the world built memorials to local people killed. The one on the left is in Noto, Sicily. On the right is an example of a memorial to a Moroccan Division. These memorials are usually found close to where the men on them fought.

THANK YOU!

Nicolai Eberholst
Heather Klem
Bethany Moore
Jim Smithson
Dr. Philip Weir

Ryan Gearing
Kamal Hyder
George Morton-Jack

And the many, many people who supported our crowd-funding campaign to ensure that we could make this book as fat as we liked!